Fourth Shore

Studies in Imperialism
Robin W. Winks, Editor

Fourth Shore

The Italian Colonization of Libya

Claudio G. Segrè

The University of Chicago Press
Chicago and London

Claudio G. Segrè is assistant professor of history at the University of Texas at Austin.
[1974]

The University of Chicago Press, Chicago 60637
The University of Chicago Press, Ltd., London

To My Mother

Contents

Series Editor's Preface

Imperial historians may well be prime imperialists themselves, if by "imperialism" one means, in part at least, the expansive questing after that which traditionally has been thought to belong to others. For imperial history, as written and taught today, must embrace political science, economics, anthropology, sociology, and law, and may well require formal training in one of these disciplines in the future; and imperial history, and those who profess it, must be immersed in areas conveniently and even fashionably labeled African, or Southeast Asian, or West Indian, or South Asian History. For the imperial experience was a shared one, between the Western, thrusting, encroaching power, and the cultures and people thrust upon, who in turn—whether through collaboration, primary resistance, or collapse—were shaped by the imperial experience. Indeed, it is the thesis of this series of volumes that the imperial experience is one best approached as an aspect of intellectual history, of what European and indigenous peoples came to think was true of each other, fully as much as being aspects of economic or political realities. An hypothesis buried within the conception of the series as a whole (although not necessarily explicit in each volume) is that the imperial experience, as a meeting between high- and low-technology cultures, turned predominantly upon four variables present in all such encounters: the cultural baggage borne by the encroaching white settlers, administrators, missionaries, or traders; the incredibly various natures of the indigenous cultures themselves, which helped promote widely different responses; the degree of commitment the imperial power had to the retention or exercise of power over an area, which changed; and the physical nature of the landscape in which the confrontation between the cultures was to be played out. It is, further, an implicit conclusion of this series that it might be well were we to call a moratorium on further generalizations and broad theories about imperialism until a sufficient number of case studies are available to make such theorizing more fruitful than it has proven to be in the past.

The series will, therefore, admit of volumes limited to the responses of the indigenous societies to the European and of volumes which appear to be almost solely about the Europeans themselves: of volumes which might, for those who must have tidy minds, appear to be more anthropological than historical; and of volumes which, while pointing toward theoretical conclusions concerning racism, or the exercise of power in a capitalist economy, or the problem of decolonization, are rooted in the sources. It follows that the series must contain contributions assembled in a variety of ways: works of original scholarship which grow from doctoral or postdoctoral research; translations of important statements about empire and colonies from German, or Afrikaans, or Portuguese originals; new collections of source materials not previously assembled in a single place; edited memoirs of district officers, native chiefs, and other men truly on the spot; or reprinted works of otherwise unobtainable scholarship and observation. The series taken as a whole is intended to be comparative, in that all modern imperialisms are appropriate to its purpose. No broad theory of "comparative history" is intended, however, and the series carries the bias that, baldly put, comparisons are useful only when made between the genuinely comparable: to play the nineteenth-century British game of comparing the Pax Britannica with the Pax Romana seems scarcely creditable in the twentieth century, for surely today we realize that to compare two experiences so utterly unlike in technology and the availability of resources is to engage in a fruitless metaphysical game about power and some unproven notion about the psychic unity of mankind. In short, volumes will not be self-consciously comparative, although taken as a whole, the series should provide new insights into the idea of comparative history.

Italy was never a major imperial power, and the handful of books in English on Italian imperialism affords little support to a comparative approach. Further, with the exception of writings on Ethiopia, scholars have given little attention to even the internal history of the Italian "colonies." Today imperial history, written both from the inside out and the outside in, demands a broader focus than ever before. Claudio G. Segrè's work provides precisely this broadened focus, making it possible for us to understand the role of Libya in the Italian state, and of Italian culture, business, and politics in Libya. Although Italy did not possess the high technology common to Britain, Germany, and the United States (and for this reason has been thought by some not to have been an imperialist nation), its technological power relative to the areas into which it expanded was nonetheless great. If one accepts that imperialism is essentially a strategy used by an expanding industrial state against a preindustrial one, it is the gap between the two societies, and not their specific position on some imaginary column dominated by GNP figures, that helps determine the actual imperial relationship. Then, too, there is an imperialism of the mind, a desire to expand one's ideas, culture, and normative modes of existence to and over another people, and in this sense Italy shared certain characteristics with the major imperial powers. Nonetheless Italian imperialism was distinctive, and it is by showing us the nature of that distinction, as well as illuminating the comparative elements, that Professor Segrè's book tells us so much.

Robin W. Winks

Preface

Can a nation conquer and administer huge blocks of overseas territory, call itself an empire, and still not be "imperialist"? Yes, claim the defenders of Italian colonialism. As one might expect from an admirer of Mussolini's regime, a Fascist apologist writes that Italy's African empire was not an exercise in "mere greedy imperialism," but an unavoidable alternative to unemployment and starvation. The Fascists, however, are not alone in making these claims. A prominent postwar Christian Democratic politician like Alcide De Gasperi also argues that Italy never considered her African colonies as a "tool of imperialism" but thought of them as an outlet for her excess manpower.

At this point the reader may accuse the Italians of still another distortion of that much-abused term "imperialism." But, argue the Italian apologists undaunted, generally speaking "imperialism" or an "imperialist nation" in modern times suggests an industrialized country expanding overseas in search of raw materials and new markets. Italy does not fit this description. On the contrary, between unification and the fall of Fascism, the period of modern Italy's history as a colonial power, she was a poor, backward—at least by the yardstick of economic development—nation whose chief economic resource was her labor force. Yet, because of her internal poverty she could not make full use of even this modest asset. Through emigration, Italian labor went to the benefit of other nations. In short, far from being an imperialist nation, Italians see their colonial history as that of a "proletarian nation"—a term coined during the Libyan war—desperate for colonies in which to settle her emigrants. As a proletarian nation, Italian colonialist apologists argue that their country's imperial history was very different from that of other European powers. Is there any validity to these claims?

Taken as a whole, there were certainly distinctive aspects to Italian imperial policy. To begin with, as far as was known at the time, the colonies in Libya and East Africa were poor—"a collection of deserts," according to the more malicious anticolonialists in Italy. Moreover, the mother country lacked the financial resources to develop these territories. Thus the Italians were forced to practice a kind of preindustrial form of imperialism in which agriculture was the chief source of wealth. Colonization, in the original sense of the term—settling men on the land—was one of the major concerns of Italian imperial policy. The great hope was that through emigration the empire could be transformed from a collection of remote colonies to a *magna Italia*, an extension of the mother country.

The Italians, however, were not content with a typical plantation colony in which a thin strata of Europeans operated large concessions with the labor of the indigenous peoples. For political, social, and ideological reasons, the Italians dreamed of "proletarian" or "demographic colonization" (*colonizzazione demografica*) for their empire. Their colonies were to be settled by large influxes of emigrants who would work their own farms with a minimum of help from the indigenous peoples. This dense network of small, independent landowners was to form the backbone of Italian society in the colonies.

As this book illustrates for Libya, there were enormous practical difficulties in carrying out this program. Private capital was not easily attracted to colonial agriculture. Those who did invest in a concession found that settling colonist families was a financial burden and a hindrance to their operation. Thus the concessioners showed no interest in "demographic colonization" unless the government was willing to provide handsome subsidies. Then there was the problem of the emigrants. The general assumption was that they would welcome the opportunity to start a new life under the Italian flag and that with their industrious habits they would make good colonists. In practice, neither assumption proved true. Quite often the emigrants preferred to follow relatives to the United States or South America or even to seek temporary work in Europe. Nor did they always make good colonists. Even those from rural backgrounds usually had no experience in managing a farm. Once in the colony, they preferred to settle in urban centers. To resolve these problems, the state intervened more and more with financial and technical aid. In East Africa, as in Libya, the government, especially under Fascism, organized colonization programs which provided farms, houses, village centers, livestock, seeds, fertilizers—whatever was necessary to help transform the emigrants into independent farmers.

To the British, French, and Germans, this type of settlement policy on a large scale was essentially foreign. For political reasons the French had practiced state colonization in Algeria at the end of the nineteenth century and Algeria was incorporated into metropolitan France. The British, too, from time to time—for instance, with aid to veterans after World War I—helped emigrants resettle in the dominions. Yet these cases were more exceptions than the rule. One need only think of Delamere in Kenya, with his dream of creating an elitist utopia of big plantation owners, to see how alien the British vision was from Italy's "proletarian colonization."

Perhaps the closest parallel to the Italian case is Portugal. Like Italy, Portugal is relatively poor and backward. Like Italy, the Portuguese felt the problem of emigration acutely, and their colonial policy reflected much concern with emigration outlets and colonization programs. In 1943, for instance, Salazar spoke of developing the rich, extensive lands of Angola and Mozambique in order to complement metropolitan agriculture and take care of Portuguese emigrants which Brazil would not accept. Like the Italians, the Portuguese wavered over whether to adopt government colonization programs. Finally, in the 1950s they applied them with some success in Angola and Mozambique.

Yet the uniqueness of Italian or Portuguese imperial theory and policy should not be exaggerated. For instance, the argument that colonies were necessary as an outlet for emigrants was also used by colonialist thinkers of the other imperial powers to justify their nations' expansion. Nor were Italy and Portugal, as examples of proletarian nations, unique in their colonization techniques. Many other examples of state colonization could be listed. The French settlement in Algeria is only one instance. Moreover, land colonization and resettlement projects were common throughout the depression world of the interwar period. The Americans, for instance, experimented—without much success—with settling ruined Midwestern farmers in Alaska. In all these cases the decisive factor in determining policy seemed to be not so much economic and technical considerations as politics. If the security of the flag demanded intensive settlement, or if times were hard domestically and the government needed to recoup its prestige, then a form of proletarian colonization, subsidized by the state, followed.

Finally, one might ask if proletarian nations like Italy and Portugal pursued policies toward the indigenous peoples in their colonies significantly different from those the other imperial powers followed in their possessions. Were the Africans exploited any less? Italian colonialists would have us believe—as the biographer of an Italian financier and colonial governor wrote recently—that Italy's emigrant families and laborers went to Africa bringing with them only their labor and their spirit of "peasant and Christian benevolence." African and Italian worked side by side to develop the colony for the mutual benefit of both peoples.

It is certainly true that the Italians—unlike the British—were not ashamed to work in the fields with the indigenous peoples when necessary. But in Libya, for instance, because Italian labor was relatively scarce and expensive, Libyans built much of the Fourth Shore—at wages considerably lower than those of Italians.

As for "peasant and Christian benevolence," there is no way of knowing how relations between Africans and Italians would have developed in the long run. However, throughout their country's imperial history the Italians were as preoccupied as any other colonial power with maintaining their prestige and dominance, as Italians and as Europeans, over the Africans. During the last days of the Fascist regime, all signs pointed toward an overt policy of racism. In Libya, Balbo's proposal for a first-class citizenship for the indigenous peoples was rejected. The Fascist regime, allied with Nazi Germany, embarked on a policy of domestic racism which would surely have sharpened color lines even more in the colonies.

As an indication of what might have happened in the long run if the Italian empire had survived World War II, Portugal can again serve as an example. During the postwar period the Portuguese government lavished investments and attentions on its nationals to induce emigration to Angola and Mozambique. The influx of emigrants reduced opportunities for the Africans and tended to harden color lines. Ultimately these tensions exploded into the recent successful struggle of the colonies for independence.

Finally, it is difficult to see that the Italians were any less "imperialist" in their search for raw materials than other colonial powers. In the colonies, where agriculture was the chief economic activity, land was the most valuable resource. Quite naturally the Italians sought to gain control of the best lands for their own colonists. In many cases they did so by compensating the indigenous peoples. But the Italians were also quite capable, when it suited their purposes, of confiscating territories with the excuse that the lands belonged to "rebels."

All in all, then, Italian colonialism, in its concern with emigrants and with colonization, did show certain distinctive traits. Were these traits unusual enough to conclude that Italy was somehow less "imperialist" than other European colonial powers? As the reader examines in detail how the Italians tried to build their *quarta sponda* in Libya—a fourth shore to add to the peninsula's Tyrrhenian, Adriatic, and Ionian coasts—he can judge for himself.

Acknowledgments

I began this study partly in response to an evening's conversation with an old family friend, Laura Fermi, who long after she emigrated to the United States from the Duce's Italy, has retained a lively curiosity about Italian Fascism. Among the topics we discussed on that particular evening were the bombastic celebrations of empire in the Fascist press. What, if anything, Mrs. Fermi wanted to know, had the Italians really done in their colonies?

Many librarians and archivists in the United States and Europe provided generous assistance in my research on the Italian experience in Libya. I am especially indebted to the following persons and the staffs of their institutions: Professor Renato Mori, director of the historical archives of the Ministry of Foreign Affairs, Rome; Doctor Mario Gazzini, archivist for the Comitato per la Documentazione delle Attività Italiane in Africa, Rome; Doctor Leopoldo Sandri and the staff of the Archivio Centrale dello Stato, Rome; Professor Arturo Marassi and the staff of the Istituto Agronomico per l'Oltremare, Florence; Doctor Armando Ceppollaro and the staff of the Istituto Italiano per l'Africa, Rome; the librarians of the Biblioteca della Camera dei Deputati, Rome. In the United States I was aided by Peter Duignan, curator of the African Collection, and the staff of the Hoover Institution on War, Revolution and Peace, Stanford, California; and the staffs of the New York Public Library, the American Geographical Society Library, and the Library of Congress.

Many persons helped me with personal interviews or extended other courtesies. I would particularly like to thank two members of the late Marshal Balbo's family—Donna Emanuella, the marshal's widow, and Avvocato Paolo Balbo, the marshal's son, for helping me to arrange many interviews. I am also much indebted to Professor Armando Maugini, director emeritus of the Istituto Agronomico per l'Oltremare, and Doctor Giuseppe Minnucci and Doctor Giuseppe Palloni, formerly with the Ente per la Colonizzazione della Libia, for sharing with me their many years of experience with the colonization projects in Libya; to Avvocato Giuseppe Bucciante, Professor Ardito Desio, Doctor Giuseppe Daodiace, and Senator Alessandro Lessona for insights into political and technical aspects of colonization; to Signor Pino Fazio and the colonists at the village of Sacida (Anzio) for their reminiscences about the colonist's life in Libya; to Professor Renzo De Felice and Professor Carlo Giglio for valuable bibliographical insights; to Professors Gary L. Fowler and Robert W. Brown, two young American geographers, for enthusiastically sharing their ideas and perspectives on Libya; to Professors Martin Klein, Davis McEntire, Richard A. Webster, Aldo Mei, Steven T. Ross, and R. L. Hess, who read the manuscript at various stages and provided many useful comments. My wife Zaza helped me with many stylistic criticisms and contributed much patience and sympathy. The late Raymond J. Sontag taught me many lessons in what it means to be a scholar—and a gentleman.

For financial support, I should like to thank the American Philosophical Society, the Hoover Institution on War, Revolution and Peace, and the University Research Institute, University of Texas at Austin.

Parts of chapters 5 and 6 have been published in the *Journal of Contemporary History*, vol. 7 (July–October 1972). I would like to thank the editors of this journal for permission to reproduce this material here.

The problem of transliterating Arabic names and places is always a vexing one, and Libya presents special problems. Libya is unique among Arabic-speaking countries in having followed rules of Italian orthography for transliterating Arabic into Roman script. French rules were imposed in other Arab Maghreb countries and in Syria-Lebanon; English became the standard in Egypt, Sudan, Palestine, and Iraq. Since this book presents Libya as the Italians saw it, I have not hesitated to use Italian spellings of place names. However, the first time that a place is mentioned, I have added in parenthesis the current Arabic equivalent, according to usage in the *Times Atlas of the World*, comprehensive edition (1971), 2d edition, revised, which conforms to rules recommended by the Permanent Committee on Geographical Names in London and the United States Board of Geographical Names. With certain commonly used geographical expressions or places, such as "wadi" or "Cyrenaica," I have adopted English usage over the Italian.

All translations are mine unless otherwise noted.

Abbreviations

General abbreviations

ATI	Azienda Tabacchi Italiani
BMA	British Military Administration
CMCI	Commissariato per le Migrazioni e la Colonizzazione Interna
DG	Decreto governatoriale (decree of colonial governor)
ECC	Ente per la Colonizzazione della Cirenaica
ECL	Ente per la Colonizzazione della Libia
ICLE	Istituto di Credito per il Lavoro all'Estero
INFPS	Istituto Nazionale Fascista per la Previdenza Sociale (after the fall of Fascism known as INPS)
ONC	Opera Nazionale per i Combattenti
RD	Regio decreto (royal decree)
UCIA	Unione Coloniale Italo Araba

Abbreviations used in footnotes

ACS	Archivio Centrale dello Stato, Roma
APCD	Atti Parlamentari. Camera dei Deputati
ASMAI	Archivio storico, ex-Ministero dell'Africa Italiana (Ministero degli Affari Esteri), Roma
CDIA	Ministero degli Affari Esteri, Comitato per la Documentazione delle attività italiane in Africa, *L'Italia in Africa*
CSC	Consiglio Superiore Coloniale
FAO	United Nations Food and Agricultural Organization, Rome
IAC	Istituto Agricolo Coloniale, Firenze
IAO-OR	Istituto Agronomico per l'Oltremare, Firenze, Osservatorio Rurale
ORIG	United States National Archives, Official Records of Italian Government Agencies (1922–44)
PCM	Presidenza del Consiglio dei Ministri

I. Origins of the Fourth Shore

1

Emigration and Empire in Liberal Italy

Italian Colonialism and the "Demographic Myth"

During her sixty-year cycle as a modern colonial power, Italy never cultivated a lasting taste for empire. To be sure, there were brief peaks of enthusiasm for the Libyan war in 1911 and for the conquest of Ethiopia in 1935. But these peaks were succeeded by long troughs of public apathy, hostility, and indifference. All in all, as Italy's tiny band of colonialist enthusiasts lamented endlessly, the nation never developed a genuine *coscienza coloniale*—a "colonial consciousness."

Italy's tepid interest in empire is not difficult to explain. She came to the colonial realm late and inexperienced. The nation that emerged in 1861 was weak, divided, and concerned primarily with whether the "miracle" of unification would last. She had nothing to invest overseas: her economic and financial position was so precarious that at moments the national government feared it might teeter into bankruptcy. Another obstacle to colonial expansion was the problem of the unredeemed territories, the *terre irredente*, of the Trentino and Trieste, which aroused far more interest than colonies overseas. Finally, the ideological factor of the Risorgimento's Liberal ideals acted as a restraint. If Italy had been created on the principle of national self-determination, what right did she have to impose her rule abroad? For these reasons, the small band of colonialist enthusiasts—the explorers, travelers, missionaries, businessmen, intellectuals, and politicians—found that their message of overseas expansion was generally received with indifference.

As Robert Michels noted in 1914, only two aspects of the colonialist message aroused any widespread national interest.[1] The first was the value of colonies as symbols of great power status. If Italy was to improve her "Cinderella" image—her standing as the last among the great powers, a position held largely by courtesy—she could not stay out of the scramble for Africa. Once in the race, for fear of losing prestige she could not quit, no matter how costly and fruitless the competition might seem.

The second aspect of the colonialist appeal to arouse widespread interest was the hope that colonies could provide at least a partial solution to Italy's emigration problem. From Italy's first expansionist adventures in East Africa under Crispi and Mancini to Mussolini's invasion of Ethiopia, colonialist apologists have defended Italian expansion as an economic and demographic necessity. In the view of these apologists, Italy was unlike other imperial powers such as France or Britain, for Italy was a "proletarian nation"—rich in manpower, poor in natural resources. She sought a colonial empire to find outlets for her emigration and resources to support her population. In the words of Luigi Villari, an apologist for the Fascist regime, Italy's desire for colonies was "not mere greedy imperialism, as unfriendly critics made out, but a compelling necessity for the Italian people, an alternative to unemployment and starvation."[2] At the other end of the political spectrum the same argument appears. Alcide De Gasperi, the great Christian Democratic leader and architect of Italy's immediate postwar recovery, wrote to American Secretary of State Byrnes in 1945: "Democratic Italy never considered colonies as a tool for imperialism, but rather as a means for absorbing Italy's surplus manpower."[3] Even in contemporary Italy, the "demographic myth," the image of colonies as major population outlets, persists. Carlo Giglio, one of Italy's best-known scholars on colonialism and African affairs, observed that "In Italy, when speaking of Africa, the minds of most people run instinctively to the idea of an outlet for excess emigration."[4]

As a source of new homes and new opportunities for the "proletarian" nation's dispossessed, Italy's colonies never matched the promises of the demographic myth. East Africa and Libya proved to be mostly barren areas unfit for European settlement. Those regions which seemed suitable for colonists, the Ethiopian highlands and Libya's Mediterranean shores, required enormous investments before they would support heavy immigration. Even those colonies in which Italy had an opportunity to make long-term investments, such as Libya and Eritrea, never became important outlets. Eritrea, where colonization plans were drawn up in 1890, had perhaps 72,500 Italians in 1940, most of them employed in the bureaucracy or the military.[5] After thirty years of Italian rule, which included a period of state supported-colonization, Libya in 1940 had a total Italian population of about 110,000. The combined Italian population in the entire empire at its pinnacle in 1939 totaled about 305,000, considerably fewer than the estimated 500,000 Italians living in New York City. At its peak, the empire could not absorb the average annual natural increase in the Italian population, which totaled about 400,000 betwen 1935 and 1940. Nor could the colonies absorb more than an infinitesimal fraction of the annual average Italian overseas emigration before World War I. In short, as demographic outlets African colonies proved to be dismal failures, and the "necessity" of an empire to resolve the nation's population problems was simply a fable.

Neither the facts nor the conclusions to be drawn from them deterred Mussolini or earlier generations of colonialist enthusiasts from preaching the "demographic myth." Nearly half a century after the failure of colonization experiments in the Eritrean highlands, a Fascist colonial minister argued that the experiment had been perfectly sound in its conception: it merely lacked energetic state financing and Fascist leadership.[6]

With the colonies' poor record as emigration outlets, how could Italians persist for so long in the belief that empire would provide an important solution to emigration?

Sometimes international political and economic conditions worked to give the imperial solution to emigration a certain plausibility. Mussolini's demands for colonies came in the bewildering and uncertain conditions of the interwar period. With trade and industry in a slump and major emigration outlets closed, empire appeared to be the only remaining alternative. In the same way Crispi, nearly half a century earlier, had made colonies seem an attractive solution to a country that was burdened with agricultural slumps, tariff wars, and massive emigration.

More important in accounting for the durability of the demographic myth is the question of national pride. In seeking colonies as population outlets, Italy was searching as much for a psychological solution to her social problems as for a physical answer.[7] Perhaps an empire could never absorb the nation's emigration stream. Nevertheless, the pride and prestige of empire could assuage the humiliation which Italy felt about her emigrants. As Corrado Gini, Italy's most eminent demographer, concluded in 1941, imperial expansion was less a policy based on seeking rational solutions to social problems than a simple will to power. Like individuals, Gini observed, peoples "reach certain stages of development when they feel an overwhelming desire to express their personality, to assert their desire to command in the world."[8]

Gini's remarks were certainly applicable to the Fascist regime that he had observed for nearly twenty years. Fascism added little that was new to Liberal Italy's colonialist ideology. Under the guise of seeking to resolve the nation's demographic problems, Fascism too sought empire and great power status. In practice, however, the Duce's regime behaved quite differently from its predecessors. Liberal Italy had always shown a certain caution in confronting the great powers directly. Diplomatic prudence, as well as Liberal ideology, for instance, led to renunciations in Tunisia and Egypt. Liberal regimes also avoided direct state involvement in regulating emigration or colonization. Fascism, however, had no such sense of limits. The Duce, after a cautious start, quite literally planned to realize Italy's aspirations for great power status and colonial emigration outlets. In this way, he carried the Italian colonialist tradition to its logical conclusion.

This chapter and the following one examine how the colonialist tradition in Liberal Italy, with its stress on searching for demographic outlets, colored Italy's hopes and expectations for Libya. The succeeding chapters illustrate the way Fascism, as heir to the "demographic myth," carried it out in the colonization of Libya.

Liberal Italy and the Emigration Issue

Among the many problems the new kingdom of Italy faced in the decades after 1870 was a population pressure of increasingly worrisome proportions. Although after 1870 Italy entered the period of demographic transition, the annual crude rate of increase, which had been 6 to 8 per thousand, moved up to levels of about 11 per thousand annually.[8] Between 1861 and 1911 the population increased by about 10 million, from 25.7 million to 35.9 million. The meaning of this population upsurge becomes vividly clear from the statistics on population density. The population increased from 63.2 persons per square kilometer in 1800 to 87 persons per square kilometer in 1861. Between 1861 and 1911 the density increased from 87 to 123 persons per square kilometer. During the period 1901–11 alone the density increased by 10 persons per square kilometer.

In a poor country like Italy, in which industry did not develop extensively until the turn of the century, the natural solution to this demographic phenomenon was emigration. The annual mean emigration during the first two decades after unification was 100,000 to 150,000 emigrants.[9] The massive Southern exodus began in the mid-1880s as the annual crude rate of population increase coincided with a series of agricultural crises. The conjunction of these two factors produced some of the blackest years in the economic history of the new kingdom. By 1887 the emigrant stream had grown to more than 200,000 and by 1896 to about 300,000. By the turn of the century, the emigration reached the proportions of a major exodus. Between 1901 and 1910 the mean annual rate of emigration was 602,669, with peaks of nearly 800,000 in 1906 and 872,598 in 1912.

The dynamics of the emigration stream are extraordinarily complex. In part the Italian emigration fed the great exodus from Europe during the nineteenth century, a massive movement that has been described as the most important migratory movement of the modern era and perhaps one of the largest in all human history.[10] Changing social structures, the new technology of the industrial revolution, and political and social persecution created an unsettling complex of push-pull factors. Thousands were freed—or were driven—to seek new lives abroad. Average annual overseas emigration from Europe amounted to about 377,000 from 1846 to 1890; about 911,000 from 1891 to 1920; and about 366,000 from 1921 to 1929.

In Italy the emigrant surge varied from region to region and shifted with the economic tide.[11] Until the agricultural slump of the mid-1880s, Northern Italy provided the bulk of emigrants. Liguria, Piedmont, Lombardy, the Veneto, and certain communes around Naples were areas of high emigration. Even with the industrial development of the North in the 1890s, certain towns and districts such as Rovigo and the Friuli retained very high emigration rates. The Southern emigration of the 1880s reflected the world agricultural depression and the government's vindictive tariff policies against France. Italy was slowly discovering that she was far from being a "natural garden" or one of the most fertile regions in Europe. Nearly four-fifths of the peninsula's area is mountains and hills. Other factors like the social structure and land tenure systems compounded the misery of the Southern peasantry.

TABLE 1. ITALIAN EMIGRATION (Annual Means)

Years	Expatriated	Repatriated
1861–70	121,040	. . .
1871–80	117,596	81,832
1881–90	187,920	. . .
1891–1900	283,473	. . .
1901–10	602,669	. . .
1911–20	382,807	. . .
1921–30	257,844	137,814
1931–40	70,265	58,986
1941–50	163,539	63,801
1951–60	300,651	141,561

SOURCE: S. B. Clough, *The Economic History of Modern Italy* (New York: Columbia University Press, 1964). For certain periods, data is lacking on repatriates.

Potential solutions such as birth control, reclamation, and industrialization were either blocked or developed very slowly.[12] For the Southern peasant, emigration was the easiest and most natural solution to his problem.

While the emigrants followed their own interests and departed, the nation as a whole wondered about the effects of the emigrant stream on the new Italy. Some argued that emigration was a natural phenomenon, disconcerting and sad perhaps, but beneficial in the long run.[13] Restrictive legislation was both impractical, because it would be ineffective, and immoral, because the state had no right to impose unnecessary restrictions on the individual. Those who defended a laissez-faire policy of unrestricted emigration argued that emigrant remittances from abroad were important in helping to balance Italy's international accounts. Another benefit was that emigration functioned as a "safety valve" against internal discontent. Through emigration the nation rid itself of malcontents and revolutionaries.

The opponents of unrestricted emigration included special interest groups such as big landowners and the military. The landowners worried about labor shortages and rising agricultural wages. The military feared that the manpower needed for national defense might be seriously drained. Other opponents of emigration argued that despite the remittances, the nation still suffered serious economic losses. From birth to the time of emigration, the nation contributed to feeding and educating the emigrant—only to lose that investment to some other country. As for the "safety valve" argument, opponents of unrestricted emigration agreed that emigration provided a fine outlet for discontent. But relying on emigration to answer such problems left Italy at the mercy of other nations. What would happen if one day these nations closed their outlets?

Perhaps what counted most heavily in the discussion was not so much the calculus of economic and social benefits as the emotional factor of national pride. In the popular mind, as well as in the minds of scholars, economists, and statesmen, emigration was associated with humiliation. The plight of the emigrants was widely publicized. Edmondo de Amicis's description of the life of emigrants in *Sull'oceano* went through six editions by 1889, a decade after its publication. Newspaper articles described the misery and disillusionment of Italian emigrants in the United States and South America. Incidents like an attack on Italian mine workers at Aigues-Mortes in France (1893) or an American lynching episode in New Orleans (1891) stung the national conscience. What kind of country was this that could not even feed its citizens and which forced them to seek a living abroad? Equally humiliating was the poverty, misery, and abuse the emigrants encountered overseas. Why couldn't the government in Rome at least do something to ensure respectful treatment of its citizens in foreign countries? Thus for the small band of colonialist enthusiasts preaching their cause before an often hostile parliament and an indifferent country, emigration was always a major issue.

Emigration and the Italian Colonialist Movement

In their backgrounds and interests, the Italian colonialists during the first decades after unification resembled their counterparts in other European countries.[14] As in France and Germany, they consisted of a tiny band of intellectuals, explorers, missionaries, scientists, politicians, scholars, and sailors. They organized themselves into societies, principally the Società Geografica Italiana of Florence, founded in 1867, the Società d'Esplorazioni Commerciali in Africa of Milan, founded in 1879, and the Società Africana d'Italia of Naples, founded in 1882. They subsidized colonial journals, such as Manfredo Camperio's *L'Esploratore,* and they sponsored expeditions to Africa. With the support of these societies, Italian explorers like Romolo Gessi, Carlo Piaggia, Pellegrino Matteucci, and many others contributed to Europe's knowledge of the Dark Continent.

For the first two decades of unity, the expansionist arguments of the Italian colonialists were ignored. Their appeals resembled those which colonialists also used in other countries: the search for markets and raw materials, the demands of international power balance, the civilizing mission. To an economically backward and divided Italy, however, these arguments meant little. The Italian colonialists eventually found that their most effective appeal was the theme of colonies as population outlets, especially when the scramble for Africa coincided with the beginnings of the mass Southern emigration.

Italian colonialists were not unique in arguing that their country's population pressures made overseas colonies imperative. Colonialist circles in Germany and England played on the same demographic theme. German colonialists went so far as to indicate North Africa—including Tripolitania—as one of the possible outlets for their nation's excess population.[15] Nevertheless, the rapid pace of industrialization in England and Germany helped to absorb their potential emigrants. Italy, on the contrary, developed more slowly, while her emigrant stream grew and grew. Italian colonialists could thus argue their case with a special fervor. For them, colonies under direct Italian sovereignty were the only humane and honorable solution to the nation's demographic pressures.

But where was Italy to acquire these colonies? In casting about for suitable geographical areas in which to establish population colonies, the colonialists turned again and again to Africa. "Africa attracts us irresistibly," commented Cesare Correnti in founding the Società Geografica Italiana.[16] Africa appealed especially to Southerners, who were particularly numerous in the colonialist movement.[17] They thought of Africa as a continent of vast lands and space. The Sicilians, especially, remembered how their friends or relatives had prospered under the French protectorate in Tunisia. Nevertheless, these emigrants still worked under a foreign flag. Where could Italy find areas not already claimed by a foreign power? How was Italy to acquire territories without violating the rights of the indigenous peoples to national self-determination?

One argument was that Italy should exploit her existing "free" or "spontaneous" colonies, such as the large emigrant communities in Argentina and the Plata republics.[18] By a little adroit gunboat diplomacy and a program of strengthening the local consulates in these areas, the colonies might become the equivalent of a Canada or an Australia, argued the Lombard geographer Cristoforo Negri as early as 1850. A free trade and laissez-faire economist like Luigi Einaudi also subscribed to the theory of "free colonies," especially in the Plata region. In *Il principe mercante,* he pictured the emigrants as following the tradition of the Italian merchant princes and entrepreneurs of the Renaissance, who made their fortunes while also spreading Italian culture.

The theory of "free" or "spontaneous" colonies was easy to criticize. Italy was not exporting merchant princes. The majority of emigrants were peasants without capital and without education. The few merchants who actually ventured abroad usually had a narrow technical education and had little interest beyond enriching themselves. They spread neither culture nor influence beyond their immediate community.

Those who ridiculed the "free colonies" theory often went beyond criticizing its impracticability. Their demand for emigration outlets abroad was little more than a thinly disguised appeal for Italy to assert herself as a great power. Economists like Leone Carpi, an Italian counterpart to France's Leroy-Beaulieu, and Girolamo Boccardo were willing to abandon laissez-faire doctrines in the interest of gaining government backing for colonies abroad.[19] Boccardo in particular was eager to shake Italy from its lethargy and direct her toward "the glorious perils of colonization."[20]

Until the scramble for Africa began, the government and Parliament preferred to ignore colonial issues entirely. In 1883, for instance, under Depretis, the government was unsympathetic to a plea in Parliament for Italy to establish agricultural colonies in Tripolitania and Cyrenaica.[21] As the government knew only too well, such a request to resolve the problem of emigration was also a demand for the nation to act as a great power, to claim her share of the decaying Turkish empire. Once the partition of Africa began, however, Italy's leaders could not resist joining in the competition. They justified Italy's entry into the colonial race by appeals both to the demographic theme and to the nation's sense of honor.

Such was the story of the conversion of the Neapolitan foreign minister P. S. Mancini to the imperial cause and of his authorization of the nation's first major colonial commitment, the expedition to Massawa in 1885.[22] Mancini was an expert on international law and had been opposed to colonial expansion for ideological reasons. Yet he could not bear the sight of Italy remaining on the sidelines while the other European powers advanced in Africa. Before a hostile Parliament, he defended his expedition to Massawa on the grounds that the government could not ignore "its duty to seek outlets for emigration, which has now reached alarming heights."[23] Beyond Massawa, Mancini told Parliament, he had sent the explorers Giacomo Bove and Antonio Cecchi to seek further population outlets in the Congo and Somalia. Mancini also tried to defend his expedition by citing Massawa's advantages as a port and naval base. He concluded with a mysterious allusion to Massawa's importance for Italy's position in the Mediterranean. "The keys to the Mediterranean lie in the Red Sea," he asserted. The comment brought jeers from the anticolonialists, who invited Mancini to find Moses and ask him to drain the Red Sea and produce the keys.[24] Clearly the nation was in no mood to be hoodwinked by the vague allusions of a formerly anticolonialist minister who had suddenly caught colonial fever.

Even Francesco Crispi, despite his reputation as the most expansionist of Liberal Italy's prime ministers, failed to arouse the nation from its uneasy and vacillating pursuit of African empire.[25] Crispi himself pursued an erratic policy which lacked conviction. His chief concern was to defend Italy's status as a great power.

In his speeches, the fiery Sicilian prime minister sounded the call for Italy to expand and to seek demographic outlets. At Palermo, on 14 October 1889, for instance, in accents that suggest later Nationalist and Fascist rhetoric, Crispi spoke of Italy's historical mission in Africa. This mission was dictated by her geography and maritime tradition, he said. The nation was "set in the middle of Europe," yet was close to Africa and to the "doors" to the Atlantic Ocean and the Red Sea. On these seas "our fathers cleared the path to new civilization." He concluded that "we would be failing our country if we did not enlarge our field of activity."[26] In expounding on the demographic theme,

Crispi described Ethiopia as a land with

vast zones of cultivable land which will offer an outlet in the near future to
that overflowing Italian fecundity which now goes to other civilized countries
. . . [and] is lost to the mother country.[27]

At the same time, in Parliament he showed little enthusiasm for the colonialist cause. He claimed that he had inherited Italy's colonial situation and that he had never voted in favor of the initial enterprises. He had persisted in his African policies, he declared, only to the point necessary to preserve the nation's honor.

His actions confirmed his hesitations. He never launched a truly ambitious and expansionist colonial program during his two ministries. He confined himself to consolidating the Italian position in East Africa and pursuing the local intrigues that he had inherited from his predecessors. Even in the case of Tripolitania—despite his concern with Italy's prestige in the Mediterranean—he was content to preserve the status quo.

Crispi's fall with the defeat at Adowa indicated how little headway he made in arousing the nation's colonial consciousness. Adowa need not have meant a general retreat from Africa. Other nations had suffered similar defeats and continued with their expansionist policies. The Italian retreat illustrated once again the nation's diffidence toward colonial matters.

The profound psychological shock of the Adowa disaster almost totally overshadowed another important legacy of the Crispi era: Italy's first major attempt to create population colonies in Africa. Under the leadership of Baron Leopoldo Franchetti, a philanthropist and expert on the rural problems of the South, Italy attempted to direct emigrants to Eritrea's highlands. In the long run, despite government support, the experiments failed. In the short run, however, the experience so impressed a number of important anticolonialists that they converted to the colonialist cause. Nor did the impact of the Eritrean experiment cease then. For two generations afterward, Italy sought to create an empire which, if it offered little else, at least provided settlement possibilities for her emigrants. Thus, whether in her East African colonies of Eritrea, Somalia, and Ethiopia or in Libya, land colonization programs were always a major concern in Italian imperial policy. The classic point of reference in formulating these programs was often the example of Eritrea.[28]

Agricultural Colonies in Eritrea: "Capitalist" or "Demographic" Colonization?

In contrast to the steaming, desolate port of Massawa, the Eritrean highlands offered an ideal climate for European settlement.[29] The area, which ranged in altitude from 1,400 to 2,300 meters, appeared to be thinly populated and the climate was attractive. Following a tortuous and conflicting policy, the Italians gradually began their expansion inland. The massacre of an Italian column at Dogali in 1887 served only to strengthen the government's determination to remain in the area, if only to uphold national honor. By 1889, the Italians had occupied an extensive stretch of the highlands and had come to a confused and ambiguous political agreement with the Ethiopian emperor in the Treaty of Uccialli. The situation seemed sufficiently stable for the king to proclaim the formal creation of the "colony of Eritrea" on 1 January 1890.

In his Palermo speech of October 1889, Crispi had alluded to the possibilities for agricultural settlements in the new colony. At the same time, he had sent Baron Leopoldo Franchetti to explore the highlands and make recommendations for future colonization. Franchetti, scion of a wealthy Jewish banking family from Florence, was well qualified for the mission, for he had devoted his life to philanthropic projects and to the study of economic and social problems of the rural South.[30] As a young man, in 1876 he had distinguished himself as a coauthor with Sidney Sonnino of a famous report on agricultural conditions in Sicily. Together with Sonnino, he also edited the *Rassegna Settimanale,* a journal devoted to social and agricultural problems.

Franchetti saw colonies less as power symbols than as an opportunity to fulfill his philanthropic ideas. His goal was to develop Eritrea as an outlet for the landless Southern peasantry. His Eritrean program would not resolve the nation's emigration problems, but at least the colony would provide a beginning and an example, he thought. Franchetti favored a "peasant" or "demographic" colonization based on small family-sized concessions, aided by the state if necessary. He opposed a "capitalist" colonization based on large privately financed estates. Colonist families would create a dense, stable, and productive population which could defend itself militarily and which would soon bring the colony to financial autonomy. Private initiative, he feared, would lead only to the rural phenomenon he knew so well from his studies in Italy: land speculators and large estates. Unless his program was followed, Eritrea would remain little more than an unproductive desert where "a little private wealth would flourish on public misery."[31] "If this type of state support and direction is socialism," declared Franchetti, who by temperament and background was a classical Liberal, "then I declare myself to be a socialist."[32]

The conflict between "capitalist" and "demographic" colonization policies—a controversy which later also lay at the heart of Italy's erratic colonization policies in Libya—perpetually plagued the settlements in

Eritrea. The government was opposed to Franchetti's idea of excluding private initiative entirely. Crispi's own reaction to Franchetti's plan was:

You would close the door on honest speculation. What inspires you is a poem. A noble poem but [one] that would not bring about any useful results.[33]

A parliamentary commission, appointed in 1891 to investigate rumors of colonial administration scandals and abuses toward the indigenous population, shared Crispi's conclusion. The commission's report was generally positive about the colony's future as an "outlet for part of Italian emigration." The report expressed faith that "little by little" the colony would reach financial self-sufficiency.[34] However, the commission did not favor excluding private initiative from Eritrea's agricultural development:

In order to prevent the colony from developing in any way different from the most desirable fashion, the colony has been prevented from developing at all, and an orthopedic apparatus has been imposed on it which has preserved it from the perils of adolescence by perpetuating its infancy.[35]

Franchetti's schemes did not fare very well.[36] Colonization began in earnest at the end of 1893 when twenty-nine Lombard, Sicilian, and Venetian families settled in stone houses near Godefalassi. Not long afterward, an additional two hundred settlers received land at Ghinda near the edge of the Eritrean plateau. Each family was provided with twenty to twenty-five hectares of land, agricultural implements, cattle, and enough provisions to tide them over until their first crop. The families were expected to repay these advances, the equivalent of a four thousand lire loan, at 3 percent interest. After five years, if the families cultivated the land, they would receive title to it.

The fate of these colonization projects is clear from the 1905 census in Eritrea. As an outlet for emigration, the colony was not very successful.[37] Between 1890 and 1905 an estimated 8.5 million Italians emigrated. Yet the European population of Eritrea totaled 3,949. As an agricultural colony, the experiments were also a disappointment. Of the 1,617 European males in the colony, only 62 classified themselves as agriculturalists. Of the rest, more than half were related to the military. The dream of the small farmer's paradise also evaporated as the area under cultivation slowly declined. In 1902 there were 126 colonists, of whom only 36 cultivated more than 5 hectares. By 1913 the total area under cultivation had declined from 1,524 hectares to 1,146 hectares and the number of colonists had slumped to 61.

What went wrong with the colonization in Eritrea? A host of troubles, common to most such colonization projects, troubles that also appeared later in Libya, combined to thwart this first major attempt by the Italians to establish an emigrant's paradise in Africa. First, there was a confused and misguided land policy. Land on the plateau appeared to be plentiful only because the local populations had temporarily abandoned the area in 1890 after a series of local wars, famines, and epidemics. When the Eritreans drifted back to their lands, they clashed with the colonists. Until the Italians made themselves masters of Ethiopia and Eritrea, the colonists feared for their security. The Italian disaster at Adowa was scarcely a reassuring sign. Some families repatriated in fear and discouragement, and the remaining colonists had little confidence in their future.

Administrative confusion and incompetence compounded the colonists' problems. Baron Franchetti was constantly at odds with the colonial administration, especially General Baratieri, the governor of the colony.[38] In 1895 Franchetti finally resigned his post as head of the colonization.

Mistakes in planning the settlements plagued the colonists. Often there was an acute shortage of supplies. In some areas drinking water was not available and had to be shipped from Naples on special boats. The colonizing families had been poorly selected in some cases. Factory workers from Milan with no experience in farming, old persons too inflexible to change their patterns of life, and families from rival regions in Italy all contributed to a confused sense of purpose and to low morale. Another discouraging factor was the isolation of the plateau and the poor communications with Massawa. Without easy access to markets, the colonists could not sell their products.

A number of the colonists abandoned their land and went to work for the government at wages that were higher than their anticipated earnings from the land. Finally, with Franchetti's resignation, the state's subsidies to attract colonists were cut off. The government warned that the cost of establishing an average family would range between 2,500 and 3,500 lire. The government would do no more than provide temporary lodging. In short, the prospective family was invited to spend 2,500 or more lire with very uncertain future prospects. As one anonymous critic commented:

What farmer in Italy possessing such a sum would decide to emigrate? And if he did, would he wish to risk his life and savings in a country where the results of European farming were still unknown? Would he not prefer to go elsewhere?[39]

Although Eritrea was a long-term failure in terms of the numbers of emigrants who settled there, the experience proved to be an important benefit for the colonialist movement. The experiments in land colonization won over a number of influential anticolonialists to the African cause. Among them were two future foreign ministers, the Marquis Antonino di San Giuliano and Baron Sidney Sonnino.[40] A third important convert was the writer and politician Ferdinando Martini, who later served as governor of Eritrea and then briefly as colonial minister. Together with Franchetti, these men constituted an important lobby in Parliament and at court in favor of colonial expansion.

The four men shared similar backgrounds and a number of common experiences and political views. All were members of Parliament. All had been strongly opposed to Italian involvement in Africa. All had favored unrestricted emigration. Martini and di San Giuliano had been won over in 1891 to the colonial cause after serving on the parliamentary committee looking into the Eritrea colony's affairs. Franchetti and Sonnino, like Martini, were Tuscans, and di San Giuliano was a Sicilian. Except for Martini, all were large landowners. All four had studied the problems of emigration and the "Southern question." By background and by temperament, Franchetti, di San Giuliano, and Sonnino were agrarian conservatives. For them the solution to Italy's social problems lay in awakening the consciences of their peers to the need for agrarian reform. Implicit in this approach was a suspicion of industrial development. As wealthy landowners and members of Italy's ruling elite, they favored an enlightened and benevolent paternalism to the specter of socialism. In their view, the experiences of Britain, France, and Germany had shown that with the development of industry the old order could not prevail. With these thoughts in mind they turned to imperial expansion as a solution to Italy's social problems.

What they had glimpsed in Eritrea was a new vision of colonies. The colonization experiments had shown that East Africa need not be simply a source of futile and expensive military adventures. With careful planning the region could become an important asset. As di San Giuliano remarked, Italy needed an empire suitable to her development. The nation's chief export was not capital but peasants.[41] Thus agricultural colonies seemed to meet Italy's needs. Finally, as diplomats and patriots who believed in Italy's future as a great power, these men looked with favor on the creation of a *magna Italia* in Africa.

Italian Colonialism after Adowa: The Coming of the Libyan War

In the aftermath of Adowa and of Crispi's downfall, Italy retreated momentarily from her expansionist course. In Parliament the Ethiopian emperor was cheered with cries of "Viva Menelik," and a petition bearing 91,490 names calling for withdrawal from Africa was presented.[42] Nevertheless, colonialism was far from a dead issue. Scarcely fifteen years later the nation was once again in a frenzy. This time the issue was the conquest of Libya, and this time, in contrast to similar occasions in the past, the nation seemed to give overwhelming support to the enterprise.

Among the factors that contributed to the revival of the colonialist movement and a favorable attitude toward overseas expansion was a Giolittian decade of unprecedented peace and prosperity.[43] During the first decade of the new century, Italy blossomed both materially and spiritually. But with this progress came a sharpening of social tensions. As Giolitti understood clearly, a host of new social and political forces were emerging during the nation's rapid development, forces that threatened to upset the primacy of the bourgeoisie that had ruled Italy since unification. Giolitti planned to meet the challenge through a program of moderate reform. He hoped that his social welfare and electoral reform measures would win over the working class, the Catholics, and the Socialists. Opposed to the Giolittian system was an array of landowners, business elite, and nationalists. The anti-Giolittian forces were angry and were contemptuous of Giolitti's welfare "socialism," his seemingly unprincipled pragmatism, and his unconcern with Italy's status as a great power. For them the challenge of the new forces should be met not by reform and integration but by exclusion. In their opinion, a powerful and authoritarian state should keep order at home and make Italy respected overseas.

In this context of struggle against the Giolittian system, the old colonialist forces launched into new activities. The geographical societies, the Naval League, the Dante Alighieri Society all took on new life. In 1906 the Italian Colonial Institute was created with government subsidies. A series of congresses spread the colonialist theme. Prominent in the leadership of these groups were the agrarian conservative "converts" to colonialism from the early days of the Eritrean colony. Among the members of the governing board of the Italian Colonial Institute, for instance, were the Marquis di San Giuliano, Baron Sidney Sonnino, and Baron Franchetti.

The expansionist cause gained much impetus and publicity through the literary movements of the period.[44] Italy's status as a great power became a major theme in a cultural revolt against the cautious, modest *Italietta* that had emerged from the Risorgimento.[45] Poets like Carducci, d'Annunzio, and Pascoli, and minor literary figures like Oriani and Corradini, revived the great myth of the Roman past and recalled the high hopes for the "Third Italy" that had inspired the Risorgimento. If the Third Italy persisted on its prosaic and dreary path, then they favored the creation of a Fourth Italy.

The Nationalists, one of the most influential forces in the revival of

Italian expansionist aspirations, originated as a literary movement at the turn of the century. In magazines like *Il Regno* and *Leonardo*, men like Enrico Corradini, Giuseppe Prezzolini, and Giovanni Papini expressed the sentiments of a generation revolted by Positivism, shamed by Adowa, and dazzled by the works of d'Annunzio. Luigi Federzoni, a disciple of Corradini and a future minister of colonies under Fascism, wrote of Corradini that his vocation was "the reaction to Adowa, the revenge for Adowa."[46] Of the Risorgimento, the Nationalists remembered only Italy's hopes for becoming a great power and a world leader and recalled nothing of the movement's Liberal ideals.

The literary revolt gradually began to take on political substance in 1910 when the Nationalists held their first national congress. Even then the adherents were a highly heterogeneous group of syndicalists, irredentists and imperialists. Only after a series of congresses in 1912 and 1914 did a clearly defined ideology emerge, a program which favored a powerful, authoritarian state and expansion abroad. From the Nationalists, Fascism borrowed generously for its expansionist program, its rhetoric, and even its personnel.[47] For example, the Fascist image of the "proletarian nation" and the exaltation of war as a path to greatness were concepts and slogans popularized by the Nationalists.

The Nationalists made the emigration problem one of their major themes.[48] Despite the new opportunities emerging in Italy, emigrants were leaving in greater numbers than ever before. Even some members of the Left now began to look favorably on possible African solutions to Italy's emigration problems.[49] For the Nationalists, emigration was a shame and a disgrace. Enrico Corradini, one of the Nationalists' best-known ideologists, visited Italian communities in Tunis, the United States, and South America. For him, emigration was a phenomenon "if not of an inferior people, at least of a people at an inferior stage of existence."[50] Far from being a necessary evil, for Corradini emigration was no more beneficent than death.

Italy's condition, Corradini wrote, could be remedied only in one way: only when the spirit of emigration had been converted to the spirit of colonialism and imperialism would the Italians be a great people.[51] Corradini distinguished himself from an older generation of colonialists such as Ferdinando Martini, who, on the basis of his own visit to Argentina, was content to limit colonial policy to improving conditions in "free colonies." For a nation of emigrants, Corradini argued, "free colonies" were neither "free" nor "colonies": they were a form of subjection. For Corradini, only when Italy acquired colonies under her own direct sovereignty would the nation emerge from an "inferior stage of emigration" to a genuine "superior stage of colonization."

Corradini synthesized his ideas in his theory of the "proletarian nation," which he presented to the first Nationalist congress in 1910. Corradini combined his hatred for socialism and class warfare with his aspirations for Italy's status as a great power in a theory that turned Socialist doctrine on its head:

Our point of departure should be this: there are proletarian nations just as there are proletarian classes—nations, that is to say, whose standards of living are immeasurably lower than those of other nations. . . . As Socialism teaches the proletariat the value of class struggle so must we teach Italy the value of international struggle. . . . If the international struggle means war—then let there be war.[52]

With his slogan of Italy as a proletarian nation, Corradini gave a powerful new ideological impetus to the Italian colonialist tradition which emphasized the nation's right to empire in order to fulfill her demographic needs. For Corradini—and for much of Italy—the conquest of Libya was to be the first major test of Italy's revived expansionist spirit after Adowa.

In the campaign to justify the war, to arouse the nation to conquest, the demographic theme played a major role. Corradini and the Nationalists—but also many of the Giolittian papers—predicted that Libya would become the long-awaited *terra promessa*, the promised land for emigrants in Africa. Only a tiny minority of dissenters resisted the nation's expansionist euphoria and challenged these rash predictions.

2

Libya and the Demographic Myth

"La grande Proletaria si è mossa"

As Gaetano Salvemini, the maverick Socialist, remarked in 1911, Libya had been an idée fixe in Italy for almost three decades.[1] Italy began coveting Libya in 1881 as a "consolation prize" for the loss of Tunisia to the French. However, for two decades Italy took no diplomatic steps to secure the Turkish possession for the Italian sphere.[2] In 1905, alarmed by British and French penetration of the Libyan hinterland and by possible German competition in Tripoli, the Italians initiated a policy of peaceful economic penetration. Under the leadership of the Banco di Roma, which had a branch in Constantinople and close ties with the Vatican, Italy began to build a network of banking, shipping, and agricultural enterprises.[3] Pressures for government action mounted as Italian business interests encountered opposition from the Turkish government. The Bosnian crisis and then, more immediately, the French penetration of Morocco and the Agadir incident inflamed public opinion. Despite her diplomatic hold on Libya, Italy could no longer afford to waver in the face of possible French and German rivalry. Many agreed with the journalist and politician Andrea Torre, who commented that if Italy lost Libya, her prestige would be reduced to that of a "maritime Switzerland."[4]

Because the Libyan conquest had been a national idée fixe for so long, when the time came for action in the summer of 1911, the expansionist majority followed no particular party or sectional lines. Left and Right, Republicans and Catholics, Nationalists and Socialists, North and South all contributed to the enthusiastic majority who favored conquest.[5] Among the Socialists, for instance, the reformist wing led by Bissolati and Bonomi favored the Libyan conquest and argued that showing solidarity with the nation helped reinforce class solidarity. They were joined by revolutionary syndicalists like Arturo Labriola, Paolo Orano, and Angiolo Olivetti, who hoped that the war would awaken the Italian proletariat and prepare them for the revolutionary struggle by teaching them how to fight. The Sicilian Socialist Giuseppe De Felice Giufridda favored the Libyan war for the sake of his native island. In De Felice's view, with Libya as part of Italy, Sicily would be transformed from a national appendage to a vital internal commercial link. Salvatore Barzilai, a Republican, favored the conquest for a number of reasons ranging from political-diplomatic considerations to the importance of the conquest for forging a national conscience. Many moderate Catholics, too, favored the Libyan enterprise out of religious and patriotic convictions. Even Don Luigi Sturzo, the future leader of the *Popolari,* viewed Libya with a certain optimism as a solution to the problem of the *mezzogiorno.*

Each group, however, also had its minority of dissidents. The extreme left wing of the Socialists, including Lazzari, Mussolini, De Ambris, and Corridoni, opposed the war, gained control of the party, and eventually expelled the reformists and war sympathizers. The Catholic conservatives hoped that the war would weaken the Italian secular state. Even the Nationalists were split between those who favored the Libyan conquest and those who feared that it might detract from the battle to reclaim the *terre irredente.*

The poet Giovanni Pascoli, in his famous oration "La grande Proletaria si è mossa" (the great proletariat has stirred), summed up the mood of the expansionist majority.[6] The speech, which the poet delivered at Barga on 26 November 1911, about two months after hostilities had begun, had a special meaning for the nation, for Pascoli was the successor to Carducci as Italy's *vate,* the secular guardian of the nation's ideals and aspirations. Speaking in this role, Pascoli dedicated his oration to the dead and wounded who had sacrificed themselves in the Libyan campaign.

The poet touched on the major themes which the expansionists invoked to justify the war: the humiliations of emigration; Libya's potential as a fruitful colony and a population outlet; Italy's legal-historical right—as a successor to the Roman Empire—to Libya; Italy's aspirations as a great power; the war as a test of national unity.

Pascoli began by summarizing the frustrations and humiliations of the emigrants who journeyed beyond the Alps and the oceans to furnish labor to the world. In a long catalog, the poet recited the feats of Italian emigrant labor. They had "built cities where once there had been virgin forest" and had "planted vineyards in the desert." Yet the world showed little gratitude. The emigrants were treated badly, paid poorly, and dismissed as "Carcamanos! Gringos! Cincali! Degos!" In America, these countrymen of Columbus were treated no better than the Negroes and suffered the same lynchings.

Now, however, in Libya the Great Proletariat had found a solution for the emigrants, the poet proclaimed. Pascoli pictured the future colony as a vast region which at one time, thanks to the work of Italy's Roman forebears, had been "abundant with water and crops and green with trees and gardens." For some time now, because of the "inertia of the nomadic and slothful population," the land had become in large part a desert. Yet in Pascoli's vision the emigrants would soon turn the colony into "a continuation of their native land." They would build roads, till the fields, erect houses and ports, "always seeing our tricolor on high, stirred by the immense throbbing of our sea."

What right did the Italians have to this land? All men, Pascoli argued, have the right to feed and clothe themselves with the products of the land they work. But the nomadic Libyans, he claimed, were:

creatures who sequester for themselves and leave uncultivated land that is necessary to all mankind.

To this Libyan soil, "so ignobly subtracted from the world," the Italians had a right because of their geographical proximity and because of their Roman heritage. "We were there already," Pascoli asserted,

we left signs that not even the Berbers, the Bedouins and the Turks could erase; signs of our humanity and civilization, signs...that we are not Berbers, Bedouins and Turks. We are returning.

For Pascoli the war was also justified in view of Italy's civilizing mission, "her duty to contribute her share to the humanization [umanamento] and civilization of peoples." He sounded a slogan that was later so dear to Fascist imperial thinking: Italy's right "not to be suffocated and blocked in her seas." He praised the virtues of the military as a school for valor and duty, and he concluded on the great theme of unity. Fifty years earlier Massimo D'Azeglio had commented, "Now that Italy has been made, we must make Italians." For Pascoli, the nation's response to the Libyan war had proved that at last—even sooner than the leaders of the Risorgimento had anticipated—"Italians, too, have been created."

Thus, as Benedetto Croce pointed out, "sentimental reasons" played a major role in arousing the nation to conquest.[7] The Libyan war, coming as it did on the fiftieth anniversary of unification, was a kind of national initiation rite.[8] Victory in Libya would exorcise the fears of two generations of Italians who had worried over the nation's strength and unity. For years Italian patriots had been embarrassed by the dubious military tradition of the Risorgimento and the disaster at Adowa.[9] The nation had also fretted about Italy's cautious and uneasy international alliances. A victory in Libya, without the benefit of external help, would prove the valor of Italian arms and the nation's independence as a great power. For many Italians still concerned at the regional and cultural divisions within the country, a victory in Libya would prove that Italy was a nation at last. As Giustino Fortunato, the great student of the "Southern question," remarked with joy, the war showed how much things had changed from the days of his youth: peasants from the Basilicata and Puglie now fought together and considered themselves Italians.[10]

Libya's Future: "La Terra Promessa"

Giolitti, prosaic and pragmatic as always, showed no enthusiasm for the rhetoric of the expansionists.[11] As the Nationalists complained bitterly, Giolitti was not in the least excited by the prospects of the war. His primary concern always remained domestic politics. Eventually, however, because of what he later termed "historical inevitability" (*fatalità storica*) he knew that he would have to find a solution to the Libyan problem. The nation, flushed with pride at the progress made in the fifty years since unification, would not have tolerated seeing Libya go the way of Tunisia. Yet even after the war began, in the same speech in Turin in which he spoke of the *"fatalità storica,"* he expressed the hope that foreign policy would have no influence on internal politics, except if possible to speed internal reform.

Thus, during the press campaign that prepared the nation for war, the Giolittian papers showed a certain prudence as well as enthusiasm.[12] In the columns of the pro-Giolittian *La Tribuna* and *La Stampa,* prominent scholars like the ancient historian Guglielmo Ferrero and the sociologist Gaetano Mosca analyzed the potential benefits that Libya might offer Italy. At the same time, reflecting Giolitti's cautious approach, Ferrero and Mosca warned of the difficulties and dangers of colonial enterprises. Ferrero, for instance, predicted that in the future Africa was destined to become "the great reserve and the great colony of Europe."[13] In particular, European Mediterranean nations were likely to be most influenced by the North African territories that had once been under Roman dominion, he claimed. Certainly a Mediterranean nation like Italy had the "duty to face the risks and the right to enjoy the benefits" of colonizing these territories. Yet Ferrero warned that the benefits might be a long time in coming. In colonial matters, "one generation sows and another reaps," he wrote, and he concluded that colonies offered "neither marvels nor miracles."[14]

On one theme of the press campaign, however, there was little restraint: the promise of Libya as a land of "Bengodi"—an El Dorado for Italian emigrants.[15] It was more than coincidence that the Giolittian papers sent correspondents to Libya who had a reputation for being experts on the problems of emigration. Giuseppe Bevione, for instance, the correspondent for *La Stampa*, had written articles on Italian emigration to Argentina. He assured his readers that there was plenty of water in Libya for future colonization, since the water "extended in an uninterrupted layer from the mountains to the sea" at no more than one or two meters below the surface.[16] In a dispatch from Derna in Cyrenaica, he pictured the land as a cornucopia in which palm trees, fig trees, citrus fruits, and banana plants spilled over the garden walls "like a full-bodied wine" overflows "the rim of the glass."[17]

Giuseppe Piazza, who wrote for *La Tribuna*, had also described the problems of South American emigration. Piazza delivered the most memorable evaluations of Libya's future demographic potential. For him, the new conquest was nothing less than *la terra promessa* (the promised land)—the title under which he published his collected articles on Libya.[18] Regrets and recriminations over Tunisia, which was flourishing brilliantly, thanks to Italian labor, were useless, Piazza wrote. Next door there was still a great destiny in store for Italian farmers. In his opinion, agriculture was Libya's chief resource, the one most worth developing. To colonize, "that is to populate and to cultivate," was to reach the "marrow" of the territory. He warned that until large numbers of Italians emigrated to Libya the land would never be Italian except in name, "a name written on the sand dunes that a gust of wind could erase at any moment."[19] In a classic passage dealing with the indigenous populations, Piazza described them as "kindly, peaceful, friendly." "The hostility of the Arabs is a Turkish fable," he wrote.[20]

When the Nationalists joined the campaign with the first issue of the *Idea Nazionale*, they too stressed Libya's potential riches and her promise as a population outlet. Corradini, who had been touring the country giving speeches on the theme, "Proletariato, emigrazione, Tripolitania" (the proletariat, emigration, Tripolitania), claimed that "millions of men could live happily" in Libya.[21] He described the climate as "very healthful," with temperatures similar to those in Sicily.[22] As for riches, Corradini said that Tripolitania was covered with three million date palms (Bevione had claimed only two million). He pictured Cyrenaica as a land of abundant underground water, a region covered with fields of wheat and barley, forests and pastures. Minerals such as sulfur and phosphates were plentiful. "These two regions, Tripolitania and Cyrenaica, are all that remains to us as heirs of the empire which Rome established on the African coast," Corradini argued.[23] He concluded that only "Turkish barbarism" barred the way to a promised land.

Foreign correspondents remarked on the nation's euphoria. "At the time of the conquest, Libya was considered by all Italians as an earthly paradise," wrote a French observer.[24] Another French writer spoke of the Italian image of Tripoli as "a land of dreams" where work would be paid according to its true value.[25]

Some observers shared Italy's optimism about her new colony's future. As a correspondent for an American magazine wrote, "desert" was not synonymous with "worthless."[26] What the French and British had accomplished in their North African colonies could also be achieved by the Italians—especially since the French agricultural triumph in Tunisia depended so heavily on the Sicilian immigrants, he reasoned. Anyone who had seen the vineyards of Capri or the farm-steads of Calabria knew the patience and tenacity of the Italian peasantry. Thus Libya's potential lay not with "government railways and subsidized steamship lines and regiments of brass-bound officials" but with "patient, painstaking, plodding men with artesian well drilling machines and steam plows and barrels of fertilizer."[27]

Libya's Future: Some Dissenting Views

All in all, the press campaign, combined with a flood of travel books, monographs, articles, and pamphlets urging Italian expansion and promising rich rewards, proved highly successful. The opposition was scattered and attracted few followers. As Salvemini worried in the introduction to *Come siamo andati in Libia*, a collection of essays intended to counter the flood of expansionist rhetoric, future gener-ations would no doubt wonder if everyone was taken in by the tall tales and lies of the newspapers. He concluded that the answer "will not be very flattering to our generation."[28]

Perhaps the voices of those opposed to the Libyan enterprise were not as loud as those of the expansionists.[29] Nevertheless, those willing to listen heard some of Italy's leading intellectuals from all sides of the political spectrum reply with wit and irony to the expansionist argu-ments. Robert Michels, a sociologist with socialist sympathies, and Napoleone Colajanni, a politician and journalist who had served with Garibaldi, ridiculed the legal-historical argument that the Roman occupation had given Italy a "right" to Libya. Why shouldn't Italy claim old Roman territories from England to Turkey? What if other countries decided to claim these "rights"?[30] What if the French demanded parts of Sicily on the grounds that France, with the occupation of Tunisia, assumed the claims of the old Carthaginian empire? Arcangelo Ghisleri, a geographer and a staunch Republican, wondered why Italy should ignore her Mazzinian heritage—her mission to defend a people's right to self-determination—when it came to discussing Arab rights in Libya. As for Italy's civilizing mission, a socialist organizer from the Abruzzi pointed to the misery of the peasants in his region and asked how Italians could presume to teach "civilization" to the Arabs of Libya. Other critics were skeptical that the imperialism of Corradini's proletarian nation would turn out differently from any other kind of imperialism. More than likely, the critics argued, the Italian proletariat would shed blood and sweat to conquer and develop the colony—ultimately for the benefit of the capitalists. As the journalist Luigi Barzini reminded the nation in a dispatch from Calabria, the peasants of the South, the proletariat who were nominally to be beneficiaries of the victory, were so alienated from the government, so oblivious of official Italy, that they seemed to belong to another race and another epoch. Of the war, of the new colony, they understood nothing.[31]

Given their rhetorical nature, demolishing the moral and legal arguments of the expansionists was a relatively easy task. The opposition, however, also showed much insight in assessing Libya's practical value as a colony for Italy. At the time of the conquest Libya was largely unknown to Europeans except for the scattered reports of travelers. Nevertheless, enough information was available to an inquisitive and critical investigator to suggest the dubiousness of the colony's future as a *terra promessa*. Leone Caetani, a Roman landowner and renowned Oriental scholar, minced no words before the Chamber of Deputies during a debate over the Foreign Ministry's budget in June 1911.[32] For reasons which Caetani found "incomprehensible," Italy wanted to occupy Tripolitania. As a result, the nation would have "to lavish incalculable millions in military operations" and then invest many more millions in building the colony. As Caetani pointed out,

This country [Tripolitania] has no roads, no ports, no railroads, no buildings, nothing, nothing, nothing!

Even after these heavy investments, as Salvemini, Mosca, Einaudi, and others argued in great detail, the new colony would not have any real economic or military-strategic importance for the mother country. Libya could offer neither mineral wealth nor new markets nor important trade benefits. Even as a population colony, as an outlet for emigration, the region was a poor prospect.

What, for instance, Salvemini wanted to know, was Libya's contribution to Italy's military security?[33] The expansionists alluded to a potential threat to the *mezzogiorno* if an enemy nation were to occupy Libya. Why was the occupation of Libya any more of a threat to national security than the French bases at Bizerte or the English positions at Malta? Salvemini argued that for Italy the acquisition of Libya simply meant adding another long coastline to defend in addition to the peninsula. He also pointed out that Italy would have to scatter troops in the colony at the expense of the garrisons at home—and ultimately he believed that the fate of the colonies would be decided not in Africa but in Europe.

Libya's future riches were also an illusion, the critics argued. The area's potential as a trade center seemed remote. The Lombard patriot and explorer Manfredo Camperio (1826–99) had predicted a brilliant future for Tripoli as an outlet for the trans-Saharan trade.[34] Camperio made trips to Tripolitania in 1879 and to Cyrenaica in 1881 and returned with the conviction that "whoever possesses these lands will dominate the trade from the Sudan."[35] By the turn of the century, however, Camperio's predictions were far from being realized. As Augusto Medana, the Italian consul at Tripoli, reported, trans-Saharan trade was on the decline, a victim of British and French partitions of the hinterland, shifting trade routes, and the Italian colony's own lack of initiative.[36] Not only was the trans-Saharan trade declining, Medana reported, but the total volume of trade had decreased during the years 1899–1902. Despite the large and influential Italian community in Tripoli, Italy was well behind Great Britain, France, Austria-Hungary, and Turkey in terms of trade volume with Tripoli. By 1910 the Italians, through a determined effort, had increased their share of Libya's international trade from one-twentieth to somewhere between one-third and one-half, Einaudi pointed out.[37] However, the total volume of Libya's trade was steadily diminishing. The Libyans would have to increase their trade volume from eight to fifteen times to reach Italian levels, and Italian levels were far from impressive.

At the time of the Libyan war there was still much talk of reviving the trade through the construction of railroads. A Tripoli-Kano route might revive trans-Saharan commerce; or a Cairo-Tripoli line might capture the Indian trade, it was said. Such schemes were little more than fantasies, as Mosca pointed out.[38] In the first place, the technical difficulties of a trans-Saharan link were enormous. Besides, if such a railway were feasible, why hadn't the French built one to link their West African colonies with Algeria? The Cairo-Tripoli line to carry traffic from India seemed equally preposterous. Why should the line end at Tripoli? Why, Mosca wondered, shouldn't it extend as far as Tunis, a natural shipping point to Marseilles?

Libya as a market for Italian products did not seem at all promising. Libya had little to offer beyond the products of her primitive agriculture. To Italy she exported eggs, dates, hides, and other agricultural by-products. To England, Libya exported barley and sparto grass. In turn, the Libyans bought cottons, cheap silks, and flour. Robert Michels speculated—without much conviction—that the Libyan market for cheap cottons might be developed in the same way that India became a vast outlet for Lancashire cottons.[39] Few shared even this faint hope. Mosca dismissed the Libyan market as one that would always remain secondary for Italy, even in the best of circumstances.

The prospect of developing any industries also appeared remote, according to the critics. The country offered neither fuel nor water power. As for mineral resources, Mosca commented laconically, "There is little to be said about the mines of Tripolitania because very little is known for certain."[40] Traces of various minerals had been reported, including deposits of sulfur in the Sirte. Yet the possibilities for commercial development were unpromising. In any case, the sulfur would have offered disastrous competition to the mines in Sicily, Einaudi pointed out.[41] In his view, the discovery of phosphates for agricultural purposes would prove far more beneficial. Yet even phosphates would face enormous competition, since there were no shortages on the world market.

Even if Libya had had great economic potential, where would the enormous investments needed to develop the colony come from? Despite the Turkish policy of minimal development, the colony was still probably a drain on the Ottoman treasury, Einaudi speculated.[42] If the Italian government were to limit its investments to building an infrastructure, schools and administration—and if it avoided "follies" such as subsidizing colonization and agriculture—the colony would not begin to pay for itself for at least three decades.

Yet, who, if not the state, would invest in Libya? Einaudi warned that Italy's savings barely covered the needs of domestic agriculture and industry. He was in favor of inviting French capital to help develop the colony. Salvemini painted a gloomy picture of the business abilities of Italian capitalists.[43] They had neither the means, the skills, nor the interest to compete with foreign investments. Italian businessmen ignored quality controls and did not study local consumer patterns and tastes. They did not pay attention to the advice of local consuls. If Italian business had been serious about developing Libya, Salvemini wrote, then Italy would have become first in volume of commerce while the area was still a Turkish colony. For him, the real meaning of the Libyan war was that businessmen wanted state protection. The Libyan enterprise, he complained, once again revealed the old Italian vice of "not knowing how to do anything without the help of the state."[44]

As for the great hope that Libya would turn out to be a major demographic outlet and an important agricultural colony, the critics were equally pessimistic. In the first place, the physical environment was forbidding. The example of classical antiquity was totally misleading, Salvemini pointed out. Classical authors were not always acute observers, and they sometimes became carried away with their rhetoric. The most recent advances in archaeology indicated that classical times, far from being a golden age, were not too different from the present. Nor did the analogy with Tunisia hold.[45] One did not need to be an agricultural expert to see that the climatic parallel was only approximate. Libya was considerably farther south than Tunisia or Sicily, and Tripolitania's summer droughts in particular were likely to be much worse. *La Voce*, which had consistently opposed the war and warned that Libya had no future as an important population outlet, cited a report of the Jewish Territorial Organization which rejected Cyrenaica as a suitable area for Jewish colonization because of a lack of adequate water.[46]

Critics like Einaudi contrasted Libya with conditions in the United States, Canada, and Argentina, which had successfully absorbed mass emigration.[47] Libya's potential as a population colony, according to Einaudi, was severely limited by the availability of land. The colony was already well populated in the areas that were best suited for agricultural development. Furthermore, in Einaudi's view the type of agriculture that flourished in Libya—small, intensive plots centered around oases—required considerable capital and patience. By contrast, in the United States, Canada and Argentina the colonist could count on successful wheat harvests thanks to the rich, deep virgin soil. In a few years the colonist, who perhaps began his career as a day laborer, could accumulate enough capital to buy his own land, Einaudi said. Tripolitania, on the other hand, would have to rely for its development on the olive and the vine—cultures that took a long time to reach maturity. Einaudi ridiculed the hope of raising wheat in such a climate. He challenged Bevione's claims that Tripolitania might follow the path of Tunisia in raising wheat. According to Einaudi, far from the "incredible yields" Bevione claimed, the actual yield per hectare of wheat in Tunisia was much lower than the average yield of the poorest area in Italy.

Thus Libya could never replace America as a promised land for the poor emigrant, Einaudi affirmed. Libya's colonists would need suffic- ient capital to invest in the vineyards and olives and to support themselves until the trees reached maturity. Salvemini, writing in 1913, pointed to emigrant reaction to Libya: the war, far from attracting emigrants to the colony, had resulted in increased emigration abroad. However painful it might be to the naive and ingenuous, he concluded, it was necessary to "abandon the illusion that Libya will now, later, or ever attract a notable mass of emigrants.[48]

Both Salvemini and Einaudi anticipated the argument that if colonists did not flow to Libya on their own accord, they could be induced to emigrate to the colony if the state would finance them. Already, Einaudi pointed out, the newspapers carried stories implying that "the providential help of the state won't be lacking" in Libya.[49] In Einaudi's view such programs of subsidies and credits could lead only to waste, as the French example of state colonization in Algeria indicated. Salvemini, too, warned that government-aided colonization would not resolve the problem of attracting colonists. "Grandiose public works projects" and "more or less forced state colonization" would lead only to an "artificial agglomeration of immigrants to whom the government would be forced to give work even when there was no longer any."[50]

If, then, the occupation of Libya could not be defended on any military-strategic or economic grounds, what was to be done? What possible benefits could there be? For Salvemini, the best that could be done now would be for the nation to cut its losses through a program of minimum development. The government should not spend a cent for capital improvements. Let private enterprise build the roads, railroads, and harbors. In his view the Italians should remain on the coast and eventually win over the tribes of the interior by controlling the trade through the ports. "Our feeling of national solidarity does not extend beyond the borders of our country and the needs of our countrymen," he wrote.[51] To the Nationalists he left the folly of "loving the Berbers of Tripoli more than their Italian brothers."

Despite their often scathing attacks on the Libyan enterprise, the critics were also patriots, despondent at seeing the nation involve itself in such follies. Thus the majority ultimately gave grudging approval to the conquest and desperately searched for some positive benefits that Italy might derive from the undertaking. Einaudi tried to comfort himself with the notion that Italy would spread civilization, that she would stimulate "the hidden energies of primitive peoples" and prepare "the political greatness if not the future wealth of our grandchildren."[52] Giustino Fortunato, the famous *meridionalista*, wrote, "Who more than I [is] convinced that Tripoli will be a fruitless and expensive undertaking, even though necessary and inevitable?" In spite of this, he was willing to cry *viva la guerra* if the Libyan war meant that after fifty years of national life "something new, beautiful, and promising" was stirring in the nation.[53] Salvemini, too, hoped for some national moral benefit. Perhaps, he speculated, the war would help cure Italy's "perpetual ignorance and thoughtlessness."[54] He hoped that perhaps the campaign would instill in Italians "a greater seriousness of purpose, a better sense of discipline so that future adventures like Libya might be avoided."

Yet some critics did not even cling to vague hopes of a moral resurrection for Italy. Ghisleri commented that "This war over Tripoli has been more devastating—morally—than an invasion of barbarians."[55] Another critic, the economist Edoardo Giretti, in answer to Einaudi's hopes that Italy meant to spread civilization in Libya, saw the war as simply a revival of "the least noble instincts of the Italian people."[56] Salvemini cited a speech in which a deputy paralleled the Libyan adventure to the "blindness" that had led to Italy's earlier involvement in East Africa. Significantly, the speech concluded that the nation should turn away from its "empty dreams of great power."[57]

For the three decades of Italian occupation following the conquest, Italy's policymakers thrashed over the problems and issues raised at the time of the Libyan war. Like Salvemini and his allies, a later generation of the more level-headed agricultural experts, colonial officials, and politicians warned against overestimating Libya's real geographical and economic possibilities. They too listed the factors which would prevent "beautiful Tripoli" from becoming another "America"—as a peasant from the Puglie had so confidently predicted at the time of the Libyan war.[58] They too spoke of the dangers of initiating a "proletarian" colonization at state expense. This later generation learned—as Salvemini and his allies had learned before them—that their ideas were generally discarded in favor of policies based on political expediency and propaganda effect. The objections and warnings of the critics were almost irrelevant to a regime bent on grandeur and conquest as ends in themselves.

Already at the time of the Libyan war, there were expansionists like Corradini, who in moments of candor admitted that the entire discussion about Libya's material value was superfluous. To make the olive trees and the oases flourish would be "our great work in this century and their fruits will be our reward," he wrote.[59] But he also said, "to cross the sea would be a duty for us, even if it were to be a [material] sacrifice."[60] Carlo Galli, the last Italian consul in Tripoli, also saw the

colonization as the first step in a broadly expansionist program. With
the Libyan war, he remarked with satisfaction, Italy had opened "a
window in the wall" opposite Sicily, a wall that threatened Italy with
"suffocation."[61] Whether or not this first breach in the wall would lead
to additional space for Italy's expansive powers remained to be seen.
His hopes for further expansion were unequivocal: "We wish it, believe
in it, are certain that it will come."[62] In the meantime, Italy must wait
and work to settle the new colony. Perhaps the colonization would take
hundreds of millions of lire and several decades, but the result would
be certain. Beyond the Sea of Sicily, the little white houses of the
emigrants would form a new Italian region, an extension of Sicily.
Joyfully he concluded that the "fourth Italy of our youthful dreams"
was beginning.

II. Building the Fourth Shore

3

The Volpi Era:
Colonization and Capitalism

The "Mediocre Bargain": Libya's Geographical and Historical Heritage

Italy found herself in the position of "having to put up with a mediocre bargain to avoid a mediocre image," Gaetano Mosca concluded about the Libyan War.[1] At best, Mosca's assessment was generous, for Italy's military and diplomatic status was scarcely enhanced by the North African conquest, and Libya's geography and history promised little in the way of present or even future economic rewards.

From a military and diplomatic aspect, the conquest of Libya turned out to be far more complicated and expensive than Italy had anticipated. The "military stroll" that had been predicted in the press became a long march extending over three decades.[2] Like many of Libya's previous conquerors, the Italians managed to control little more than the coastal towns by the time peace was made with the Turks at Ouchy in 1912. Accords with the Ottoman empire, of course, did not mean peace or authority over the indigenous peoples of the interior. That struggle was resolved only in 1932 after nearly twenty years of guerrilla war, interrupted by temporary treaties and truces. In the meantime, the costs of the original war with the Turks proved to be a severe financial strain.[3] Most humiliating of all for the Italians, the great powers were more annoyed at the potentially explosive diplomatic repercussions of Italy's actions than impressed by her victory over the declining Ottoman empire.[4]

If the acquisition of Libya did little for Italy's diplomatic and military image, the new colony offered even fewer economic rewards. The Italians became masters of a vast, impoverished, thinly populated region inhabited largely by nomads who eked out a precarious existence by following their flocks.

The present Libyan state, which is slightly smaller than the Ottoman territories the Italians annexed in 1912, encompasses nearly 1.8 million square kilometers and ranks as the fourth largest country in Africa.[5] More than 90 percent of this vast territory is desert, and the majority of the population lives along the northern coast on less than three percent of the country's total area. This northern coastal strip was the only region of interest to the Italians. They had no hope of developing the deserts of the interior region known as the Fezzan.

Geographically and climatically the northern coastal area falls into two distinct zones separated by one of the world's most formidable natural barriers, the Sirte desert. The western half of Libya, Tripolitania, is part of Africa; the eastern half, Cyrenaica, is more like a Greek island surrounded by the Sahara and the Mediterranean. Before the Italians completed a border-to-border coastal road in 1937, the two halves of Libya had far closer ties to Tunisia or Egypt than to each other.

Cyrenaica is a multiterraced plateau that protrudes between the Gulf of Sirte on the west and the Gulf of Bomba (Bunbah) on the east. At the western end, each terrace is sharply differentiated and the plateau rises steeply in giant steps. First comes Benghazi's coastal strip, then the Barce (al-Marj) plain, and finally, on the highest level, the Gebel Akhdar (Jabal al-Akhdar), or Green Mountain. At the eastern end of the plateau, the terraces taper off, and near Derna (Darnah) they lose their differentiation; to the south, they roll gently into the Libyan desert.

Cyrenaica's shape helps to explain its relatively mild climate and abundant rainfall, in contrast to Tripolitania.[6] The altitude of the plateaus and the mitigating sea winds produce a climate that is less subject to extremes. The summers are cooler and more humid than in Tripolitania; the winters in Cyrenaica are comparatively cold, and snow and fog sometimes cover the Gebel Akhdar. Except for the Soluk-Benghazi strip, Cyrenaica never suffers from the blistering ghibli winds of the Sahara as Tripolitania does. The rainfall is relatively less plentiful, especially on the Gebel, and is somewhat less irregular and torrential than in Tripolitania.

The most attractive area for agriculture is the Gebel Akhdar, a plateau that extends about 140 kilometers east and west and 25 to 30 kilometers north and south. Groves of pines, cypresses, holm oaks, junipers, and wild olives grow in isolated groves and along the ravines. The typical vegetation includes thickets of shrubs alternating with asphodel-covered plains. The soil is primarily *terra rossa* (red earth), which contains considerable clay and does not retain moisture easily. However, some pockets of black earth, rich in humus, exist around Cyrene.

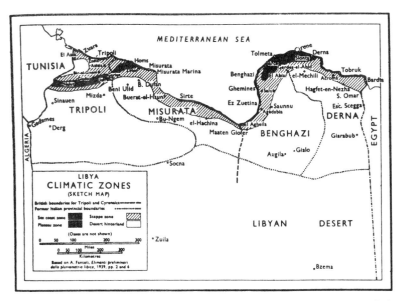

Map 1. Libya: Climatic zones. From C. L. Pan, "The Population of Libya," *Population Studies* 3 (June 1949): 101.

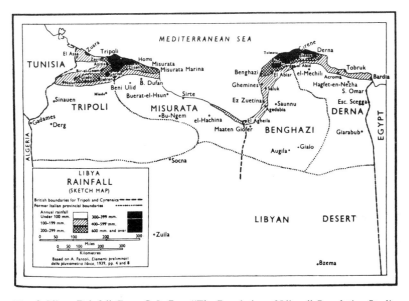

Map 2. Libya: Rainfall. From C. L. Pan, "The Population of Libya," *Population Studies* 3 (June 1949): 101.

Tripolitania's location creates a climate which, although still Mediterranean, suffers from extremes. Tunisia often screens out the northwest winds which bring moisture-laden clouds to the French Maghreb. By the time these clouds reach Tripolitania they bear little or no humidity. At the same time, Tripolitania is north and west of vast deserts and thus is subject to the ghiblis, the hot southern winds which eventually reach Italy as the sirocco and France as the mistral. The result is a climate of extreme temperatures, droughts, and rainfall. Tripolitania boasts the world's highest recorded shade-temperature of 136 degrees Fahrenheit, registered in September 1932 at Azizia (Al-'Azīzīya) on the northern edge of Tripolitania's coastal plain. Droughts may occur once every five or six years and last as long as two seasons. Rains, when they come, are often torrential and the waters quickly disappear underground, for Tripolitania has no perennial rivers and streams. The ghiblis may blow at any time of year but are most frequent between April and June and at the end of the summer.[7] A classic ghibli can raise the temperature along the coast by 30 or 40 degrees Fahrenheit and leaves a wake of ruined crops and deposits of fine dust even in tightly shuttered buildings.

Northern Tripolitania, the only region that was extensively developed by the Italians, falls into three geographical areas: a coastal strip, an inland steppe, and the plateau, or Gebel. The coastal plain, including the coastal strip and the steppe of the hinterland, forms a triangle with its internal vertex at Nālūt and its coastal vertexes at Gabès in Tunisia and Misurata (Misrātah) on the east.

The coastal strip proper consists of a series of densely populated oases extending from the Tunisian border to Misurata. The oases are interspersed with sand dunes, steppe, and salt marshes. Beyond the coast, extending inland for sixty to seventy kilometers south, are the monotonous plains of the Gefara, consisting of asphodel-covered steppe. Finally comes the Gebel, a line of escarpments and hills that strikes a northeastern line from the Tunisian border to Homs (al-Khums). The Gebel is divided naturally into distinct segments—Gebel Tarhuna (Tarhūnah), Gebel Garian (Gharyān), and Gebel Yefren (Yafran)—by narrow gorges and ravines. To the east, it rolls gently toward the sea in low hills which form fertile basins for agriculture. Trees, especially olives, flourish on the Gebel.

In contrast to Cyrenaica, less than half of Tripolitania gets more than an average of two hundred millimeters of rain (the lowest limit for dry farming).[8] Only Tripoli and a small part of the central and eastern Gebel get three hundred millimeters annually. Theoretically, the rainy season extends from October to April. Usually, however, the season is shorter and sometimes the autumn and spring rains fail completely. To some extent the lack of rainfall is compensated by the sandy soils, which readily absorb moisture. Although the surface water disappears rapidly through evaporation and the soil is often swept away by the winds, much of the water filters away underground where it can be tapped by wells.[9]

Despite this unpromising environment, Libya's reputation for richness and fertility dated from the ancient world. At the time of the Libyan War, colonialist enthusiasts frequently cited passages from the Greek and Roman classics as evidence of Libya's great potential wealth. To the ancients, Cyrenaica was known as the "garden of the Hesperides."[10] Corradini quoted Herodotus: "For eight months continuously the people of Cyrene do nothing except harvest."[11] Pindar also celebrated Cyrene as a land "encircled by beautiful fields, adorned with vast pastures and forests."[12] The *Odyssey* refers to Libya as

Libya, where the ewes bring forth lambs with horns on and bear them thrice in the cycle of each year. No Libyan, be he lord or shepherd, goes short of cheese or meat or sweet ewe milk, for the flocks give milk all year round.[13]

In addition to the literary references, the ruins of Leptis Magna (Labdah) and Sabratha (Sabrātah) in Tripolitania and the Pentapolis of Cyrenaica all testified that these areas had known stable agriculture and urban living.[14] Yet when the Italians arrived, the fabled pastures and forests, the traditions of stable agriculture, and the urban centers had largely disappeared. Tripolitania still offered a fairly stable population with agricultural traditions, particularly in the areas immediately surrounding Tripoli.[15] Cyrenaica, however, was populated by wild, nomadic tribes which relied almost entirely on a pastoral existence.

What had happened to bring about the change? Was the transformation due to climatic variation? Most authorities have concluded that the changes depended on historical circumstances rather than on any fundamental natural mutations.[16] Stable agriculture in Libya demands a constant struggle against the desert. Any slackening in the reclamation effort invites the return of the sands. Libya's prosperity under the Romans, for instance, was in large part due to the careful conservation measures the Romans practiced. They built cisterns, wells, dams, and drainage canals which the Italians found useful nearly two thousand years later. When these systems decayed during the successive wave of invasions that followed the decline of the empire, the desert returned.

For geographical reasons, Tripolitania and Cyrenaica followed different patterns of development in the ancient world.[17] However, stable agriculture formed an important part of the economy of both areas. Cyrenaica developed as an annex to the Greek world, with Crete and the Peloponnesus as neighbors. The area's most famous agricultural asset, advertised on Cyrenean coins, was the mysterious silphium (known to the Greeks as *silphion*), an umbelliferous plant whose root was prized for uses as varied as cattle fodder, flavoring, and medicine. By late Roman times, heavy demand for the plant and waves of devastating invasions had turned silphium into a rarity and eventually led to its extinction.

Tripolitania's prosperity depended primarily on trade with the Sahara and the Sudan. Contrary to popular belief, Tripolitania never became a "granary" for the Roman world.[18] During the first and second centuries, the Romans developed agriculture, especially wheat. The ruins in the eastern Gebel and parts of the Gefara attest to the Roman effort. More likely, however, the local population absorbed Tripolitania's production. The real granaries for metropolitan Italy were Tunisia and Egypt. Olive oil was probably Tripolitania's most important agricultural export. The ports of Sabratha and Leptis Magna—part of the original *tripolis*—flourished on these exports of olive oil and on the trade in ivory, gold dust, and precious stones from the Sudan.

In Libya's characteristic age-old struggle between the peoples of the desert and the peoples of the sown, the Romans had temporarily tipped the battle in favor of the sown. With the decline of the empire and the Vandal invasions of the fifth and sixth centuries, nomadism began recurring along the coast. Despite successive invasions, however, the decline was gradual until the catastrophic appearance of the Bani Hilal and Bani Sulaim tribes in the eleventh century. Ibn Khaldun likened them to a swarm of locusts which destroyed everything in its path. Perhaps as many as a million men, women, and children spent nearly a century traveling across North Africa from the Nile Valley to Algeria. The Sulaim tribes formed nuclei that were strong enough to change the country's ethnographic composition. The Berber language gradually disappeared except in the extreme southern oases. The *pentapolis* decayed, more from neglect and anarchy than from systematic destruction. By the fourteenth century tents flourished on the former sites of cities and the Greek tombs in Cyrene became the homes of troglodytes. By the nineteenth century Cyrenaica's population was almost completely nomadic except for small communities at Benghazi and Derna, which were based on an immigration of Jews and Moslems from Tripolitania. The only other permanent settlements were the *zawiyas* or religious lodges founded by the Sanusi in the Gebel Akhdar near Cyrene.

In Tripolitania, Tripoli alone survived as an island in a nomadic sea. The city flourished as an entrepôt for Mediterranean and trans-Saharan trade and acquired a reputation for cleanliness and whiteness. Whether the regime was Norman, Spanish, or Ottoman made little difference to Tripoli's role as a trade center. Even Tripoli's reputation as a haven for pirates, which made "God preserve you from the Tripoli galleys" a standard farewell among Christian sailors, did not disturb trade relations between the city and Europe. Beyond the city walls the authorities, whether Christian or Moslem, had little control. Occasional travelers who ventured among the tribes of the hinterland painted a picture of poverty and desolation.

By the late nineteenth century, Tripolitania and Cyrenaica were little more than two sleepy Turkish provinces peopled largely by nomads. Cyrenaica's population, of little more than 100,000, consisted of restless bedouins.[19] The Sanusi, a religious order founded in the early nineteenth century, ruled on behalf of the Turks. The Sanusi provided education, security, and justice. As long as the order collected taxes for the Turks, Sanusi authority remained undisturbed. In Tripolitania, with a population of about half a million, the Turks ruled with an indifferent hand.[20] Tripoli, deprived of its best sources of income in the form of piracy and slavery, went into a slow decline. The country existed meagerly at best on its resources of fishing, farming, and livestock.

The Italian colony in Libya before the occupation consisted largely of traders and businessmen in Tripoli.[21] In 1911 Tripoli had a population of 29,869, of whom 19,409 were Moslems, 6,460 were Jews and about 4,000 were Europeans, mostly Greeks, Maltese, and Italians. The Italian community, many of whom were Sicilians, was very influential. At the turn of the century, the 660 Italian citizens were second in number only to the large Maltese community of 1,900 fishermen, artisans, and builders. Italian was the foreign language of the business and commercial community. Italians also operated the largest commercial bank, and in 1907 Italian shipping lines controlled 45 percent of the commerce entering the port. By the time of the occupation in 1911, the Italian community in Tripoli numbered 819. The community had developed its own hospital, schools, and cultural organizations. However, consular officials complained that the Italian population grew very little. Between 1908 and 1910 emigration from Italy to Tripolitania varied between 230 and 260 emigrants; during the same period Algeria absorbed 1,500–1,700 emigrants from Italy, Tunisia 2,300–3,100, and Egypt 1,700–2,000.[22] With the Italian victory in 1912, the emigration from Italy to Tripolitania jumped to 7,428, but the emigration to the other North African countries dipped only slightly.

Italian emigration to Tripolitania was not extensive, because emigrants found few opportunities for employment. Consular reports lamented that the few laborers who from time to time sailed from Tunisia to Tripoli in search of work usually departed the same day on the same steamer or left the following week with the help of a charitable organization.[23] The consuls also remarked that the Italians in Tripoli kept to themselves and were concerned strictly with business opportunities. They showed no interest at all in raising the "moral and civil standards" of the country and peoples they were "exploiting." In practice they had nothing in common with the indigenous peoples with whom they dealt: "neither soul, nor heart, nor religion, nor political ideals."[24]

In Cyrenaica a few hundred Italians lived in Benghazi and a dozen or so in Derna. They were employed by the Banco di Roma and the Società di Navigazione Generale Italiana, which operated a coastal shipping service from Syracuse to Khania on the northwest coast of Crete. Others worked in the post office, schools, or with medical and charitable organizations. The only agricultural activity was that of a religious organization which operated a farm near Benghazi, and the Banco di Roma's experiments on four thousand hectares near al-Guarscia.[25]

Libya as a Population Colony: Early Surveys

What was to be done with such an unpromising colony? Although a number of Italian travelers and technical experts had visited Libya and written of their impressions, the Italian government made little systematic effort to study the country ahead of time.[26] Official planning was largely improvised, superficial, and confused.[27] The exaggerated claims made during the propaganda campaign that preceded the conquest were soon disproved. From the little that was known about the area, the plans for trade, for mineral wealth, and for industry had no real basis. Public opinion, so optimistic at the time of the conquest, swung to the extremes of pessimism. A French writer noted that "at the time of the conquest, all Italians considered Libya as an earthly paradise; today they call it a desert and an inferno."[28]

The chief remaining hope—for many, the chief justification for the conquest—was that Libya could become a major population outlet.[29] Only if the new colony fulfilled this role could "the painful sacrifices which Italy is undertaking" be justified, remarked Ausonio Franzoni, an authority on emigration and a president of the Istituto Coloniale Italiano.[30] Unlike other European powers in North Africa, Italy had the demographic resources to create a population colony. He added that

without a program for intensive colonization the Italians could renounce any hope of conquering or controlling the colony's interior.
Thus, he concluded, all factors pointed to "a work of colonization and
demographic expansion" in Libya.[31]

What policies should be followed to transform Libya into a population colony remained a subject of much debate. Einaudi, for instance,
argued that the government should intervene only indirectly, by
limiting itself to the construction of roads, railroads, and agricultural
experiment stations (for, he pointed out, the agriculture of Tripolitania
was even more of an unknown than that of the *mezzogiorno*.)[32]
Franzoni, on the other hand, favored "official colonization"—programs "initiated, directed, controlled, and, where necessary, also
materially subsidized by the state."[33] Franzoni argued that in a country
that lacked even the minimal necessities for economic development, the
state should initiate enterprise as well as ensure stability and order.
Afterward, private initiative could be encouraged. Even more fundamental was the problem of attracting immigrants in the first place. As
a visitor to the Banco di Roma's farms at Guarscia in 1910 remarked,
the vast majority of emigrants thought of sailing for America, not for
an unknown Africa which their imaginations sometimes peopled with
"monsters" both human and animal. Subsidies, "at least a year of
support," would be needed to attract peasant families. Unless and until
the government gave colonization full support "it won't be possible to
see these lands flourish," the visitor concluded.[34]

The government, however, as radical newspapers complained, took a
dim view of encouraging mass emigration to Libya and rejected any
state support for emigrants.[35] Obstacles such as special passports or
proofs of financial independence discouraged potential colonists. To
preserve economic order and stability in the colony, land transactions
were forbidden. The ban was not lifted until 1914. In that same year,
the government created an Agricultural Office (Ufficio Agrario) to
conduct agricultural experiments and to encourage colonization.

Government policy reflected the recommendations of three important technical missions which explored the agricultural possibilities of
Tripolitania in 1912 and 1913.[36] All the reports took a cautiously
optimistic view of the area's agricultural potential and urged extensive
research and experimentation. Yet the reports also agreed that the
country was not suited—at least not yet—for a massive influx of
colonists.

The most influential report was that of the Bertolini Commission,
which did its fieldwork in Tripolitania between March and June of

1913. The commission made clear that, at least initially, population schemes were not appropriate for developing Libya. The trouble with the term "colonization," warned the report, was that in the popular mind it had only one meaning: the transfer of emigrants—mostly landless peasants—to areas where extensive lands would be available for cultivation.[37] Colonization in the popular mind was a surrogate for emigration, a surrogate which the government was expected to promote and organize with appropriate measures. Colonization as an association with indigenous populations to develop local resources "is the aspiration of scarcely anyone."[38] Yet in the commission's view the collaboration of the indigenous peoples would be crucial to the colony's development.

The commission members were wary of opening the colony to land speculators. For this reason the report recommended that colonization be restricted to lands in which the state had clear property rights.[39] The state would rent the lots to Italian colonists and provide them with limited technical and financial aid. Private enterprise and private capital were to be the dominant modes of development.

The report recommended three types of development: (1) small farms devoted exclusively to irrigated agriculture; (2) large farms of two to three hundred hectares devoted to a mixed scheme of cultivation that emphasized tree cultures and cereals; and (3) pastoral estates.[40] Although the first type might be developed by Italians alone, the other two would function only if there was a close association with the indigenous population. The Libyans were to provide the labor, the Italians the technical expertise and the capital. According to the report, this close association would yield both economic and political benefits. A close economic tie between Libyans and Italians would help promote political security in the colony.[41]

As a complement to the Bertolini Commission's investigations, Leopoldo Franchetti, well known for his studies of the *mezzogiorno* and for his abortive colonization attempts in Eritrea, led a privately sponsored mission in February 1913. Since the Bertolini Commission had covered the coastal plain, Franchetti's group visited the Tripolitanian Gebel, especially the areas around Tarhuna, Msellata, and Garian.

In his report Franchetti showed his deep interest in the possibility of peasant colonization:

From the beginning of the Libyan enterprise one of the dearest wishes of all Italians has been that our emigrants could find economic independence in the new land through the ownership of a plot which he could develop with his own work and that of his family.[42]

On the basis of his investigations, however, he could express only the most cautious optimism. It would be "premature to affirm or to deny" whether the land and climate would be suitable for small landowners.[43] Certainly establishing small landowners in Tripolitania would be far more difficult and far more expensive than on the Eritrean highlands. From his observations of the colony's natural environment it seemed that the farms in Tripolitania would have to be at least double or triple the size of plots normally cultivated by a family in Italy or in Eritrea. As for the extent and form of government aid, Franchetti felt that this should be determined when more was known about the best methods of cultivation. However, there was no doubt in his mind that state aid would be justified, since he felt that colonization was in the interest of the nation as a whole.

For more than a decade the debate over colonization policy remained largely academic. Little or nothing could be accomplished while Libya remained in political turmoil. The Libyans showed no great sympathy for the Italian invaders, and the Italians failed to prove themselves definitive masters of the colony.[44] In 1921, after a series of indecisive campaigns punctuated by ambiguous truces, the Italians were scarcely more secure than when they first landed. Their sovereignty consisted of a few toeholds along the coast—Tripoli, Homs, and Zuara (Zuwārah) —and an "advanced" outpost or two such as Azizia, fifty kilometers south of Tripoli. In Cyrenaica their position was even more tenuous.

The weakness of the Italian military and political position is not surprising, considering that the war in Europe alone badly strained the nation's capacities. Moreover, Italy's divided internal state at the end of the European war left no energy to prosecute a colonial conflict. Even without the European war Italy would have had trouble maintaining order in the colony. She began the war on the assumption that she was grabbing territory from a tired Turkish empire and that the fighting would end after a rapid campaign and peace treaty. Libya, however, had a long history of foreign invaders like the Turks, who contented themselves with nominal sovereignty over the entire area but real authority only over the coastal towns. When the Italians pressed for control over the interior, the war developed into a full-scale colonial guerrilla battle against insurgents who rallied around the Sanusi religious order.

By the time the Fascists came to power, the real nature of the war had become apparent. To the credit of the Fascists, they had learned from the previous ten years of confusion. Truces, agreements, bribes, and experiments with dual sovereignty had led to nothing except a deterioration of Italian prestige. If the Italians claimed sovereignty over

Libya, they had to prove their authority by force of arms. The task proved relatively easy in Tripolitania: the country was peaceful by 1924. Cyrenaica demanded nearly another decade of bloody and barbarous campaigning before the Sanusi resistance was finally extinguished.

Early Experiments at Colonization

Despite the political uncertainties of the first decade, the recommendations of the Bertolini Commission were carried out on a small scale in the immediate area of Tripoli.[45] Under RD 2 March 1914 no. 169, two types of lots, large parcels of fifty to sixty hectares and small ones of three to thirty hectares, were available for long-term rent or lease from the government. By setting these conditions, the colonial authorities retained control over the land and could discourage speculators and colonists without suitable agricultural experience. On the other hand, qualified tenants would benefit from government technical assistance. The contracts provided for long-term leases that could eventually be turned into ownership. The large grants were to be developed with the help of Libyan labor, and the small grants were to be worked by individual families, much as the Bertolini Commission recommended. A total of forty lots totaling about 1,250 hectares were granted in the immediate vicinity of Tripoli during the nine months the program was in operation. All the concessioners were residents of Tripoli, and many held jobs or owned businesses within the city. None of them had emigrated especially to become colonists.

The program was started again in October 1920. By the end of 1921 when it was again suspended, sixty lots, or about 1,250 hectares, had been granted. However, at this point the supply of land available in the state domain was almost completely exhausted.

According to the 1921 census, the number of people involved as colonists or agriculturalists represented less than 1 percent of the total labor force and less than 1 percent of the Italian families in Tripolitania.[46]

Even more discouraging was the pace of development in Cyrenaica. During the war, the Italian military garrisons experimented with a program to raise cereals for their own needs.[47] The soldiers furnished the labor. Although the quantitative results were not impressive, the experiments were useful in gaining a better understanding of the area's agricultural possibilities. During the decade after World War I, despite the dangers of Sanusi raids, private individuals made isolated attempts at colonization beyond the military outposts. At the end of 1931, however, the Italian agricultural population totaled only 429 colonists.[48]

The Volpi Era in Tripolitania: Conquest and Land Policies

After a decade of vacillation and uncertainty, Italian policy in Tripolitania took on consistency and direction under the governorship of Count Giuseppe Volpi.[49] Volpi was appointed governor 3 August 1921, more than a year before the March on Rome. Nevertheless, his decisive policies contrasted markedly with the vacillations of the earlier Liberal regimes. By profession Volpi was a financier whose empire was based on electric power in his native Venetia. He was also founder and director of several companies with interests in the Balkans. In addition to his business activities, he had carried out a number of important diplomatic assignments. He had served as Italian consul to Serbia in 1912, negotiated the Treaty of Ouchy, which concluded the Libyan war, presided over the Committee on Industrial Mobilization during World War I, and attended the Versailles conference as a member of the Italian delegation. He was one of the first of the major industrialists and bankers to join the Fascist party. Hence the Fascists liked to celebrate him as one of their own. When Mussolini took power, he gave his blessing to Volpi's programs.[50]

Volpi made two major contributions to the development of Tripolitania. First, he resolved the ambiguities and the stalemate in the political situation by directing the military reconquest of the area. Second, he resolved the problem of creating a public domain for colonization purposes. The two moves complemented each other in Volpi's thinking. Force and repression alone were not a sufficient basis for the colony's development. Politics and economics had to work hand-in-hand.

Volpi soon broke with the earlier government policy of temporizing with tribal chiefs. As he explained his decision, "When I arrived in Tripoli, I found things worse than I had thought."[51] The homages of the tribal chieftains during a state visit by the heir to the throne struck him as disingenuous; schemes for collaborating with the Libyans on a basis of equality impressed him as unrealistic. In September 1921, while on a brief visit to Rome, he proposed the military occupation of Misurata Marina. Permission was refused because of the delicate internal Italian political situation and because of the expense involved. Eventually the occupation—the first step in the military reconquest of the colony—was carried out 26 January 1922.

Volpi pursued his goal of undisputed Italian domination over the colony through a series of relentless military campaigns. His success depended in part on a shift in military tactics. The army in Tripolitania of thirty thousand men remained relatively small, but now, through the use of mechanized transports, the Italians struck with speed and flexibility. The "essential secret" of his victories, Volpi reported in 1924, was the use of strong columns of native troops, light and highly mobile, capable of using Arab tactics against Arabs.[52] Marshall Graziani directed attacks against the enemy's camps instead of against their fixed posts or forts. The offensive of the winter of 1922-23 led to Italian control over the agricultural zone from Zuara to Misurata, including the Garian massif. The offensive of the following year led to pacification from the Tunisian frontier to Tauroga (Tāwurgah). The southern oases of Sinaoun (Sīnawān) and Ghadames (Ghudāms) were also occupied. On the eve of Mussolini's visit to the colony in April 1926, the northern area of Tripolitania, the zone most valuable for agricultural purposes, was entirely under Italian control.

These military successes were combined with political and economic policies that often suggested Lyautey's programs in Morocco.[53] Volpi totally abandoned the politics of "humility, fraternity, favors" of the immediate postwar period which had allowed the indigenous leaders to "take advantage of our weakness and our naiveté." Volpi insisted that rebellious tribes hand in their firearms to the Italians at the time of surrender. Indigenous military or administrative leaders were always to be under the direction of an Italian, and Libyans were to be confined to minor posts. Volpi played on tribal antagonisms and rivalries between chiefs in his campaign to divide and conquer.

As part of his pacification program, Volpi also brought economic factors into play. He confiscated the lands of rebellious tribes, either those lands that were "uncultivated or at any rate those lands that exceeded the needs of the natives." These seizures offered "new affirmation" of Italian authority and sovereignty, he wrote. These policies also proved to be an "efficacious method" for swelling the public domain available for colonization from the 3,600 hectares declared when he first took office to 55,000 hectares at the end of 1924. Another way of applying economic pressures on the indigenous peoples was through favorable treatment of "pacified areas." As the Italian troops moved south, they built wells and roads in areas under their firm control. The unpacified areas remained impoverished and isolated from outside aid.

Volpi's second major contribution was the creation of a public domain.[54] The Italians faced an enormously difficult task in determining which lands could be considered public property. In the first place, as in nearly all Moslem countries, most lands were fundamentally common property of a family or tribe. Single individuals could not claim permanent rights to a particular piece of land. Furthermore, "title" to land often rested more on custom, habit, and long use than on any formal document. The Ottoman government had made some effort to bring formal order into the Libyan land system through a cadastral survey, but these efforts were neither very rigorous nor very complete. The records were often descriptive, based on the word of a prominent local official. No attempt was made to actually survey the sites, and the investigation was confined to the towns and their immediate surroundings. In the countryside the tribes were left to resolve their own disputes. Furthermore, the Turkish records were destroyed during the Italian invasion.

Initially, the Italians proceeded in scrupulously logical fashion. The Italian Land Office (Ufficio Fondiario), founded in 1913, tried to reconstruct and expand the work done by the Turkish cadastral survey. The process, impossibly slow and complex under the best of conditions, was hindered by the perpetual political uncertainty. After nearly ten years of labor, only 3,600 hectares had been definitively declared part of the public domain.[55] The bulk of this land had already been declared from the Turkish registers.

Volpi's answer was to cut the Gordian knot. The Land Office had proceeded on the assumption that all uncultivated lands were private property. Volpi, with the decree of DG 18 July 1922, ser. A, no. 660, simply reversed the assumption: all lands that were not cultivated were presumed to belong to the public domain.

For the Italians, eager to amass lands for colonization, Volpi's decree was designed to avoid as many legal complications as possible.[56] The Land Office posted notices of Italian claims on the land. After two months, if no objections or counterclaims were advanced, the land reverted to the state. If claims were made, the government worked out a scheme of compensation. In this way the question of establishing ownership was avoided as much as possible.

Two other decrees supported the work of the Land Office. The first (RD 15 November 1923 no. 3204) was designed to deal with owners who could show legal claim to their lands and yet refused to develop them and held their properties as speculation. The new law provided that lands which had lain fallow for three years would revert to the state. A second decree (DG 11 April 1923, ser. A, no. 320) provided for confiscation of lands held by "rebels" or by those who aided "rebels." Thanks in large part to this legislation, by the end of his term as governor Volpi had amassed a public domain totaling 68,000 hectares, compared with the 3,600 hectares gained during the entire decade before his governorship.

Like any other colonial power, the Italians were eager—indeed, still are eager today—to justify their methods of creating the public domain for colonization. The defenders of Italian policy claim that the Italians made no fundamental changes in the existing laws, but faithfully followed the laws and customs of their Turkish predecessors.[57] All indigenous property rights and compensation claims were fulfilled. Confiscations were few and occurred only in extreme cases. Even from a technical view, Italian apologists claim, the creation of the domain was sound: the proper balance of oasis, steppe, and pastoral and nomadic lands was maintained.

To refute these claims in detail would be a long and arduous process. However, needless to say, this pristine image of fairness and concern for indigenous land rights simply does not square with reality.

From a legal point of view, for instance, the Italians liked to point out that Volpi's decrees followed Moslem law. Broadly speaking, they did. Moslem law and the Ottoman code were premised on the concept that all land belonged to God and to his representative on earth, the government.[58] Although the individual could enjoy use of the land as long as he cultivated it, the land would revert to the public domain if it lay fallow for three years. On this premise Volpi based his major decrees of 18 July 1922 and 15 November 1923. Yet one could also raise the question whether it was proper for a Christian and secular government to apply a code designed for a Turkish state led by the titular head of Islam. Even contemporary Italian experts admitted that although Volpi's decrees had a veneer of legality, they were "legally as well as morally debatable."[59]

A second claim the Italians make in defense of their land policies is that outright confiscations were few and were used only in extreme cases. Count Filippo Cavazza, the head of the Colonization Office in Tripolitania, for instance, pointed out that only 1,700 hectares of the 68,000 hectares in the public domain at the end of Volpi's governorship were acquired by means of direct or indirect expropriation.[60] Thus he hoped to reassure those "philanthropists or democrats in colonial policy (if they still exist)" that the government of Tripolitania had used its powers of expropriation only "with the most scrupulous sense of propriety as well as justice."[61] Cavazza, of course, was speaking only of his own work in Tripolitania and ignored the case of Cyrenaica.[62] There, between 1923 and 1932 the Italians had registered 120,790 hectares for the public domain. Well over half of this land, some 68,225 hectares, came from confiscations from "rebels" and the Sanusi estates. Cavazza would no doubt have justified these confiscations—as he did those in Tripolitania—as necessary to keep order and to curb the "anarchic tendencies" of the Arabs.[63] As a mitigating factor, he argued that Italian policies were far less harsh and repressive than comparable legislation used by the French in Algeria. That defense alone seems dubious enough. There is little comfort in knowing that Italian thieves are less exacting than French thieves. Cavazza's defense of the expropriation decree as an emergency measure to be used only against rebels seems even more hypocritical in view of his office's frank admission that the decree could be used at the pleasure of the Italians. If the Italians were to need "some pieces of cultivated land in the eastern oases" in order to initiate colonization experiments with metropolitan immigrants, "it will be necessary to make use of this [expropriation] decree," the Colonization Office admitted.[64]

A third claim is that the Libyans were in most cases compensated fairly for lands which were appropriated for the colonization. The ethical or philosophical problem of arriving at a "fair" price could be argued endlessly, for the two parties had utterly different concepts of land values and land usage. However, it is legitimate to question the good faith of the Italians in seeking a fair and legal settlement of land questions. In the first place, as the Italians boasted, the beauty of Volpi's decrees were that they avoided questions of rights and ownership as much as possible.[65] The Italians appropriated the lands by default, often because the Libyans were either unaware of or indifferent to the Italian decrees.[66]

Those who did put forth claims were not compensated according to a free market price. The RD 2 September 1912 no. 1099 provided that compensations were to be based on the average price during the five years preceding occupation (1907–12). The Italians argued that any increase in land values since that time was due not to the owner's improvements but to the investments and improvements introduced by the Italian occupation. Thus, according to the Italians, the Libyans should not benefit for having done nothing.[67] As a practical matter, too, the Italians generally dictated the prices that were to be paid. In Cyrenaica, the lands to be taken over by the state were usually surveyed in a nontechnical way by employees of the Land Registry Office. The owners of the lands were then summoned and told how much their land was worth. The Italians drew up tables of succession showing the shares to which each member of a group or tribe was entitled. The Libyans were likely to lose their land whether or not they took their compensation. Thus, most of them accepted their money.

Finally, the Italians claim that from a technical view the creation of the public domain was sound. The proper balance of oasis, steppe, and pastoral and nomadic lands was maintained. In the first place, if the proper balance was maintained, this was less by design than by accident. The lands that were expropriated depended on political considerations and not technical plans.[68] The Italians could not simply appropriate the best oases, for the resistance would have been too great. Initially, they had to confine themselves to the lands in the Italian zone of penetration, the areas that were politically secure around Benghazi and Tripoli, lands where Italian colonists would be close to markets. Second, whether the creation of the domain was technically sound depends on the type of agriculture to be practiced. What was sound for the Italians, interested in establishing settled agriculture, was not necessarily beneficial to the Libyans, who were primarily interested in pastures for their livestock.

A behind-the-scenes glimpse into Volpi's land policies in Tripolitania reveals how much Italians really worried over Libyan land rights. A confidential Land Office memorandum of 13 November 1923 gleefully boasts of recent mass expropriations and illegal acquisitions in Tripolitania.[69] Strictly speaking, Libyans received compensation for their lands. Yet, as the report boasts, from the Italian view the average price of fifty lire per hectare was so low—even below the prices of half a century earlier—as to constitute expropriation. Furthermore, not all the money was spent on the land. Some went to tips or bribes, "to smooth the path of the transaction and guarantee the tranquility which we certainly did not dare to hope would be so full and absolute." Thus in reality "thousands of persons were expropriated":

I said "thousands of persons expropriated" because that is the truth. In appearance the transfer is voluntary—in practice it is what must not be admitted: robbery.

Yet, the report noted with satisfaction, among the indigenous authorities, the notables, the heads of the *cabila* "not one has raised his head in sign of protest." The indigenous leaders "bow, smiling, satisfied (and in effect they are satisfied with very little.)" Thus the process is "a real and genuine pillage which saves appearances and gives satisfaction to both parties." Nor did the Land Office confine its operations to steppe land. As the report admits, "With perfect tranquility," non-steppe land, property with "authentic and perfectly valid title" and lands owned by or entrusted to religious foundations or orders (*waqf*) were also appropriated. The report commented:

Perhaps these are things that everyone knows, but they are things which cannot and must not be talked about officially except to deny them.

The Land Office report suggests that Volpi always got his way, that officials in the ministry ignored or condoned Volpi's methods. The governor's proposals, however, always had to pass the scrutiny of the Consiglio Superiore Coloniale, the colonial ministry's senior advisory board.[70] The council's opinions—although ultimately ignored in some cases—indicate that there were experts with a sympathetic and intelligent understanding of the Libyan view. An example of the council's opposition to Volpi's methods came in its opinions on the expropriation proposal which was ultimately issued as the RD 15 November 1923 no. 2304.

Volpi—with the concurrence of the Land Office—wanted the decree as an ultimate legal weapon against any indigenous owner who might refuse accommodation. As Volpi wrote to Federzoni, in November 1923 about 2,500 hectares of scattered plots around Tripoli still remained to be claimed to fill out the domain. Could he now cut back or stop his program for the sake of a few indigenous owners who left their lands uncultivated year after year? Should he sacrifice his program for a few proprietors "who would never in any way have collaborated in the work of developing the country's resources?"[71]

Volpi's draft legislation gave him the right to expropriate steppe land, whether privately or collectively owned, which had not been cultivated or reclaimed for the past three years. Cultivation was explicitly defined to exclude the indigenous custom of sowing scattered and irregular patches of cereals while following the herds. Volpi assured Federzoni that the proposed decree would not be misused against the Libyans. As an example, he claimed that his proclamation of 11 April 1923 had been applied sparingly to confiscate the lands of a few rebel leaders.

The council, in its opinion, opposed giving the governor such broad powers of expropriation, for Volpi's decree seemed to threaten the very concept of private property. In the council's view, the sacrifice of private property could be justified only in the face of some actual or demonstrated public utility. As the council pointed out, under Volpi's draft the land could be expropriated even when no requests for it had been made, and even when there were no concrete plans for future development. The effects of such a decree on the indigenous population would be disastrous, the council argued. The Libyans would see the measure as designed to carry out

not the goal of agricultural development and improvement but the political goal of stripping them of those lands to which they feel particularly attached by sentiment and tradition.[72]

Thus, to Volpi's annoyance, the council wanted to insert the phrase that the governor would have the right to expropriate steppe land "whenever purchase by mutual agreement is not possible." As Volpi remarked sourly to Federzoni, it was one thing to include this phrase in bureaucratic reports and regulations and another thing to insert it in the text of the decree.[73]

Volpi's proposal also established a ceiling on the indemnity to be paid for the lands. The price was to be based on the RD 2 September 1912 no. 1099 which provided for compensation on the basis of the average price of the land for the preceding five years (1907–12). However, under Volpi's proposal, in view of inflation and changing values, the indemnity could be increased to a maximum of 100 percent beyond the 1907–12 base price. The council, after considerable debate, sided with Volpi but recommended that the indemnity ceiling be raised to a maximum of 200 percent of the 1907–12 average. The council favored a ceiling price rather than simply paying the prevailing price for fear of lawsuits if no maximum was established. The council also felt that the value of the land might have increased because of the Italian government's investments and improvements. "It would not be right that this increased value should be only for the benefit of the owner," the council concluded.[74]

In the end, however, the council's opinion was purely advisory, and Volpi got his way in the final drafts. The council's clause that the powers of expropriation should be used "whenever purchase by mutual consent is not possible" was stricken, and the indemnity ceiling remained at no more than 100 percent of the 1907–12 average prices. With the problem of the public domain well on its way to resolution, Volpi also elaborated a program of colonization.

Volpi's Program for Colonization

Volpi recognized the political importance of populating Tripolitania as rapidly as possible, and he was optimistic about the colony's potential. Following the Italian reoccupation of Tarhuna, Volpi wrote to Federzoni on 17 February 1923 that "tens and tens of thousands" of Italians would be able to find work there "if we can find an economic solution."[75] The image of Libya as a big sandbox (*scatolone di sabbia*) was nonsense in his opinion. He described the Gebel of Tripolitania as "a marvelous territory for agriculture" and added that "it is understandable how the Romans developed it so extensively."

On the other hand, he was firmly opposed to any programs of state colonization, even for political ends. As he wrote to Federzoni in a letter of 17 November 1923, Volpi did not even want to discuss such programs because he considered them "an economic and social error and an excessive expenditure of funds on the part of the state."[76] Count

Filippo Cavazza, director of the Colonization Office in Tripolitania under Volpi, also warned Federzoni of the perils of demographic colonization supported by the state. "If, for *political reasons*," Cavazza hypothesized, the government wished to settle a large nucleus of small landowners, then state backing would be necessary. Without state financing, a policy of granting small concessions would result in "hundreds of deluded and cursing poor wretches . . . to be repatriated at state expense."[77] Thus he urged Federzoni to use his influence and authority to favor the formation of large private companies in Italy which would have the means to develop large-scale concessions in the colony. Both Volpi and Cavazza made frequent references to French colonization in Algeria and Tunisia. In their opinion, the Algerian experience with state colonization had proved enormously costly and had yielded meager results.

A model far more attractive to them was the colonization in Tunisia. There large-scale French capital had initiated the infrastructure and had yielded naturally to more and more small farmers. Volpi's technical advisors assured him that there were strong parallels between the Tunisian environment and Tripolitania.[78] In Volpi's opinion, the Italians in Libya would do well to imitate the French colonization plan in Tunisia.

Thus Volpi's goal was to attract large-scale Italian capital to Tripolitania by offering cheap land, favorable tax advantages, and government assistance in the form of credit and technical help. In return, the concessioner had to develop the land or face revocation of his grant. Since it was estimated that development of the raw steppe would take 1,500 to 3,500 lire per hectare, and there would be no yield from tree cultures for ten to fifteen years, only capitalists could afford such an investment.[79]

Volpi's plan was developed explicitly in the decree of 10 February 1923.[80] This legislation provided for two types of concessions. Under type A the concessioner could pay a small annual rent with the option to purchase his grant as soon as he had completed the improvements. This contract was designed for large-scale development. The concessioner, since his rent was small, could devote most of his capital to improvements. Ultimately, parts of the developed large-scale farms might then be broken down into small, single-family farms. Type B concessions favored the single-family farms. The concessioner made a down payment equivalent to half the value of the land. He received ownership when he had completed his improvements and paid the remaining balance. The required improvements varied from contract to contract, depending on the land to be developed. In general they included digging wells, planting trees, constructing buildings, and settling a certain number of Italian families. Volpi's system was quite similar to the recommendations of the Bertolini Commission and the experimental colonization programs in the Tripoli area of a decade earlier.

Having taken care of land and labor, the Volpi regime faced the problem of credit with the creation of the Tripoli Savings Bank (*Cassa di risparmio per la Tripolitania*) the first credit institution created in the colony especially for agricultural needs.[81]

The Volpi regime marked a period of renaissance in the turbulent decade of Libya's history as an Italian colony. Volpi's ideas were not new. His goals and methods were those that had been expressed a decade earlier by the Bertolini Commission, which had concluded that the agricultural development of Libya must depend, at least initially, on private enterprise and initiative. Political goals must be subordinated to economic means. Volpi's main achievement was that with the reconquest of northern Tripolitania, he had created conditions in which these plans could be carried out. Volpi also had the advantage of firm support from the government in Rome.

Volpi's resignation in July 1925 and Mussolini's visit to Libya in April 1926 proved to be important turning points in the Italian plans for Libya. Volpi had insisted on subordinating political goals to economic means. The young Fascist regime, once it had survived a period of consolidation, tended more and more to disregard Italy's economic resources in the quest for empire and glory.

4

The De Bono and Badoglio Eras: Colonization in Crisis

Colonies and Italy's Fascist Future

In April 1926, Mussolini made a five-day tour of Libya. As the Duce took pains to emphasize, his visit was not to be interpreted as an "act of routine administration." The trip was intended as a "violent shake" (*un violento scossone*) designed to "focus the attention of Italians overseas" and to exhibit the Italian colonial problem before the world.[1] Mussolini summed up his intentions at a speech in Tripoli. His visit was, he declared, "an affirmation of the force of the Italian people," who once again were to repeat the history of their Roman ancestors and "bear the triumphal and immortal lictors of Rome on the banks of the African sea." He concluded:

It is destiny which pushes us toward this land. No one can check our destiny and above all no one can break our infallible will.[2]

The trip and Mussolini's speech signaled a turning point in the regime's plans. The Duce's remarks showed that he was keenly aware of the nation's long-standing distrust for colonial adventures. He knew that Fascism would have to work hard to arouse the nation's enthusiasm for colonies. His widely publicized trip—the first visit an Italian prime minister had made to the colonies—was followed by the first celebration of "Colonial Day," 21 April 1926. Italians became aware of their imperial destiny in many other ways: in new journals, magazines, and newspapers devoted to colonial problems, in the activities of the chambers of commerce, in the creation of special academic chairs, and in the organization of trips to Africa.[3]

The trip also indicated that Mussolini himself was taking a new interest in colonial problems. As a Revolutionary Socialist, the Duce had been a violent opponent of the Libyan war. In 1915, during the crisis over intervention, he had expressed his contempt for both the Libyan war and the colonial campaigns in Eritrea, dismissing them as "one more disastrous than the other."[4] His stand in favor of intervention had nothing to do with Italy's overseas ambitions.

In the immediate postwar years, the colonial question became one of Italy's major concerns, and Fascism rallied to the imperial cause.[5] "Imperialism is the eternal and immutable rule of life," Mussolini wrote in the *Popolo d'Italia* in 1919. At Bologna, two years later, he made imperialism one of the constituent elements of Fascism with the boast that "We Fascists had the supreme courage to declare ourselves imperialists." References to Italy's need for "living space" and to the Mediterranean as an "Italian lake" studded his speeches.

Once he was in power, the declarations became even more aggressive. In 1923, Mussolini spoke of Italians as "restricted to a divine but too narrow peninsula from whence comes our human, fatal, and irresistible need for expansion." In a report on foreign policy to the Chamber of Deputies that same year he declared that Italy could not allow herself the "luxury of a policy of altruism." Prominent in his rhetoric was the familiar theme of overpopulation which gave Italy the right to place her citizens on "new territories acquired for the purpose." By 1926, for the Fascist magazine *Il Tevere* Mussolini had become "*condottiere* of a people thirsty for grandeur and forced to waste away within frontiers inadequate to their numbers and quality." The magazine applauded the Duce for having "placed the colonial problem in the foreground, on an equal footing with the most burning problems of foreign policy."

In formulating its colonial program, Fascism relied heavily on the Nationalists for men and ideas. The first Fascist minister of colonies was Luigi Federzoni, one of the founders of the Nationalist Party and a former editor of *L'Idea Nazionale*. Federzoni held the portfolio twice (1922–24 and 1926–28) before retiring to a role as senator and elder statesman.[6] Another prominent former Nationalist, Roberto Cantalupo, who once defined himself as "a Fascist who made Italy's colonial needs the passion of his life," served as colonial undersecretary.[7] Cantalupo became one of the most vigorous and prolific of propagandists for the Italian colonialist cause.

What were the goals of Fascist expansionism? To a large extent, the Duce pursued Italy's traditional political-diplomatic goals of seeking hegemony in the Mediterranean and empire in East Africa. Colonialist writers like Francesco Coppola—another prominent former Nationalist—argued that despite Italy's victory in World War I, her position in the Mediterranean was worse than before the war.[8] Now she was surrounded either by French and British possessions or by their satellites, Yugoslavia and Greece. Italy could not allow herself to be "stifled,"[9] Coppola wrote.

In the minds of Italian strategists, Libya had an important role to play in the struggle to expand Italy's Mediterranean position. Through Tunisia, the French controlled the straits of Sicily; through Egypt the British controlled the Suez Canal and the routes to East Africa. Libya, with borders on each colony, could become a source of pressure to advance the Italian position.[10] As Italy conquered the Fezzan, colonialist writers anticipated that Italian influence would radiate more and more into central and East Africa.

Libya also had a central role in the Italian plan to launch a strong pan-Islamic policy—a key to successful Mediterranean expansion.[11] The Italians reasoned that unlike the British and French, Italy had never conquered or dominated the Maghreb or the Middle East, and thus had made no enemies among the Islamic peoples.[12] In the struggle to woo the Islamic peoples, Libya could become an important center for propaganda and agitation as well as an example of Italy's liberal policies toward indigenous peoples.[13]

Beyond the importance of empire in enhancing Italy's status and prestige as a great power, the Duce viewed the colonies as necessary in resolving Italy's demographic problems. The Duce's approach to Italy's population problems reversed most popular assumptions. His theory was simple: many Italians would make a greater Italy; and only a great and powerful Italy could marshal the respect and resources necessary to resolve the nation's social problems. His goal, therefore, was not to reduce the number of mouths that Italy had to feed but to increase them. The "demographic problem" became an obsession with Mussolini.[14] For him, the birthrate was a crucial index of national moral and material energies. "All nations and all empires have felt the bite of their decadence when they saw their birthrate decline," he declared.[15]

By 1926 Mussolini began to realize some of his demographic ideas. First there was the "battle of the births."[16] This consisted of a series of measures to bolster the declining birthrate through special legal and financial incentives. Bachelors and heads of families with few children, for instance, faced higher income taxes. Laws were passed against birth-control propaganda, contraceptives, and abortions. Second, Mussolini made every effort to "ruralize" Italy.[17] Migrations from country districts of high birthrates to urban areas of low birthrates were severely restricted. Under a law of 24 December 1928, prefects had the authority to return to their former place of residence all persons who arrived in cities without means of support and who remained unemployed.

Finally, the government made every effort to discourage permanent emigration, particularly after major outlets such as the United States closed their doors. As Grandi, the foreign minister, rationalized the new restrictive policies in 1927:

Why should our race form a kind of human reservoir for the replenishment of the small or declining populations of other nations? Why should our mothers continue to bring into the world children who will grow up into soldiers for other nations? Fascism will cease to encourage emigration which saps the vital forces of race and state.[18]

Despite these measures, in the long run the "battle of the births" was a failure. Between 1921 and 1941 the Italian population grew from 37,452,000 to 44,357,000, well under the increase necessary to reach the 60 million that Mussolini had prophesied for 1950.[19] Even more humiliating was the decline in the birthrate from 27.5 per thousand to 23.4 per thousand between 1927 and 1934, the very years when the impact of Mussolini's campaign should have been most in evidence.

Even if Mussolini's demographic plans had succeeded, how could Italy, which had faced an enormous emigration problem for forty years, pretend to maintain such a burgeoning population on her pensinsula? For Mussolini there was only one solution: more land. Through internal reclamation and especially through overseas expansion, Italy would finally resolve her problems.

Mussolini's "solutions" to Italy's population problems strike us as odd, particularly coming from an ex-Socialist. Why didn't the Duce appreciate the productive capacities of an industrial society? Why did he insist on his agrarian conservative policies? There is no easy answer.

In part, no doubt, he was moved by purely political interests and considerations which ran counter to any genuine solutions. Fascism triumphed initially as an instrument of counterrevolution. Big landowners and industrialists backed the Fascist *squadristi* as a means of smashing the growing Socialist labor and agrarian reform movements. Since Mussolini depended on the support of big business and the big landowners, he did little to alter the status quo. Agrarian reform was quickly shelved and the labor movement was stifled behind the facade of the corporative state. Instead of resolving problems, Mussolini turned to realizing Italy's imperial aspirations. Fantasies of power and glory, rationalized by "demographic needs," diverted the nation's attention from its real problems.

But there are also indications of a genuine agrarian conservative strain in Mussolini's personal thought. His background as a *romagnolo*, the classical region of land reclamation in Italy, might well have impressed him with the notion that power and wealth lie only in land.[20]

In his speeches he referred to "an old and intimate conviction" that rapid industrial development constituted a "very serious peril for civilization" and that "the only true and durable wealth is that which comes from the land."[21] The world depression merely served to reinforce his ideas. The Duce also liked to moralize about the softness and decadence of urban living. "Peoples who abandon the land are condemned to decadence," he said.[22] Only a return to the soil would breed a nation of hardy, sturdy, frugal Italians.

Mussolini's battle for more land to feed Italy's growing population began with an ambitious program of internal reclamation and land settlement projects.[23] These efforts were widely publicized and Mussolini took a personal interest in them. Foreigners were invariably shown the regime's achievements in the Pontine Marshes south of Rome. Although critics attacked them as expensive and wasteful "Potemkin villages," foreign visitors usually came away impressed with Fascism's vigor and discipline.[24]

The reclamation projects were one of the main tools in the regime's plans to "ruralize" Italy. The new agricultural colonies that sprang up throughout the country offered at least a partial solution to the problems of urban unemployment and rural overpopulation. Projects such as the Pontine Marshes provided permanent settlement opportunities for landless peasants from overpopulated areas of the Po Valley. At the same time, these projects were always useful in providing at least temporary construction jobs for the unemployed during the hard times of the Depression.

The Fascists described their projects as total or "integral reclamation" (*bonifica integrale*).[25] In theory, at least, Fascism's approach was far more comprehensive than that of the Liberal regimes which contented themselves with draining swamps and marshes. Fascism's program included reclaiming the land, creating homes and services for new villages, and finally transporting colonists to the newly reclaimed areas.

In practice there was little new about the regime's projects. Critics like Salvemini pointed out that Italy had always been a land of reclamation. Long before Fascism, the Liberal regimes had achieved some impressive results in reclaiming and repopulating vast areas.[26] Fascism gave this tradition a new impulse through a centralization and coordination of the scattered legislation, and through a vast increase in the government's financial contribution to the projects.

In general, the regime's plans were far too grandiose for the financial resources that were available. It was true that Fascism extended the areas officially under reclamation to 9 million hectares by 1938, about nine times the area under reclamation in 1922. Yet the projects "completed"—a nebulous term at best—amounted to only 220,000 to 250,000 hectares.[27] A disproportionate amount of funds was spent on a showpiece such as the Pontine Marshes and the entire program had to be curtailed for lack of funds in 1934.

Libya's role in this broad design became increasingly clear in the year or two following Mussolini's visit of 1926. More and more frequently Libya was referred to as an extension of metropolitan Italy, another area that could be integrated into plans for resolving the problems of unemployment and rural overpopulation. De Bono's legislation of 1928, providing new sources of government support for agricultural reclamation and colonization in Libya, was developed almost at the same time that the Mussolini law governing internal reclamation in Italy was passed. In 1930, the Commission for Internal Migration and Colonization, a body created specifically to direct and coordinate the movements of unemployed agricultural workers, had its authority extended beyond metropolitan Italy to the colonies.

In this way Libya was expected to play a key role both in Fascism's plans for Mediterranean hegemony and in the regime's internal social policies. For the sake of prestige and Mussolini's demographic policies, "which had as a corollary the myth of population colonies," Italy remained tied to "the most archaic and expensive form of imperialism," as the contemporary historian Giampiero Carocci has remarked.[28]

The De Bono Laws: The Debate over Policy

Yet in Italy the enthusiasm for colonies and colonialism did not extend far beyond official pronouncements. Federzoni, as Fascism's first minister of colonies, wrote confidently in 1923 about the new interest with which the public was following colonial matters. He contrasted the spirit under Fascism with the attitude of twenty-five years earlier when an "Africanist" was "one who was viewed with execration."[29] Nevertheless, three years later, at the conclusion of Mussolini's visit to Libya, Federzoni indicated privately that there was still much work to be done in educating Italians about colonial problems. He praised Mussolini's trip for having a "tremendous effect on the minds of Italians who were until then indifferent or negatively inclined" toward colonial expansion.[30] At the same time, he worried that too much of the enthusiasm generated by the Duce's trip was superficial. The newspapers, for instance, had talked much of Italy, colonies, and empire,

but always, it must be confessed, with rhetorical amplification and journalistic approximation rather than with a sufficient understanding of problems.[31]

Federzoni feared that such campaigns did not really help further the government's plans and might lead to public satiation on the topic of colonies. In Parliament, a colonialist deputy remarked that on the whole, despite the regime's aggressive propaganda, the country remained suspicious of colonies. Too many Italians still remembered that in Libya, for instance, the promises of a "military stroll" and a *terra promessa* for emigrants had never been fulfilled.[32]

Even more worrisome was the corollary to Italy's lack of imperial enthusiasm—the reluctance of private Italian capital to invest in the colonies. Italian business tolerated Mussolini's foreign adventures for the sake of the Duce's domestic policies.[33] Italian capitalism, however, showed little inclination to invest in the colonies without heavy government subsidies or guarantees. In the case of Libya, as Federzoni warned in 1923, the colony would never develop seriously until "Italian capital feels that it is its duty and in its interest to provide large investments in our colonies."[34] Five years later the same themes were reiterated with increasing bitterness. Italian capital, "lazy and sluggish, still shuffling about in its household slippers, has understood nothing of our colonial future and what is worse, doesn't want to understand anything," complained a correspondent of the colonialist periodical *L'Oltremare*.[35] The situation was so disheartening to colonialist enthusiasts that many suggested cooperative ventures and schemes to pool capital for colonial investment.[36]

Equally disturbing to those who dreamed of a small landowner's paradise or an outlet for the Southern peasantry was the emerging pattern of investment and landownership in Tripolitania.[37] At the end of 1928, Tripolitanian agriculture was dominated by North Italian capital (Piedmont, Liguria, Lombardy, Venetia, Emilia) which controlled large estates. North Italians held about 44 percent of the concessions (41,211 hectares), but they made up only about 25 percent of the total number of concessioners (405). The largest single regional grouping of concessioners (166, or about 45 percent) were Sicilians who controlled only 14,179 hectares, or about 15 percent of the total land in concession. Thus their farms averaged about 86 hectares.

Nor was the colonization developing in a balanced and healthy manner. Even a staunch colonialist like Emilio De Bono, the old *quadrumvir* who succeeded Volpi as governor, expressed misgivings about the pattern of colonization. On the one hand, De Bono boasted of a rush for concessions. In his diary and in an enthusiastic year-end report in December 1926, he referred to shortages of land available for colonization and claimed that the Land Office in Tripolitania could not keep up with the flood of demands for concessions.[38] He pictured the colony as "crowded with serious and energetic people" who were willing to invest large sums in agricultural development with "truly attractive prospects" for future profit. Yet in public and in private, he also showed much suspicion about the concessioners' plans and capabilities. After a visit to the Zavia-Zanzur area at the end of the summer of 1926, he fulminated against the concessioners who "have done almost nothing" with those "magnificent lands," and he cattishly labeled them favorites of his predecessor, Volpi. In a March 1927 speech to landowners in Cremona, De Bono complained that most of the concessioners were short-sighted, too easily attracted by the "mirage of handsome and immediate profit."[39] Rather than developing extensive agriculture, with a stress on planting olives, almonds, and vineyards, the concessioners planted small market gardens and sold their produce in Tripoli. "That, in my opinion, is not colonizing," De Bono grumbled. He also expressed disappointment that too many southerners were still emigrating to Tunisia when they could just as easily have gone to Libya.

Far more pessimistic was the report to the Consiglio Superiore Coloniale at the end of 1927.[40] The author of the report was Professor Armando Maugini, an expert on the agriculture of Cyrenaica, and later one of the chief technical advisors responsible for the programs of mass colonization. Maugini painted a picture of near crisis. In his view, the number of concessions to be granted should be sharply reduced—if not stopped entirely. As he saw it, most of the concessioners had overextended themselves financially and lacked adequate credit facilities. The rapid expansion of the concessions had created such a demand for indigenous labor that now the colonists faced a severe labor shortage. The colony had also suffered from late rains and then extreme drought. Finally, Maugini echoed De Bono's skepticism about the capabilities and goals of the concessioners. He called for a "purge," a careful weeding out of those concessioners who were not fulfilling their contracts.

What was to be done? How could the pattern of colonization be altered—if, indeed, it should be modified? In colonialist journals, in Parliament, among the colonists themselves, the old question of settlement policy was debated anew. Men like Volpi and Cavazza had already warned of the dangers and expenses of extensive government intervention.[41] They had pointed to Tunisia as a paradigm for Libya. Agricultural technicians joined the fight against facile slogans that the "order of the day" was to "populate."[42] The real physical possibilities of the Libyan environment had to be taken into account. A veteran of life in the colonies evoked Baron Franchetti's "generous dream" for Eritrea, but concluded that the state-subsidized colonist was not simply an error, but "the worst of all errors."[43]

Yet a lack of state intervention or guidance was also fraught with dangers. Baron Franchetti had pointed them out. Who would guard against speculators? Who would ensure that the concessioners would hire Italian immigrant labor rather than the cheaper indigenous workers? If the concessioners followed their economic interests and hired local labor, how would Libya achieve a dense Italian population?

Cavazza had summed up the matter very simply.[44] If colonization was to take place according to economic criteria, then state colonization was a mistake. If, on the other hand, the colonization of Libya was to be a political act, if the goal was to create a large Italian population to counterbalance the indigenous population, then state colonization was the answer.

In the highest policymaking circles, the political consideration weighed very heavily. As Federzoni wrote to Mussolini in an April 1927 memorandum:

The colonization of Libya must be a means more than an end: it must allow us to place a few hundred thousand of our countrymen there who will make a part of Africa's Mediterranean shores Italian in fact as well as in law. [This is] A problem of colonial politics in that its solution is the only means to guarantee our definitive possession; and [thus it is] a problem of foreign policy.[45]

Large concessions of 10,000 to 20,000 hectares made him suspicious, Federzoni continued, "because if the steppe land doesn't cost much in Tripolitania, it costs a great deal to develop it."[46] For nonirrigated cultivation the costs would range from 1,000 to 1,500 lire per hectare or 15 to 30 million lire for a 10,000 to 20,000 hectare concession. The minister of colonies added, "I don't believe that at this moment in Italy it is easy to find such large sums of capital." He also worried that the large concessions would create a serious obstacle to Italian emigration. He concluded rhetorically,

Do we want to create latifundia in Tripolitania and burden the national government in 15 or 20 years with the grave problem of combatting it and breaking it up as we are doing in Italy?[47]

Clearly the government's concern with demographic goals meant that a revision of Volpi's policies was forthcoming. What form would the new laws take? How many immigrants could be settled in Libya? Federzoni provided a clue in his speeches on the colonial budget in March and April 1927. "If the means are not lacking," he said, within twenty-five years at least 300,000 Italians would be "living, working, prospering" in Libya.[48] This should be enough to counterbalance the indigenous population in the same way that the 824,000 Europeans in Algeria counterbalanced the 4.5 million Algerians and the 156,000

Europeans in Tunisia counterbalanced the 900,000 Tunisians. Such an emigration to Libya, of course, would not equal even one year's population increase in Italy, Federzoni said.

But if we do not achieve at least this result, we will have compromised not so much the economic development of the two colonies as the very goal of our rule.[49]

Agricultural experts gave official endorsement to the government's shift toward more intensive settlement goals at a congress in Tripoli in May 1928. The technicians' estimates of settlement possibilities in Tripolitania, however, were comparatively modest. As a twenty-year goal, one expert projected that 20,000 colonists might be settled in northern Tripolitania.[50] De Bono was considerably more visionary. He called for a five-year program that would grant 400,000 hectares for development and a state contribution of 300 million lire to settle 53,000 colonists in Tripolitania alone.[51]

Just how these political goals were to be reconciled with the realities of the Libyan environment and the nation's financial resources was left to the technical experts. Their conflicting views are recorded in the series of reports and resolutions of the Consiglio Superiore Coloniale's second section for the period extending from December 1927, to the spring of 1928.[52]

The outcome of their deliberations was the "De Bono laws," a new series of provisions dealing with the colonization. The council based its investigations on two premises. First, as experience had shown, agricultural transformation could not be undertaken solely by private capital. Second, the political importance of the colonization justified some form of government intervention:

agricultural and demographic development based on colonization with Italian peasant families, is a task of such vast political importance that the State cannot remain disinterested and cannot fail to assume a part of the burden.[53]

The question remained what the state's burden should be. Early drafts of the legislation proposed two approaches. The first was a series of subsidies which the state might offer to private capital to encourage the construction and development of various facilities needed on the concessions, such as wells, fencing, houses, barns, and livestock pens. In practice, this was an extension of Volpi's measures and—as members of the council noted—a parallel to legislation used to encourage reclamation in metropolitan Italy. The council members had no objections to these provisions, and they formed the core of the De Bono legislation.

The second approach in the draft legislation contained three articles which would have provided for free land, free passage, and long-term credit. Under the proposals, the colonists would have been given fifteen-hectare plots and would have repaid the state's loans in ten years. These provisions for state-subsidized colonization the council rejected.

Maugini made three points in arguing against the proposals. First, the colonist should spend his own money or he would never "attach himself to the soil."[54] As long as he was spending state funds, the colonist would not take care to be frugal and economic. He might easily allow too large a debt to accumulate and then become discouraged that he could never pay it off. At the first sign of difficulty—perhaps illness or a bad harvest—the colonist would try to return to Italy. Second, Maugini argued, direct state administration could not follow the colonist's development effectively.

It is well known that direct administration by state enterprises or public corporations is the worst form [of administration] which can be applied to the development of rural land holdings.[55]

Finally, the choice of colonists was extremely difficult. There was no way of ensuring that the colonist would possess the determination and frugality to succeed in the long run. Too often, Maugini feared, the emigrant might be chosen for reasons other than his potential as a successful colonist.

Thus in 1928 the program of state colonization with landless peasants was once again proposed and rejected. Yet ten years later Maugini and others were struggling to administer the very programs they had opposed so vigorously in 1928. Maugini proved to be an excellent prophet: most of the problems he foresaw materialized.

In the meantime, colonization was encouraged under the "De Bono laws," a kind of intensified Volpi plan in which demographic goals were made explicit.[56] The colony was now divided into zones for intensive population and zones for economic, industrial, and pastoral development. Anyone seeking land concessions under the new legislation found himself saddled with additional obligations to settle immigrant families. On the other hand, he also found the government more willing than ever to share the financial burden of development through a new series of credits and subsidies.

The basic principles of the legislation were made unmistakably clear in article I of RD 7 June 1928, no. 1695, which stated that the lands included in the public domain in Tripolitania and Cyrenaica "are granted for agricultural development aimed at [*diretto al*] the coloniza-

tion of the lands by means of Italian peasant families." When the land
was unsuitable for colonization, it was available for agricultural,
pastoral, or industrial development. Concessions were "reserved for
metropolitan citizens, and national corporations or companies constituted in the colony or the Kingdom [of Italy] who have the required
technical and financial assets and capabilities."

A Committee of Colonization prepared the detailed plans for each
type of colonization, selected the areas in which they applied, and
administered the program. The area destined for agricultural development by peasant families consisted of the littoral zone in the west and
center of Tripolitania. East of Tripoli the area extended as far as
Homs. To the south it included parts of the Gebel near Tarhuna and a
section of the central Gefara between Fonduk Cherif and Suk es Sebt.
In these areas the concessioner was required to install at least one
family per one hundred hectares. On the coast in certain areas the
proportion was almost doubled. The average price of the land was fixed
at forty to fifty lire per hectare, except in the Tarhuna, where the price
was only twenty to thirty lire per hectare.

The regions south of the population zone were reserved for agricultural, pastoral, and industrial development. These areas included the
extreme eastern coastal strip that stretched from Zliten (Zlitan) to
Misurata and the central Gefara. The cost for land in these areas was
twenty to thirty lire per hectare. In the coastal zone the requirement
was to settle one family for each three hundred to four hundred
hectares in concession; for the central Gefara the requirement was
reduced to one family for each five hundred hectares.

The qualifications demanded of the concessioner were similar to
those under the Volpi laws but were augmented by the obligation to
install immigrant families. Strict financial, moral, political, and technical guarantees were required of the applicant. The owner had to live
in the colony or be represented there. The acquisition of the land was
made through immediate payment of half the purchase price, with the
balance to be paid ten years later, or through an annual rent with an
option to buy. In any case the concessioner could not gain ownership
unless he completed all his obligations.

The obligations varied with each contract. Generally the contract
stipulated that within five to seven years the concessioner must drill
wells, construct reservoirs and dwellings, prepare an area of his
concession for irrigation, and plant a section with trees. Most important of all, he had to install Italian families, lodge them, guarantee
them work, and eventually prepare them to become small landowners.
The legislation recommended a number of possible contracts that
might be arranged between the immigrant and the concessioner.

To encourage the concessioners and to help shoulder the large financial responsibilities, further legislation outlined the government's subsidies and contributions. First, the government offered attractive credit conditions; second, it paid the expenses of creating rural centers; third, it shouldered an important percentage of expenses for land development; finally, it assumed a large share of the cost of settling the Italian immigrant families.

One important group of concessioners appeared to have been forgotten momentarily—those who had obtained their lands under the Volpi regime. These colonists felt that they might be slighted. They had had the courage to invest and work under far less favorable circumstances. Now the new concessioner would come in and reap the benefits of their initial efforts. A ministerial decree of 1 March 1929 extended the benefits of the new legislation to the "old concessioners" as long as they accepted the obligations, especially the articles that concerned the settlement of Italian immigrant families. Because the 1928 laws were so exceptionally favorable, most of the "old" concessioners accepted the new conditions, although they were often hostile to employing Italian labor in place of Arab help.

The Results of the "De Bono Laws" in Tripolitania

Superficially, at least, the results of the 1928 legislation were impressive. Thanks to the state's heavy subsidies and the legislation which made demographic settlement attractive—at the same time leaving concessioners little choice to pursue any other policy—the number of immigrant families nearly quadrupled between 1929 and 1933. In 1929 some 455 families totaling 1,778 members were settled in Tripolitania. Four years later the number had increased to 1,500 families with about 7,000 members.[57]

The domain totaled 202,827 hectares, of which slightly more than half (109,858 hectares) was in concession. Of the lands in concession, about half (53,946 hectares) were developed either through irrigated crops or through dry farming.[58]

The regional distribution again showed a strong representation of Sicilians, especially from the island of Pantelleria.[59] The Sicilians made up 47 percent of the total number of proprietors and concessioners, which in 1932 had increased to 442. They were mostly small farmers with plots that averaged a little more than one hundred hectares, and they controlled about 23 percent of the land in concession. Also notable since 1928 was an influx of Italians from Tunisia. These colonists represented about 7 percent of the total number of proprietors and concessioners; they controlled about 14 percent of the land in concession.

Compared with 1921, the increase was phenomenal. Colonists were accounting for an increasingly large segment of Italians developing the agricultural zone. Although few of the concessioners had fulfilled their demographic obligations completely, at least one colonist family was located on 80 percent of the concessions. By the end of 1932, the number of colonists in Tripolitania was not even close to De Bono's ambitious total of 53,000 colonists settled over a five-year period; nevertheless, in about four years, under the De Bono laws, the Italians had settled about one-third of the 20,000 colonists which agricultural experts had projected for immigration over a twenty-year period.

These results had been achieved despite a period of consolidation from 1929 to 1932 when the colony suffered from the world depression. During this period General Badoglio, who had succeeded Marshal De Bono as governor of Tripolitania, gave directives to eliminate any concessioners who could not carry out their obligations. Land grants dropped sharply after 1929, and no new areas were added to the colonial domain. In some cases, grants were reduced in size to match them better with the concessioner's financial and technical capabilities. Between 1929 and 1932, 6,290 hectares were revoked, or about 6 percent of the total area under concession.[60]

The statistics regarding colonists settled and lands under concession indicated that under De Bono and Badoglio the colonization in Tripolitania made considerable progress. But these statistics did not tell the entire story. The colonization faced an enormous number of problems, some of them inherent in the pattern that the De Bono laws were imposing on Libya, some of them inherent in the early stage of any colonization.

One of the primary problems was the sheer expense. State contributions for development of the concessions went as high as 25 to 30 percent of the investment. In addition, credit for up to 50 percent of the value of the property was available. With the Depression and the reluctance of private Italian capital to invest in Tripolitania's agriculture, the De Bono laws may well have saved the colonization, as many observers commented.[61] A French geographer remarked, "No other country willingly spent so much to develop and populate a colony."[62]

Between 1929 and 1933 the state contributed an estimated 35.7 million lire in agricultural subsidies to Tripolitania alone.[63] Most of these funds were sucked up by the heavy subsidies to small concessions. However, the small concessions, which represented about two-thirds of the total number of concessions, also showed the most complete development.[64] Yet even these sums were considered insufficient and several new decrees were passed to further increase the state's contribution.[65]

The financial resources for these programs were not easily available. Libya, like the other Italian colonies, never paid her own way.[66] Her trade balance between 1925 and 1934, for instance, was scarcely encouraging. The total volume of trade had dropped 30 percent; exports in 1925 totaled only 18 percent of imports, and by 1934 this figure had dropped to 16.3 percent. Furthermore, Italy furnished less than 60 percent of Libya's imports and absorbed less than half her exports. The deficit in Libya's trade balance meant that the mother country shouldered an enormous financial burden. The Libyan budgets for 1930-31 and 1933-34 indicated that the colony could generate only about 25 percent of its expenses.

The perpetual laments of finance ministers reflected the problem of rising costs. By 1925 the budget for Libya of more than 400 million lire was more than double the 182.3 million of 1920-21, as De Stefani complained.[67] The increased expenses, reflecting the regular and extraordinary military expenses in the colony, had completely absorbed any income from increasing colonial revenues. In De Stefani's view, development plans for Cyrenaica and Tripolitania should be re-examined to "better bring them into line with financial means." He concluded that he was certainly in favor of a policy that would maintain Italy's prestige in the colonial field, but he wondered—perhaps with a shade of irony—if the same ends could not be pursued with "more respect for the needs of public finance, which also plays such a large part in maintaining the nation's prestige." Volpi, too, as finance minister, fought off the increasing demands of the colonial budget.[68] In a handwritten note of 1926 to Federzoni, the minister of colonies, Volpi indicated that the order to maintain the 1927-28 colonial budget on the same level as the previous year is "the precise directive willed by His Excellency the Head of the Government."

The struggle to stretch available funds led colonial ministers to appeal directly to Mussolini. In 1926 Federzoni wrote to the Duce that his requests were the "irreducible minimum necessary to maintain the current situation in the colony."[69] This meant renouncing, "especially for Cyrenaica and Tripolitania," any government programs for political and economic development. Perhaps the current economy measures were necessary, he observed, but he speculated that what was being saved currently might cost much more in the future.

First as governor of Tripolitania, then as minister of colonies, De Bono complained incessantly about shortages of funds. His diary for the years 1927 to 1930 is studded with remarks like "tragic situation," "can't go on like this," "the financial situation of the colonies is wretched."[70] The finance ministers, he charged, showed no understanding of colonial problems and allocated funds with an insensitive bureaucratic mentality. Even his colonization program, with its provisions for subsidies to encourage settlement of emigrants, was in "essence only a bluff" in which he too had been duped, De Bono noted angrily in his diary.[71] Although he did not know it until too late, he claimed, the condition for approving his program was that the funds were to be spent only if the Ministry of Finance had money left over after meeting other expenses. To Mussolini he complained that he had been forced to "all kinds of expedients" to meet the subsidies promised to the concessioners. Only his tactics, De Bono claimed, had prevented the concessioners and colonists from suing the government for fraud.

Repeatedly De Bono urged the Duce to see that Italy faced her colonies "decisively and in a truly Fascist manner."

We can no longer limit ourselves to patching and mending; the patches and the thread no longer hold and we run the risk of revealing our shame.[72]

Either the colonies should be supported—"and they should be supported with money: only money is necessary," De Bono commented caustically—or Italy should have the courage to renounce all colonial programs. In the meantime, he concluded, all the clamor over "*romanità* and empire" was ridiculous if the means for expansion were not available. In his diary he fulminated privately, "useless to speak of the Duce's promises, for they aren't worth a thing," and "interest in the colonies on the Duce's part: zero."

How effectively the money was spent among the private concessioners was another problem. Some critics have dismissed the work of the concessioners as sheer speculation and fraud. According to this view, the concessioners did nothing more than plan their development in such a way as to milk the maximum of subsidies from the government. One story has it that when government inspectors came to evaluate the progress made on farms and estates, concessioners were not above shifting plants or trees from field to field in order to maximize subsidies.[73]

There is undoubtedly much truth to the charges of speculation. Although there is no direct evidence available, perhaps there were also cases of outright fraud. To guard against abuses, the legislation governing the concessions became increasingly restrictive and minute.[74] New decrees spelled out in great detail what the government considered to be a "rational" manner for developing the concessions. The subsidies the concessioner received depended on how well he followed these guides. The legislation also provided that subsidies would be paid only if concessioners fulfilled their obligations to settle colonist families. The families now had to be "authentic peasants," and the families had to be assumed under long-term contracts, often lasting twenty years. The amount of contributions to which the concessioner was entitled was regulated by an elaborate point system.

Nevertheless, agricultural experts in the colony were outraged at how a minority of concessioners took advantage of the system.[75] For these concessioners, especially those with large grants, agricultural development was not the sporadic speculation that one might expect with any such legislation, but "open, complete exploitation of all the government's provisions," Marroni observed. In a hypothetical example, using a hectare of olives and almond trees, Marroni indicated that for an investment of 250–300 lire per hectare, a concessioner could get loans and subsidies of 800 lire per hectare. One need only extend the figure over one thousand hectares to see how attractive such a speculation could be, he added. The same type of speculation could be made on the concession's buildings and its water development. As a final benefit to the concessioner, he noted, not only was the law generous, but the local interpretation and application were even more liberal. In Marroni's view, this generosity was due in part to incorrect estimates and in part to officials who were not always "honest and disinterested."

On the other hand, as Marroni admits, the speculators formed a minority of the concessioners. The majority struggled as best they could to turn their land into a thriving concern. Like any frontier, the colony attracted a wide variety of first-generation pioneers, each with different skills, resources, and motivations.[76] The concessioners included big capitalist investors like the Venetian banker and former governor of Tripolitania Giuseppe Volpi di Misurata and the industrialist Count Gaetano Marzotto di Valdagno, who had made a fortune in textiles. At the other end of the economic spectrum were land-hungry excolonists from Tunisia and the small farmers from Sicily. The motives of the concessioners varied as widely as their backgrounds. Some considered the concessions purely as business ventures. Others were less interested in money than in ingratiating themselves politically with the regime. Still others were romantics, or discredited political figures, or simply adventurers.[77]

In a broad sense, all concessioners were speculators, for developing a farm or plantation from the Libyan steppe was an enormous gamble in itself. Some concessioners literally risked their entire fortunes on the future agricultural development. The more unfortunate ones fell prey to loan sharks. The basic technical and financial problem the concessioner faced was the long period before his investment would bear fruit. The climatic and agrological conditions of northern Tripolitania determined the narrow range of crops that the concessioner could cultivate. His primary hope—inspired in large part by the success of Tunisia—lay in planting olive trees. Olive trees resisted the climate well. Once they began to produce, the concessioner could rely on years of production without extensive further investment, and marketing prospects were promising. Almonds, especially for confectionary uses, would always find a good market. The vineyards, producing both wine and table grapes, were also considered a sound investment, although some feared that the colony's wine production might run into serious competition with that of Italy.[78] All other crops, whether cereals, irrigated fruits and vegetables, or livestock feed, were viewed as short-term investments. These short-term activities were intended to tide the concessioner over the long period until his orchards and groves reached maturity.

Together with the usual climatic hazards associated with any agricultural enterprise, the concessioners also faced many technical uncertainties. The best variety of trees and the exact methods of cultivation were all problems that remained to be worked out with "obstinate perseverance" and much trial and error.[79] In addition, some of the more innovative concessioners like Lincoln Nodari, spurred by the Duce's eagerness to find new crops that would contribute to the nation's autarky, experimented with raising varieties of tropical plants, cotton, and oranges for use in perfumes.[80] Even without his consciously introducing innovations, the life of the concessioner was one long process of uncertainty. "Must everything and everyone live and act so differently in this land!" exclaimed a concessioner's wife in frustration. Her sheep had panicked and stampeded when they were temporarily herded from a traditional Libyan walled pen to an Italian-style pen of wire and stakes.[81]

In the midst of these uncertainties, the obligation of settling colonist families and relying on their labor was a nuisance for most concessioners. Libyan labor was often scarce, and the Libyans were not as skillful in dealing with tree cultures as were the Tunisians. Nevertheless, indigenous labor had the great virtue of being cheap. Some agricultural experts felt that the ideal solution would have been the continued use of Libyan labor and increased mechanization.[82] Italian colonists could then be introduced when the colony was better developed and able to support a higher living standard.

The concessioners, however, had to deal with the De Bono directives as best they could. That they showed little interest or good will in following the government's directives is scarcely surprising. Thus the concessioners arranged to import families from Italy and perhaps greeted them with elaborate welcoming speeches. In 1931, for instance, fourteen families from Treviso, bound to work for eight concessioners in Tripolitania, were reassured that they were "neither strangers nor displaced wanderers"; although they had shifted their homes a few hundred kilometers, they were still on Italian soil.[83] Nevertheless, the concessioners did little to "root" the families to the Libyan soil.

The De Bono laws and subsequent legislation suggested a number of contractual arrangements that might regulate the concessioner's relationship to the colonist family.[84] None of the proposals were really applicable to the Libyan situation. Traditional Italian sharecropping contracts (*mezzadria*) were useless: there was little or nothing to share, and without the incentive of eventually owning a piece of land independently the colonist families never worked with much interest or efficiency. The contracts that were customarily used in Libya and Tunisia, the *enzel* and *mgarsa*, required a long period of independence and sacrifice. During this time the colonist family's living standard might drop below what the family had known in Italy. This was certainly unacceptable: the colonists went abroad looking for a life better than the one they were leaving. Furthermore, the government feared that colonists living on the same level as Libyans might undermine Italian prestige in the colony.

The result was a bastard contractual system which varied between salaried labor and sharecropping or a combination of the two.[85] Sometimes the concessioner simply acted as banker, offering land, house, seeds, and agricultural implements on credit to be repaid with the legal interest rate. These various relationships were often governed by verbal arrangements that contradicted the formal contract. Concessioners—especially small ones—tried to avoid subdividing their grants into lots for the colonist families and often excluded sharing the first-bearing crops. In some cases the concessioners paid Italians the same wages as Libyans; or the concessioner retained the colonist families just long enough to collect the government subsidies and then dismissed them in favor of local Libyan laborers. The reaction of the colonist families was often discontent and poor work. Concessioners were accustomed to replacing their colonist families once or twice a year.

Thus the colonist family's role as "collaborator and participant" in the agricultural colonization of Tripolitania was never fulfilled, as a technical expert concluded in 1935.[86] The government could easily have imposed its will through its financial pressures, he argued. Perhaps, he concluded wistfully, the situation was not entirely compromised and serious government intervention could lead to "a better social as well as economic result."

Another technician, in a private note to Maugini in 1934, summed up the situation far more harshly. For him, the major characteristics of Tripolitania's agriculture in 1934 were latifundia and unemployed day laborers. Latifundia had been created by the large concessions of the Volpi era and were being perpetuated under the system fostered by the De Bono laws, he argued. The rural day laborers were a consequence of the inappropriate contracts being used. As of 1934, he concluded, the government had spent 55 million lire on contributions to create "latifondismo" and "rural day laborers," and, he said, "we have transferred the major problem of unemployment to the colony.[87]

Early Experiments in State Colonization

Through the early 1930s, the colonization in Libya depended primarily on the efforts of private enterprise, coaxed along indirectly by the government's conditional land grants and the increasingly generous credits and subsidies. In a few selected areas, however, the state went one step further and experimented with demographic colonization by means of parastatal organizations.

The largest experiment was that of the Azienda Tabacchi Italiani (ATI) at Tigrinna, a village south of Garian on the Gebel.[88] The area was a pleasant one, famous for its troglodyte dwellings and its ancient olive trees. Some visitors were reminded of Tuscany. ATI, a parastatal company, had been formed in 1927 to develop the tobacco industry in Italy and in the colonies. For several years before the founding of the Tigrinna colony in 1931, ATI had experimented with raising oriental tobaccos in the area and had discovered two particularly successful varieties. Tobacco appeared to be an ideal crop to support colonists. Since the plant required intensive cultivation, it seemed well suited for the small farmer. Furthermore, the colonist would have no marketing problem, since the state would purchase his entire production.

Thus ATI contracted with the colonial government to initiate the scheme. The tobacco monopoly received a concession of one thousand hectares for a thirty-year period with the obligation of populating the land with five hundred colonist families within five years. ATI was to pay all expenses of recruitment, transportation, and support for the families during their first year. The tobacco monopoly also bore the expenses of raising, preparing, transporting, and marketing the crop, and paid the colonial government one lira for each kilogram of tobacco sold during the period of concession. The government's responsibility was to build the houses and the rural center and to develop the water system.

Each colonist family, depending on its size, received two to five hectares. Most of the plot was planted in tobacco; the rest was used to raise olives, cereals, and vegetables for the colonist's personal consumption. The colonist was expected to repay his debts to the tobacco monopoly out of the revenues from tobacco sales. At the end of the thirty-year grant, each colonist would own his farm.

The settlement opened late in 1931, and by the end of the year 22 families (166 persons), most of them from the Abruzzi, had arrived. The colony grew steadily but never reached its demographic goal. At the end of five years, the colony numbered 299 families (1,794 persons), and the official census of 1937 showed only 271 families (1,548 persons). A technician who visited the colony in 1936 reported "discontent and bad humor" among the colonists.

The colonists complained of bad weather and poor planning.[89] Scorching ghiblis had damaged crops in 1935 and 1936. Artesian wells could not be dug in the area, and the water had evaporated in the settlement's cisterns. Worse still, 139 of the 299 families had been assigned tiny two-hectare plots which the colonists claimed were inadequate.

The planners had not assigned such restricted plots without considerable thought and debate. Technical experts calculated that the income from the artificially high price of tobacco would more than cover the family's basic needs. The planners worried that larger plots would distract the families from the intensive care the tobacco needed. Larger plots would also require more labor than a single family could provide and might infringe on areas reserved for the indigenous economy. Finally, the planners expressed concern about treating the families too generously. Life in the colony was not meant to be easy. The colonists must never assume that credit and subsidies would always be available. The long battle toward independence for the families was to be won only through discipline, persistence, and sacrifice. Anyway, in many cases, according to the Consiglio Superiore Coloniale, the families in Tigrinna already enjoyed comforts that they did not have in the Abruzzi.[90] However, by 1935 the colonists complained that experience showed they could not make ends meet.

ATI officials played down the extent of discontent. They admitted that thirty families had asked for repatriation for "health reasons" during the winter of 1935–36. However, the company deliberately stalled on the assumption that most of the families were newly arrived and merely needed more time to adapt. In fact, of the thirty requesting repatriation, only two or three were actually sent home. Four other families were repatriated for "indiscipline." The company said that they had led a hostile demonstration against the distribution of an extra subsidy of six hundred lire to the neediest families.

ATI officials disagreed that the families could never make ends meet. The company insisted that some families now had bicycles; one had saved enough for doweries for two daughters; other families had bought land in Italy. Yet the project director also admitted that only about 50 of the 299 families—primarily those families who had been at Tigrinna from the beginning—were successful. The rest were dependent on subsidies and supplements.

Despite these harsh and discouraging conditions, the visiting technical expert concluded that the majority of colonists probably did not wish to repatriate. Most of them would have no home to return to since they had sold what little they possessed before their departure. Furthermore, some families were better off in the colony than at home. The Abruzzesi, for instance, who in Italy had perhaps made their home in a stable with their livestock, were delighted to have a nice house and regular meals. On the other hand, those accustomed to a better living standard at home, like the twenty families from around Ferrara, were sorely disillusioned with the life-style at Tigrinna. These families had hoped to "make their fortune" in the colony or at least to live "more like gentlemen." Yet Tigrinna did not even offer such amenities as a café or a movie house.

For the ATI settlement to survive, the visiting technician concluded, the project would have to be scaled down to 317 families; the size of the plots would have to be increased and the families would need additional credit and subsidies. With grants of additional land and a perpetual stream of subsidies, Tigrinna survived well into the postwar period.[91] The average population between 1932 and 1954 numbered about 280 families or 1,700 persons. The price of survival, however, was virtually perpetual subsidies. Out of twenty-two years, the colony enjoyed only seven good years in which the harvest was sufficient to take care of the families' needs. During the other fifteen years, the families required partial or total subsidy.

Another experiment—this one in military colonization—was carried out by the Fascist militia (MVSN) on 320 hectares at Fonduco on the outskirts of Tripoli.[92] Here thirty men received 10 hectares each and 20 hectares were reserved for their officer. The financial arrangement was somewhat different from Tigrinna in that the men built their own houses and water system. At the end of 1932 the grant was increased, and forty-five more militia men were installed on the 550 hectare extension. Eventually, however, the settlement was absorbed by the state's mass colonization projects.

Two penal colonies in the Tagiura area, east of Tripoli, provided another experiment in land settlement.[93] The inmates at Sghedeida developed a total grant of 175 hectares, of which 145 were sold and subdivided into five farm units. A second penal colony at Ain Zara was turned into a working farm.

Colonization in Cyrenaica to 1931

In Cyrenaica, where colonization progressed far less rapidly than in Tripolitania, the most promising developments were being watched with an eye to future peasant colonization. At the end of 1931 about 105,000 hectares were available for colonization but only 14,000 hectares had actually been granted. The Italian agricultural population totaled 429 colonists, consisting of 82 families and 44 salaried workers.[94]

The slow pace of colonization was due in large part to the unstable military situation. For twenty years the Italians fought a bitter war against the Sanusi and their allies. With the occupation of Cufra (Al Kufrah) in 1931 and the capture and execution of the Sanusi leader, Omar-el-Muktar, the Italians were finally victorious.

In addition to the Sanusi war, the few hardy Italian colonists who settled in Cyrenaica faced a number of other problems. Since the Gebel Akhdar was not safe until 1932, settlement had to begin with the least desirable areas, the coastal plain near Benghazi and Tocra and the first plateau between Barce and el-Abiar (Al Abyār).[95] In comparison with the Gebel, both of these areas presented serious environmental and water problems. Furthermore, until 1926 the colonists in Cyrenaica did not benefit from the government-sponsored technical advice and credit facilities which were available in Tripolitania. Severe droughts and the credit crisis hampered the colonization in Cyrenaica.

Despite these setbacks and difficult conditions, the hardiest concessioners survived and carried out several experiments in demographic colonization. The one that was followed with the greatest interest was a small fourteen-family colony operated by the Unione Coloniale Italo Araba (UCIA). The colony was located on the former Banco di Roma concession at el-Guarscia, a small oasis about eight kilometers south of Benghazi.[96] The company's original plans had been far more ambitious. The initial scheme embraced several agricultural villages near Barce, Derna, Tocra, Farzuga, and Cyrene, forest development, and fishing activities. The company hoped to make a profit, of course, and at the same time to fulfill a patriotic duty of attracting colonist families to Cyrenaica. The company believed that if the families practiced the strictest economy and worked with indigenous labor, they could be successful. The company also counted on the colonial government to aid the projects by underwriting public works. Although the sites had been explored as early as October 1921, the company did not settle any families until 1924, for the government proved reluctant to underwrite its share, and the original survey party returned divided on the best plan for development.

Finally, the company concentrated its efforts on el-Guarscia, where fourteen Sicilian families settled in 1924. The colonists planted vineyards, cereals, and some olives and almonds. In addition, the company raised sheep and operated a dairy which furnished milk for Benghazi. For the first three years, the colonists enjoyed good rains and good harvests. Then, with a number of drought years beginning in 1927, the colony ran into serious difficulties. The colonists had made a number of technical errors in the way they planted the trees and vineyards, and experience gradually revealed that the vineyards and trees could not survive without irrigation. The company complained that the government was diffident toward the experiment and did no more than fulfill the letter of the contract. The families began to abandon the village and seek work in Benghazi. At this point the government intervened directly. Offers of cash subsidies, livestock, and a promise to develop an irrigation system kept eight of the fourteen families in the village. By 1931 their *mgarsa* contracts had been fulfilled and they became proprietors of their plots. However, even with government subsidies and the dream of landownership fulfilled, by 1933 a company official who had followed the experiment from its inception admitted that el-Guarscia was both an economic and a social failure.[97] In nine years of operation the company had made no profits; the colonists were deeply in debt and unlikely ever to repay the company's advances. The number of families had not increased since 1924, and the few remaining families were dissatisfied with their lot.

The significance of the ATI settlement and the military colonization experiments in Tripolitania, and of the UCIA development in Cyrenaica, was the way they pointed toward the future. What could be done on a small and tentative scale might be expanded by the government for peasants eager to emigrate to the colonies. "The future will tell up to what point the methods of the UCIA are susceptible to mass application,"[98] one agricultural expert remarked as early as 1927. By 1932 the experiments began in earnest in Cyrenaica. The end of the Sanusi war opened the Gebel Akhdar for colonization. Significantly, this richest area of Cyrenaica was reserved for peasant colonization. The project was to be carried out by the Ente per la Colonizzazione della Cirenaica (ECC), a special company created for the sole purpose of promoting colonization.

By the end of Badoglio's governorship, there were signs that political

aspirations and social goals rather than cost accounting would dominate future colonization policy in Libya. De Bono's legislation had tried
to steer a compromise between opposing doctrines. Yet, as with any
compromise, the results were not wholly satisfactory to either side.
Although the De Bono laws achieved short-term results, private
concessioners often abused the intent of the legislation and pocketed
the government's subsidies. If the government was to play an increasingly large role in the colonization anyway, why should the private
concessioners benefit? All Italians had sacrificed to win Libya. Why
should the proprietors of the latifundia be the chief beneficiaries?
Thus Maugini argued in his proposal for creating the Ente Cirenaica.
These moral arguments coincided with growing unemployment in Italy
and the regime's political-strategic designs in the Mediterranean.
Experiments like the ATI and the UCIA and the Ente Cirenaica,
despite many setbacks, provided a more politically attractive path for
future colonization.

Badoglio's successor proved to be the romantic, unpredictable, and
adventurous Italo Balbo, who first made his mark as a hero of the
Fascist march to power and then as leader of Italy's nascent air force.
For political reasons, lest Balbo's exploits as an air ace rival the Duce's
own glory, Mussolini shunted the former *ras* of Ferrara off to Libya.
Balbo made no secret of his resentment. Although he had visited Libya
a number of times during the Volpi and De Bono regimes, he had no
real experience in colonial affairs. No one could be sure what direction
he would take.

5

The Balbo Era:
Origins of Intensive Colonization

The Balbo Era in Context

The colonization of Libya is invariably linked with the name of Italo Balbo. The mass settlement projects he initiated in 1938 were undoubtedly his brainchild, and under his enthusiastic and energetic leadership the colonization expanded and flourished as never before.[1] Yet Balbo's enthusiasm and energy alone cannot explain the growth of the projects in the years before the outbreak of the war. Balbo owed much to the work of his predecessors. He was also fortunate in becoming governor at an opportune moment for the colony's development.

A number of factors supported Balbo's plans. He took office after the last of the Sanusi resistance had been destroyed. For the first time in more than three decades of occupation, the Italians could concentrate on developing Libya.

Second, Italy's internal economic and social crisis favored the colonization in Libya. By the early 1930s, Italy's financial position had become precarious.[2] Her balance of trade became more and more unfavorable; tourist receipts and emigrant remittances were on the decline; the artificially high price of the lira hampered the chances of recovery. With the financial crisis went an aggravation of Italy's chronic unemployment problems.[3] Rural unemployment began to increase rapidly in 1927 and the rate did not fall until the mobilization for the Ethiopian War in 1935. During the winters of 1931–35 an estimated 10 to 15 percent of all agricultural workers were unemployed—a rate relatively higher than that among industrial workers.

Mussolini's answers to this internal crisis were programs of autarky, based in part on finding natural resources and population outlets within the colonial empire. There was little in the colonial record, after twelve years of Fascism, to encourage further pursuit of these policies.[4] By 1934 the Italian population in the five colonies of Eritrea, Somalia,

Tripolitania, Cyrenaica, and the Dodecanese totaled 70,000 persons. Thus, Italians living in the colonies made up only a tiny fraction—less than 3 percent—of the total populations in these areas. Nor did the colonies provide an effective demographic outlet for the mother country's growing population: Italy's natural annual population increase was more than three times the Italian population in the colonies. Tripolitania, where the Italians totaled 30,901, or 5.69 percent of the population, and Cyrenaica, where they totaled 18,506, or 11.5 percent of the population, were the brightest spots in the colonial demographic picture. In economic terms, the colonial trade volume in 1934 amounted to 500 million lire (385 million in imports and 114 million in exports). Italy accounted for about 60 percent of this trade; however, the colonies made up only 2.3 percent of Italy's own total trade volume. In the meantime, Italy supported the colonies with a colonial budget of between 400 and 500 million lire, of which about 400 million, evenly divided, went to Tripolitania and Cyrenaica.

The regime simply ignored this dismal record and demanded even more "living space." A nation of 42 million could not remain "confined and held captive within a closed sea," Foreign Minister Dino Grandi told the Senate in 1932.[5]

As a first step in breaking out of her "captivity," Italy had to build a modern, intensively colonized fortress in Libya. Building, of course, meant jobs, and the public works the colony needed provided temporary employment for thousands. In 1938, for instance, in preparation for the sailing of the *Ventimila*, the first of Balbo's mass emigrations, more than 5,000 laborers based in Italy worked to prepare the projects.[6] Another 4,650 Italians were hired within the colony. Once the land colonization programs began to operate, they also served to absorb the destitute and unemployed. Balbo settled approximately 30,000 colonists in 1938–39. The necessity to support, direct, and service their needs created hundreds of other jobs.

In addition to these pressures to expand the colonization, Balbo inherited a substantial legacy of ideas and institutions on which to base his policies. The type of state-directed peasant colonization that he organized on a mass scale had been discussed and rejected since the days of the Liberal regimes. Nor was Balbo original in creating the administrative institutions that governed the colonization. The companies that operated the land settlement projects were largely an extension of work begun by Balbo's predecessors, De Bono and Badoglio. With his great talents as a leader and organizer, Balbo's real contribution was to expand these ideas and institutions on a massive scale. First he vastly increased the scope and authority of the colonization companies at the expense of the private concessions; then he brought the entire land settlement program under the direction of the state. Thus, Balbo's colonization policies, favored by the circumstances of peace in Libya and Italy's domestic crisis, were less an innovation than an extension on a grand scale of the work of his predecessors. What Balbo offered to the success of the projects were his talents as a leader and organizer—a contribution which should not be lightly dismissed. As one of the technical directors of the Libyan projects remarked, colonization of new lands is ultimately a "spiritual phenomenon. The technical and economic problems can be resolved as long as the determination to succeed exists."[7] Balbo, with his infectious enthusiasm and energy, sparked the most constructive period of Italy's effort to create a *quarta sponda*.

Balbo: From Squadrista to Empire Builder

Among the Fascist *gerarchi*, Italo Balbo had few peers as an organizer and leader capable of inspiring fierce loyalty and devotion. Balbo, as a flying ace and a colonial builder, really lived the Fascist ideal of courage, deeds, and action.[8] Even his death in a plane crash in 1940 had an aura of mystery about it that set him off from the banal or sordid ends of so many of his colleagues.[9]

Balbo's polish and personal charm generally made him a favorite among both Italians and foreigners. With his background he could not be dismissed simply as one of the Duce's more ingratiating gangsters. He came from a middle-class family of schoolteachers; he held a university degree in political science from the Istituto Cesare Alfieri in Florence; and he married into a titled family. He was neither an intellectual nor a scholar, but like most Italians of his background, he knew and loved the history of his native Ferrara, could recite verses from his favorite poets, and liked to dabble in the fine arts. Throughout his life he produced a steady stream of books and articles on topics related to his wide-ranging career in politics, aviation, and colonial matters.

Few could resist his cheerful and energetic personality. Even as a middle-aged colonial governor with a growing paunch, his vivacious brown eyes radiated a boyish energy and enthusiasm. Visitors to Libya remarked that the governor's stocky figure seemed to be everywhere in the colony. One moment he might be tapping his swagger stick impatiently while he scrutinized the organization of the colonists' farms; the next moment, while stroking the *pizzo di ferro* goatee that was his trademark, he might be offering aesthetic judgments on the frescoes he had commissioned for a church in Tripoli.

As a man of action, Balbo was often compared to a Renaissance *condottiero*. Dress him in sixteenth-century armor, put him at the head of a band of daredevil horsemen, and he would look as if he had been detached live from Del Cossa's paintings in the Schifanoia palace at Ferrara, wrote one admirer.[10] Balbo lived by a code of courage, honor, and personal loyalty. His enemies and rivals, who feared his ambitious and pugnacious spirit, often accused him—usually without much basis—of being a perpetual intriguer. Yet they never questioned his personal courage and commitment. In all his endeavors, no matter what the danger, he set a personal example for his followers. Something of his patriotic and romantic credo emerges in the declaration he made to a visiting French journalist in 1936:

> We will all do our duty, all of us to the last man, whatever decisions the Duce may take. And if Italy must die she will die in beauty. I am only a soldier and the duty of soldiers is to obey without question.[11]

It was the sort of code that left room for considerable flexibility in his political views. His schoolteacher father was a Liberal who also recited his Paternosters. As a youth, Balbo was an ardent Republican. Through his older brother Edmondo, a syndicalist, while in high school Balbo met Mussolini, Corridoni, and Cesare Battisti. As a young war veteran returning home to his native Ferrara Balbo was attracted to Freemasonry and continued to advocate Republicanism. Shortly afterward he was literally hired by the big landowners of Ferrara to reorganize the local Fascist movement and to lead raids against the Socialist strongholds in the area. During the early years of the Fascist regime, there were rumors that Balbo was hatching an antimonarchist plot. Yet toward the end of his career he became reconciled to the monarchy and increasingly disenchanted with Mussolini as the Duce became ensnarled in the German alliance. Ultimately, what kept Balbo loyal was a personal allegiance to the Duce.

Balbo was always at his best as the adventuresome *capo banda*, the leader of the gang. The causes seldom seemed to matter. As a youth he ran off to fight with Ricciotti Garibaldi, son of the national hero, in an abortive Mazzinian-style expedition to free Albania from Turkish "oppression"; in 1915, shortly before Italy abandoned her neutrality and entered World War I, Balbo joined another abortive band, this time a group of volunteers who wanted to fight with the French at the Argonne. During the war he served with the Alpini. After the war, he directed Fascist *squadristi* in raiding and destroying Socialist strongholds throughout the Po Valley. Finally, he played an important role in directing and planning the March on Rome.

His style did not change under the Duce's regime. Balbo's greatest successes came as minister of aviation, when he lead a daring mass flight to Odessa and then another to Rio de Janeiro. The climax of the series came in 1933 when he led a squadron as far as Chicago. On their return to Italy, the aviators were given a "triumph" under the Arch of Constantine and Balbo was made air marshal.

Shortly afterward, however, in one of Mussolini's unpredictable "changings of the guard," the Duce himself assumed the position of minister of aviation and Balbo was shuffled off to Libya in January 1934. He was stunned and understandably bitter. "The conquering eagle of the transoceanic flights was caged among the palm groves of Tripoli," one of Balbo's admirers recorded rhetorically.[12] To visiting journalists Balbo was blunt, as usual. "Have you come here to visit the exile? Because, as you know, I'm here in exile," he told them at the opening of the Tripoli trade fair.[13]

At first glance it might appear that Balbo was right. His position was undoubtedly one of exile, and his record did not indicate that he was any better qualified for the governorship than his military predecessors De Bono and Badoglio. Nevertheless, there was some truth in De Bono's rhetorical question, raised after Balbo's death: "Who was more suitable than Balbo to carry out the new colonial program?"[14] As De Bono pointed out, at age 38 Balbo was in the prime of his life; he was universally known, and he had the aura of a hero about him. Furthermore, Balbo did know something about colonization and land settlement. His *Diary* for the year 1922 shows that he was thoroughly familiar with the problems and politics of reclamation and agricultural labor around his native Ferrara.

In the entry for 25 April 1922, for instance, Balbo recounts a discussion with Mussolini about the high rate of seasonal agricultural unemployment in the Ferrarese countryside.[15] Normally, Balbo explained to the future Duce, government public works projects helped ease the seasonal unemployment during the spring. However, because of Socialist pressures in Rome to punish Ferrarese peasants for their pro-Fascist sympathies, the government had failed to provide jobs this year. Balbo's solution was typical of his talents as a *capo banda*. With meticulous preparation of the sort he later applied to the *Ventimila* expedition to Libya, Balbo assembled some 63,000 (by his count) peasants and unemployed. Then, on 12 May at the head of his "army of the barefoot," he marched on Ferrara and occupied the town briefly until the authorities arranged for public works relief.

Once he had overcome his initial bitterness at his "exile," Balbo determined to make the best of the situation. If the glories of an air ace were to be denied him, he would turn his ever-present energies and enthusiasm to a new career as an African colonizer. He would become an Italian Lyautey. What the great French colonial leader had done for Morocco, Balbo planned to do for Libya. Perhaps the parallel was superficial, for the two men came from different generations and vastly different backgrounds. Nor, despite Balbo's remark that "No one admires him [Lyautey] more than I do,"[16] is there evidence that Balbo ever studied Lyautey's work in any depth. Nevertheless, visitors to the colony often associated the two men.

Balbo's ability to inspire fierce personal loyalty and obedience from his followers paralleled Lyautey's treatment of his subordinates. Just as Lyautey loved to be *le patron* and to have his *équipe* around him, Balbo needed to be surrounded by his pilots, junior officers, and personal friends. Balbo's influence was infectious and brought good results. One English correspondent remarked that he "has imbued all his officers with something of his own character" and concluded that "Fascism really does seem to produce a better type of man for the colonies than it does for Italy."[17]

Part of Balbo's style—as it was part of Lyautey's—was a love of grandeur and sumptuous living. Lyautey converted his officer's quarters in Hanoi into a combination of pagoda and opium den; in Morocco, he posted red-cloaked cavalry to guard his residence. Balbo enjoyed organizing Trimalchian banquets at the old Turkish governor's palace in Tripoli and decorated his office with objects from the excavations of Leptis Magna.

Like Lyautey, Balbo found satisfaction as a builder and preserver.[18] Tripoli became a handsome city with modern buildings; the Litoranea Libica linked the colony from the Tunisian frontier to the Egyptian border. The colonist villages grew up outside of Tripoli and in the plateaus of Cyrenaica. Archaeological expeditions unveiled the ancient glory of Leptis Magna and Sabratha, and Balbo turned the sites into tourist attractions. To promote tourism new hotels were built throughout the colony. Balbo encouraged the preservation and development of local handicrafts and promoted such spectacles as the auto races in Tripoli.

Balbo took a romantic interest in the life of the indigenous population and planned to improve their lot. "I admire these Africans of the north, intelligent and virile, whose word is worth as much as any written act,"[19] he declared. Whenever possible—whether through preserving their livestock from drought, or through building new agricultural villages in the countryside or modern "bedouin camps" for emigrants to the cities—Balbo was eager to show that the period of repression was over. He had embarked on a new policy that would benefit both Italians and Libyans.[20] At the same time he believed in organizing displays of splendor and power like Mussolini's entry into Tripoli in 1937 as the "protector of Islam." Such displays, Balbo felt, impressed the Libyans and reminded them that Italy's rule would be paternal but firm.

Behind the impressive new buildings, the roads, the banquets and ceremonies, the gestures toward the Libyans, lay an organic plan. Balbo's goal was to transform the northern shore from its "colonial" status into an integral part of Italy, a *quarta sponda* or "fourth shore" to add to the nation's Adriatic, Tyrrhenian, and Ionian shores. The interior of the colony was to remain a "colonial" territory under military authority. For geographic and ethnic reasons—Balbo felt that the inhabitants of the Fezzan could never achieve the cultural level of Mediterranean peoples—no transformation of the region was possible in the governor's view.[21]

When we keep in mind the goal of creating a fourth shore, Balbo's policies become quite coherent. First he aimed at administrative and physical unity. Tripolitania and Cyrenaica were unified under one government with the capital at Tripoli. The RD 3 December 1934 no. 2012 provided a new local administration for the colony by creating four provincial commissariats with seats at Tripoli, Misurata, Benghazi, and Derna. The interior remained under military direction. By 1935 the last disputes over the colony's boundaries—the southern limits—were fixed by agreement with France. The construction of the Litoranea Libica was the physical counterpart of the administrative unity.

In Balbo's mind, however, road building and administrative unity were not the key to the fourth shore. If Italy was to maintain her domination over the colony, an organic Italian community along the northern shore was an absolute necessity. Despite his admiration for the "Mediterranean Libyans" (the Arabs and Berbers), and despite his gestures of amity toward them, Balbo had few illusions about their loyalty toward the Italian conquerers. Inevitably, in his view, the example of Italian civilization and well-being would awaken in the Libyans "their consciousness and dignity as a Mediterranean people."[22] Already a symptom of that awakening—the tide of Arab nationalism—was sweeping along the entire North African coast. By the time that tide reached Libya, however, Balbo hoped that the colony would be capable of resistance—that a "predominantly Italian population, with deep and firm roots, a great italic community," would have been settled.

In building his Italian community, land colonization was fundamental to Balbo's design. He wanted to give land under the Italian flag to the emigrants he had seen on his flights abroad. More important, he also needed to encourage an intensive immigration to Libya to insure the Italian community's strength in the colony. Thus, both as a practical matter and as a question of principle, he had to attack the system of latifundia that he found when he assumed the governorship. In his estimation, he had inherited

a situation that was expensive for the state, unsuitable to the needs of the concessioners and sterile in regard to the basic goals of the Fascist regime.[23]

He concluded "there was nothing for me to do but to change course decisively." The latifundia were to give way to a colonization that would base itself "primarily on social goals," a system that would direct the government's financial sacrifices "to the true workers of the land."

The Colonization Companies: Structure

Balbo's main institutional tools were to be the ECL (Ente per la Colonizzazione della Libia) and a branch of the INFPS (Istituto Nazionale Fascista per la Previdenza Sociale), organizations whose chief purpose was to make small independent landowners of the unemployed and landless families who emigrated from Italy.[24] In concept, although not always in detail, these companies, with their mission of putting the unemployed to work on land settlement projects, were familiar throughout the Depression in Europe and the United States.[25] The companies in Libya resembled organizations such as the Opera Nazionale per i Combattenti (ONC), a veteran's organization which did reclamation and colonization work throughout Italy, including the much-publicized Pontine Marshes south of Rome.[26]

With the financial help of the government, social welfare organizations, and some private capital, these companies chose the colonists from depressed areas and relocated them on the reclamation projects. The companies provided the settlers with all the necessities for reclaiming their new farms: tools, seeds, houses, livestock, credit, technical advice, and direction. The colonist and his family contributed only their labor. Gradually, the company hoped to regain all or part of its investment. A variety of contracts between the colonist and the company provided that by stages, as the farm became productive, the colonist would repay his debts. At the end of twenty or thirty years, thanks to the company's support and direction, the colonist would be technically and spiritually prepared for independence—and he would have earned his own farm.

The close relationship between the Libyan colonization companies and Italy's internal reclamation projects is evident from the bureaucratic structure of the companies. According to its bylaws, the ECL was under the supervision of the Ministry of Colonies and the Commissariato per le Migrazioni e la Colonizzazione Interna (CMCI). The CMCI, whose task was to direct internal migration and colonization, was one of the regime's major organizations to combat unemployment and had participated in such projects as the colonization of the Pontine Marshes.[27] The CMCI's relationship to the Libyan projects included furnishing leadership for the ECL. The head of the CMCI, Luigi Razza, was the ECL's first president. The CMCI, as it did with other reclamation projects in Italy, contributed to the ECL's endowment.[28] Finally, the CMCI carried out its specific technical function of selecting the colonist families and supervising their emigration to Libya.

The ECL, when it first began operations in 1932, was known as the Ente per la Colonizzazione della Cirenaica, and its activities were restricted to Cyrenaica. In 1935 Balbo extended the company's authority to Tripolitania and changed its name to ECL. The company's purpose, according to its bylaws, was that of "developing the lands of Cirenaica by means of colonization with families from the mother country."[29] The company had its own president, a board of directors, and a board of auditors. The main office was in Rome, but the ECL maintained a field office in Barce, housed partly in some converted airplane hangars.

The ECL's assets consisted of the lands in the public domain, which the state ceded free of charge to the company for the purpose of colonization, and the financial contributions of various banks, welfare organizations, and the state. The initial endowment totaled 38 million lire. Until 1938, when the company assumed the task of colonization on behalf of the state, the ECL technically had the same status as a private concessioner and thus was eligible for subsidies under the De Bono laws. In practice, from the beginning the ECL had a privileged position. In the first place, since the company's sole preoccupation was the settlement of colonists, under the law the ECL always enjoyed the maximum amount of subsidies. Second, the company received preferential rights to any new land incorporated into the public domain and available for colonization.

Despite its favored position, the company seemed to be in perpetual financial straits. Maugini's correspondence reveals numerous appeals for additional funds. At the beginning of Balbo's governorship, Maugini advised Razza that "the financial problem is the limiting factor on the Ente's activities," and that Balbo should be made aware of this fundamental problem right away.[30] Maugini argued in favor of subsidies beyond the normal contributions for colonization. His justification was that the colonist families were not merely reclaiming land but were actually opening up virgin areas. The company, he pointed out, faced huge initial expenses of clearing land, plowing, planting trees, and searching for water. Transportation charges for the goods and materials to reach the Gebel Akhdar were another drain. He advised Razza to make it clear to Balbo that any further extension of the colonization would require new financing.

With the extension of the ECL's activities into Tripolitania, the company's financial needs became still more pressing. In May 1935 the ECL received 75 million lire, to be paid in regular installments over fifteen years. According to Maugini this was still not enough, and he watched the INFPS's projected intervention in Tripolitania with a mixture of envy and anxiety: envy at the reported 100 million lire that the INFPS had to invest and anxiety that the INFPS would replace the ECL as the major colonizing organization. For the ECL to maintain "a slackened but still appreciable reclamation activity," Maugini estimated in 1936 that the company would need an infusion of another 15 million lire for the next five years. In his memorandum for ECL officials to use in appealing for more funds, Maugini's chief argument was one of national pride. Surely, he wrote, it was not permissible "that an organization called upon to carry out the will of the Duce in a most important sector of national life should be allowed to decay and become sterile."[31] What had been done so far gave "proof of the genius of the agricultural colonization methods put into effect by Fascism." In his opinion, the problem now was whether the programs could be maintained. Foreigners, who were observing the colonization more and more, now watched closely to see if the effort could be sustained, he wrote. Maugini's appeal was successful, for the ECL received the funds in February 1937. Finally, with the shift to a policy of intensive colonization, in which the ECL operated directly as an agent of the state, the company received additional financial support.[32]

The company began operations in Cyrenaica for political as well as practical reasons. The Gebel Akhdar, the highest land on the Cyrenaican plateau, was one of the most promising zones for settlement in the entire colony. The area was also the last to be secured from the Sanusi war. To ensure firm possession of these lands, the government was anxious to settle colonists as quickly as possible. For its initial settlement in Cyrenaica, the Ente Cirenaica received 30,000 hectares in the black-soil country near Shahhat-Safsaf, 4,000 hectares near al-Zawiya al Baida, and 5,500 hectares in the neighborhood of Al Marj.[33] In 1933 the first villages began to appear among the juniper, lentisk, and cypress of the Green Mountain. First came Beda Littoria and Luigi di Savoia; then in 1934 Luigi Razza and Giovanni Berta. By the time Balbo took office, the company had already settled 150 families. When the four villages were completed, nearly 300 families had been settled.[34] On the Barce Plain, construction of Maddalena began in 1936.

In 1935, when Balbo extended the company's activities to Tripolitania, the ECL's area for colonization was initially limited to a line east of Qarabulli-Tarhuna-Beni Walid. Once the company had completed development of this area, it could extend its projects to the eastern sector. The ECL's initial grant, totaling 23,500 hectares, was scattered in three widely contrasting zones.[35] In the east, south of Misurata, the ECL held a grant of 10,000 hectares where the villages of Crispi and Gioda were developed thanks to the discovery of an artesian aquifer. In the Gebel, the ECL's grants totaled 12,000 hectares along the Tarhuna-Qussabat road where the village of Breviglieri was developed. Finally, on the Gefara plain, on the outskirts of Tripoli, the ECL took over three concessions that were already partially developed. On this area of 6,000 hectares the village of Oliveti developed. According to the 1937 agricultural census, the first major attempt to survey the development of the colonization in Libya, the ECL had settled 90 families, or 535 persons, in its first two years of work in Tripolitania.

The INFPS operated somewhat differently and on a smaller scale than the ECL. The INFPS was involved in social security and public welfare activities in Italy. The land settlement projects in Libya were restricted to Tripolitania. They were operated by a branch of the main institute and funded from the organization's accounts that were reserved specifically to combat unemployment. The INFPS expected to recover its investments in Libya over a thirty-year period, and its contracts with the colonist families were designed to throw a maximum of responsibility and risk on the colonists' shoulders. The INFPS began operations in 1935 on 4,700 hectares at Bir Terrina, about thirty kilometers southwest of Tripoli, but only ten kilometers by air from the sea.[36] After about a year and a half of work, at the time of the 1937 census the organization had developed 1,075 of the 4,702 hectares assigned. The village of Bianchi included 31 families with 249 members.

The Colonization Companies: The Politics of Change

Although Balbo vastly extended the scope and authority of the colonization companies in Libya, he had nothing to do with their origin or conception. The Ente Cirenaica, the forerunner of the ECL, was the technical brainchild of Armando Maugini, an agricultural expert who had worked in Cyrenaica during World War I and had organized the colony's agricultural service. The chief political godfathers were Luigi

Razza, one of the regime's experts on agricultural labor, and Alessandro Lessona, long an enthusiastic student of colonial problems and for many years colonial undersecretary.[37] Both Razza and Lessona fought to include the Libyan colonization as part of the regime's internal reclamation and unemployment relief projects.

With the prestige of his office as colonial undersecretary behind him and with a platform in various colonialist periodicals, especially *L'Azione Coloniale*, Lessona campaigned vigorously for more direct state intervention to encourage the colonization.[38] The gradual shift in policy was widely attributed to his efforts.[39] For economic, political, and demographic reasons, the colonization of Libya was necessary, Lessona argued. The De Bono legislation, although valid in theory, had not brought about the colonization at the "accelerated rhythm that the times advise."[40] The Depression, he observed, had created an atmosphere in which private investment could not be counted on. The government had to introduce more decisive methods "to speed the completion of the truly grandiose undertaking that is proposed."

Lessona was not always clear on how the state should intervene. On the one hand, he did not favor direct state operation of the colonization projects. Rather, he alluded to the creation of a favorable economic environment. For instance, the state was already engaged in massive public works projects at home—projects that in some cases were useless. Why shouldn't part of this budget be extended to building Libya's needs? This idea, Lessona argued, would have the double benefit of diminishing unemployment at home and resolving the problem of securing the fourth shore.

As a long-term settlement goal for Libya, based on the estimates of agricultural experts, Lessona calculated that the colony offered enough cultivable land to absorb 100,000 families, or about 500,000 persons.[41] He sketched out a financial scheme to initiate the colonization by settling 20,000 families over a five-year period. The expense, which he estimated at 900 million lire, would be met through thirty-year mortgages on each concession and through bonds secured by the mortgages and the state's investments. Lessona was never explicit about the exact administrative form that the colonization projects should take. However, writing in 1935, he appeared well satisfied with the ATI scheme and the ECL.

As Lessona remarked, there was nothing new in his general ideas. Many before him had suggested that if private means were inadequate to develop the colony, then the state should intervene. Many before him had also favored colonization companies as a means of providing the financial and technical resources that private concessioners too often lacked.[42] Forty years before, Baron Franchetti had made similar plans for Eritrea, Lessona pointed out. In his opinion, Franchetti's ideas had only one flaw: they had not been carried out with sufficient energy.[43]

If the ideas were not new in principle, neither were the criticisms. Even those who were sympathetic to the basic goals of eliminating the latifundia and replacing them with small farms were skeptical that additional state intervention would be helpful. Critics observed that organizations like the Ente Cirenaica were likely to become heavily bureaucratic and that costs would soar. The colonist families, as long as they were heavily subsidized, would not work hard to develop their farms.

Lessona answered the critics more with faith than with reason. According to Lessona, "the Fascist corporative state is not comparable to others," and thus comparisons with the French in Algeria or with other examples of state intervention were invalid.[44] For those who feared that the colonist under his system might develop a passive employee mentality, Lessona remarked that "not even we ourselves can anticipate the miracles" that would be wrought by the Italian colonist's "innate capacities and possibilities." Lessona claimed that a decade of Fascism had created a new mentality in the peasant:

The relations between the individual and the state are no longer what they once were. To affirm that the peasant has remained the old, narrow man of the fields, rapacious and egotistical, is to offend a class that more than any other has been open to Fascist influences.[45]

As for those who objected that agricultural colonization was not the answer to Italy's unemployment problem, since many of the jobless were industrial workers, Lessona replied with a vision of an urban migration in reverse.[46] He predicted that the best elements in the countryside would show the initiative and independence to take up the challenge of colonization in Libya. Their departure would leave room for the unemployed peasants in the cities, who would flow back to the countryside. Thus the colonization in Libya would contribute to the regime's fight against urbanization.

For Lessona and other colonialist writers, intensive colonization in Libya had an importance that transcended its domestic benefits. Intensive colonization impinged upon the heady world of geopolitics in which Italy had her special mission, side by side with France and England, to develop "Eurafrica."[47] This concept, which was also much discussed in contemporary French colonialist circles, stressed the economic and political interdependence of Europe and Africa. The peoples of both continents would benefit from collaboration in developing Africa's resources. As Lessona told the Second Congress of Colonial Studies in Naples in 1934:

Africa, with its huge territories, its unexplored mineral and agricultural wealth, its possibilities—in vast zones— for European colonization, its growing capacity as a market, truly constitutes a necessary complement, the supreme resource of our old continent, which is demographically too dense and economically too exploited.[48]

In exchange for Africa's raw materials and demographic outlets, Europe offered Africans the techniques of "civilization" and jobs. The colonialist writer Paolo Orsini di Camerota defined the African role a little more bluntly: "Thus, work represents the form of Eurafrican collaboration to which the indigenous peoples are called, willingly or unwillingly [*volenti o nolenti*]."[49] Without Europe's intervention, he foresaw two dismal alternatives for Africa: either intensive settlement by Asiatic hordes or exploitation by rapacious Americans.

In Lessona's view, Italy and an intensively colonized Libya had key roles to play in this "gigantic African work of penetration to the interior, of defense from the exterior."[50] Geography and history decreed that Italy and Libya would form a natural bridge that linked the two great continents. The old dreams of developing a major commercial route along a Kano–Tripoli–Italy axis were resurrected.[51]

In more narrow terms, an intensively colonized Libya was necessary to fulfill the grand design of an Italian empire which stretched from the Mediterranean to the Red Sea via the Sudan. In 1932 Mussolini was already working on long-range plans for the conquest of Ethiopia. By the following year, Marshal De Bono was asking the Duce for command of the future campaign.[52]

In the pragmatic world of the agricultural experts, Lessona's battle for intensive colonization evoked favorable but cautious reactions. Despite the technical obstacles that he anticipated, Armando Maugini, in drawing up the plans for the colonization company in Cyrenaica, concluded that there were many sound reasons for initiating Lessona's proposals.[53] Aside from the practical considerations for intensive colonization, such as securing the colony and reducing the expenses for military and police action, Maugini also considered the moral consequences of such a policy.

Maugini prefaced his views by recalling the political context of the colonization. All the problems of Libya, from the first day of the Italian occupation, took on a "distinctly political aspect," he wrote, and "it is just and inevitable that this should also happen in the matter of colonization."[54]

It is important to give great emphasis to these political factors. I believe that it will be possible to moralize, so to speak, the policy adopted so far and at the same time carry out programs that fulfill lofty national goals.

Intensive colonization would justify many aspects of Italian policy in Libya. All Italians—not just a few elite landowners—had sacrificed to win Libya as a colony; intensive colonization was the best way to ensure that the maximum number of Italians would enjoy the fruits of the national sacrifice. A prestige factor was also important, according to Maugini. Extensive capitalist colonization would lead to an elitism that made a bad impression both in Europe and among the Libyans. Finally, a program of colonization that took into account the interest of the Libyans would partially justify the repression used against them.

In the past Maugini had opposed land settlement projects that relied on state funding and direction. Once committed to the ECL, he shed these earlier doubts and theoretical concerns and threw his full energies into developing the company. From his correspondence it is clear that he wanted the ECL to dominate future development at the expense of private colonization. In October 1933, several months before Balbo took office, in a letter to a fellow technical expert, he expressed interest in extending the Ente Cirenaica to Tripolitania.[55] His chief concern was whether the moment was politically opportune, for Lessona's polemics had aroused considerable opposition and hostility in the colony. In a memorandum to Razza of February 1934, at the time Balbo was taking office, Maugini showed uncertainty and anxiety about what the new governor's policies might be.[56] He urged Razza to use his influence with Balbo to avoid any major policy changes "that might make future action more difficult." Throwing aside his usual caution, Maugini indicated what he thought the future of the colonization should be. Capitalist colonization was a failure, he declared. The majority of concessions were still in financial trouble and demographic goals were not being fulfilled. The best lands in the colony should be reserved for demographic colonization.

To continue to give land to capitalists would mean a failure to resolve the major problem [of population] and would seriously reduce lands available for colonization.[57]

Maugini also worked in other ways to increase the power and authority of the Ente Cirenaica.[58] In memorandums to Razza he opposed the introduction of any new organization to manage the colonization in Tripolitania. Additional organizations would lead only to rivalry, he feared. Most important of all, Maugini suggested that perhaps the idea of considering the Ente Cirenaica as just another private concessioner should be abandoned. In the past, Maugini had never opposed privately funded colonization companies whose goal was the settlement of colonist families. Now, however, he hinted at a new phase of colonization in which "the Ente must be the means by which the government realizes its political program of colonization." Thus, in his enthusiasm for developing the Ente Cirenaica Maugini seemed to edge more and more toward a concept of state colonization.

The Colonization Companies and Private Colonization: The 1937 Agricultural Census

The general agricultural census of 21 April 1937 summarized the status of agricultural development and colonization shortly before the regime launched its policy of "intensive demographic colonization." Like any such survey, the 1937 census had its flaws and limitations.[59] The census was restricted to farms owned, rented, or in concession to Italian citizens. Excluded were all indigenous farms, enterprises concerned solely with raising livestock, and geographical areas like the Fezzan where there were no Italian farms. A second major flaw was the lack of production figures. Initially, the census takers attempted to gather these statistics. However, they discounted their data when they realized that the concessioners were deliberately giving low figures. A third problem was the census form. The survey in Libya was based on a questionnaire used to conduct the 1930 agricultural census in Italy and thus was not always appropriate to the circumstances in the colony. Despite these limitations, the 1937 census was highly valuable, for it was the first methodical and organic attempt to survey the Italian agricultural development in Libya. Previous statistical material had often relied on the highly uncertain figures used to compute the state's subsidies and contributions to concessioners.

The census data contained few surprises with regard to the colonization's geographical aspects. The locale of Italian agriculture was restricted to a narrow belt along the Mediterranean shore, with the most intensive development around Tripoli.[60] Of the 553,940 square kilometers occupied by the four coastal provinces, farms occupied 1,877 square kilometers, or 0.3 percent of the total area. Tripoli province, thanks to factors such as political stability and the proximity of the city, accounted for about half (984 square kilometers) of the total area developed for farms.

The pattern of land use and development, according to the census, showed a predominance of dry-farming and semi-irrigated techniques, with olives destined to be the dominant crop of the future.[61] Of the 187,749 hectares in the agricultural area, 99,971 had been developed with trees, sown crops, irrigation, or reforestation. About 71 percent of this developed area was devoted to dry farming or semi-irrigated crops, in which the 1.7 million olive trees played a major role. The census included data on the age of the trees. More than half of the trees would reach fifteen years—the age of productivity—by 1945. Irrigated crops, including citrus trees and forage, occupied 3,461 hectares, of which 84 percent were in Tripoli province.

The social structure of the colonization in 1937, as the census indicated, was in a phase of transition.[62] Demographic colonization based on the creation of small family farms was making rapid progress, but the colonization was still dominated by the large capitalist concessions. The number of small farmers was increasing; and small farmers, in contrast to large concessioners, were completing their land obligations most quickly and gaining title. The census showed a total of 840 farms, with 384 still in concession and 411 owned outright. The rest were partly under concession and partly owned privately, or were state enterprises like agricultural experiment stations or prison farms on public land. Small farms of from 10 to 50 hectares made up 37.2 percent of the total number of farms. However, in terms of land area, the colony was still overwhelmingly a regime of large concessions. According to the census, 84.9 percent of the land was still under concession, and farms of more than 500 hectares occupied 75.8 percent of the total farm area.

The composition and occupation of the agricultural population provided encouraging results in the regime's battle to create small farmers who worked their own land.[63] The agricultural population totaled 2,711 families with 12,488 members. Of these families, 2,051 (10,393 members) or 83.2 percent worked directly on the land. The vast majority of these were colonist families (71.5 percent) or owner-entrepreneurs (*proprietari-imprenditori*), who totaled 11.7 percent. Only about 16.8 percent, according to the census, worked as managers, office employees, or technicians.

One of the most obvious phenomena to emerge from the census was the rapid growth of the colonization companies at the expense of private concessioners. Officially, the companies had been constituted as a complement to the efforts of private colonization. Luigi Razza, for instance, had explained in 1932 that the Ente Cirenaica

was not constituted either to carry out experiments in state colonization or to replace the large concessioner.[64]

Alessandro Lessona, speaking three years later, said that although new plans were being drawn up to further demographic colonization, a sphere would always remain in which private concessions could operate. The private concessioner and the state, he said, "were different forces called to operate along parallel lines toward a common goal."[65]

The census figures showed otherwise.[66] In Cyrenaica, the ECL was well on its way to becoming the dominant force. Of 60,738 hectares in concession, 30,358 hectares, or almost exactly 50 percent, had been assigned to the ECL. After about five years of work, the company had developed about one-third of the lands assigned to it (10,964 hectares). Private owners of the 211 farm enterprises had developed about 40 percent (10,366 hectares) of the 25,684 hectares assigned to them. In terms of geographical development, the ECL farms dominated the province of Derna, whereas the bulk of the small independent farms clustered around Benghazi. The ECL had settled fewer families (294) in 1937 than private concessions (414); however, the ECL families were far larger (2,222 members) than their counterparts on the private concessions (1,264 members). The nearly 300 ECL families also made up about half of the 538 families of colonists and owner-entrepreneurs who worked directly on the land. The families employed in managerial or clerical positions totaled 175.

In Tripolitania, where private colonization had been in operation for a longer period and under more peaceful circumstances, private concessions were considerably more developed. Private enterprises still controlled a majority of the land in concession. In contrast to the companies which had been operating in Tripolitania for only two years, the private concessions had settled more colonists than the companies and had developed more of their concessions.

The distribution of land in Tripolitania, according to the 1937 census, showed 623 concessions totaling 127,010 hectares.[67] Private concessions controlled 616 of these lots for a total of 97,165 hectares, or close to 80 percent of the land in concession. The combined colonization company holdings totaled 30,845 hectares, or less than 25 percent. The ECL was the largest concessioner among the companies, with 23,686 hectares.

The census showed that private concessions had developed close to 80 percent of the land granted to them. The ECL had developed less than one-third of its lands and the INFPS less than a quarter of its lands at the time of the census.

Private colonization had made the largest contribution toward settling colonist families, with 1,606 families with 6,665 members. This was about 75 percent of the 1,998 families (totaling 8,997 members) settled by 1937. The ATI project at Tigrinna, with 271 families, or 1,548 colonists, had absorbed the largest contingent of families among the colonization companies.

The rapid development of the colonization companies in contrast to the private concessions can be measured by comparing the 1937 census with the statistics of 1940.[68] By 1940, the land under concession for agricultural purposes in Tripolitania totaled 231,089 hectares, of which 100,363 hectares, or a little less than 50 percent, was under concession to private enterprises. Thus private concessions had received about 3,000 hectares in concession since 1937. They had developed or were developing 80,366 hectares, or about 80 percent of their concessions. In contrast, the ECL concessions in 1940 totaled 80,686 hectares compared with 23,500 in 1937, and the company was developing 28,170 hectares, or only about 37 percent of its lands. The INFPS had increased its concessions about tenfold, from 4,702 hectares in 1937 to 45,840 in 1940, and was developing 37,309 hectares. By 1940, thanks to the mass emigrations of 1938 and 1939, the ECL had settled more colonists (1,030 families with 7,986 members) than all the private concessions combined (1,639 families with 6,896 members).

In Cyrenaica much the same pattern emerged.[69] The ECL had under concession 102,778 hectares in 1940 and had developed about 60,581 hectares. Thus the company had more than tripled the land under concession from 30,350 hectares in 1937. In contrast, private concessions had increased their holdings by about 10,000 hectares, from 25,684 hectares in 1937 to 35,056 hectares in 1940. Private concessions had developed about half of their lands (15,960 hectares) by 1940. Meanwhile the ECL, after the mass migrations, had increased the number of colonist families fivefold beyond the 1937 total, from 294 families to 1,686 families, with 13,220 members. Private colonization by 1940 had added about 100 families for a total of 520 families with 1,794 members.

The conclusion of peace in Cyrenaica, the background of depression in Italy, and Fascism's imperial ambitions all combined to bring about a reorientation of the colonization policy in Libya. The 1937 agricultural census showed that the role of the private concessions was slowly diminishing. The colonization companies, still nominally private companies operating under the legislation of 1928, were becoming the dominant force in the colony's agricultural development. Initially, private investors were assured that the colonization companies would never supplant them and that the government was not interested in trying experiments in state colonization. Balbo, with his organizational genius and flair for the spectacular, extended the role of the colonization companies one step further. In 1938 he revealed plans for mass migrations to Libya organized by the colonization companies on behalf of the government. For nearly three decades the Italians had debated the wisdom of such a policy for settling Libya. Now Balbo planned to experiment with state colonization in earnest.

6

The Balbo Era:
The Ventimila

The Plans for the *Ventimila*

"Who does not remember the thousands of colonist families that Balbo led there [to Libya]," a nationalist historian wrote recently.[1] At a time when the Italian colonization efforts in Libya are all but forgotten, one moment stands out in the popular memory—the mass migration of the *Ventimila*—the twenty thousand colonists whom Balbo transported to Libya in a single mass convoy in October 1938. "A most felicitious idea, a most happy realization: the one and the other all his," Federzoni commented.[2]

Like Balbo's transoceanic flights or the draining of the Pontine Marshes, the *Ventimila* ranked as one of Fascism's spectacular feats, as important for its propaganda value as for its substance. Yet there was more to the mass emigration than a well-organized but isolated publicity stunt. The *Ventimila* was the first step in Balbo's comprehensive program to transform Libya politically, legally, and ethnically into a fourth shore.

Mussolini's visit to Libya in March 1937 foreshadowed the new program. For the Duce his second trip was no doubt the most satisfying of all his visits to the colony. Only eleven years before, on his first tour, he had stirred the Italians with promises of imperial glory. By the spring of 1937 he had realized these visions. With the conquest of Ethiopia, the Italians were lords of an empire that extended over 3.5 million square kilometers and encompassed a population of 14 million.[3]

The political achievement, however, was only the first step in Italy's imperial destiny. The nation now faced the problem of transforming the colonies into a peaceful and flourishing empire. In Libya the Duce posed as the "protector of Islam," the herald of a new period of construction and cooperation.[4] He presided over the first tangible evidences of Italy's peaceful constructive policies.[5] He attended the

inauguration of the Litoranea Libica, the coastal highway that extended across the colony from the Egyptian border to the Tunisian
frontier; and he also inspected and praised the infant colonization
programs.[6]

Shortly after the Duce's visit, more legislation to implement Balbo's
policies appeared. The first major decree, the RDL 17 May 1938, no.
701, contained Balbo's program for "intensive demographic colonization." The long-term plan was to settle twenty thousand colonists
annually for a five-year period as a first step toward realizing a
population goal of five hundred thousand Italians in the colony by
mid-century. The preface to the legislation recognized

the urgent and absolute necessity to adopt extraordinary provisions to support
the demographic colonization of [Italian] nationals in Libya by means of the
formation of small rural properties and to increase the colonization on the part
of the Libyan farmers.

The ECL and the INFPS undertook to develop the projects on behalf of
the state. The state furnished the land tax free, built rural service
centers, and provided a good part of the financing. The colonization
companies, in turn, had the task of subdividing the land into small
plots and then supervising the colonist families toward their ultimate
goal of creating their own farms.

The expenses of colonization, according to the 1938 decree, were met
in part by financing and in part by state subsidies. The state contributed outright 30 percent of the cost of development. The companies
were authorized extraordinary contributions of 100 million lire for five
years, paid through the account of the Ministry of Italian Africa. The
rest of the contributions could be drawn from public funds deposited in
the Savings Bank of Tripoli. The state underwrote the remaining
expenses in the form of first-mortgage loans that were exempt from
interest and amortization for the first five years. In the sixth year the 2
percent interest charges would begin, and in the ninth year the
companies were to begin amortization, which was to be completed in
twenty-seven annual installments.

The colonization companies thus gained new responsibilities and
fresh financial backing. However, in contracting with the state they lost
much of their freedom of action.[7] The new status rankled the
agricultural technicians in charge of the projects. They now found
themselves obeying politically inspired technical directives which often
conflicted with their professional judgment.

To encourage colonist settlement still further, the state extended the
scope of financial assistance. Under the RDL 13 May 1937, no. 1503,

all types of concessioners, whether private individuals, societies, colonization companies, or peasant colonists, were eligible for loans for the specific purpose of increasing the numbers of Italian small farmers. The Savings Bank of Tripoli was authorized to receive an additional 400 million lire in working capital. One quarter of the capital was allocated for farm improvements and one quarter for water research and development. The remaining half was reserved for the ECL and the INFPS.

The second set of provisions dealt with the status of the Libyans. For a quarter of century the Italians had vacillated in their policies toward the indigenous peoples.[8] The idealistic and militarily weak Liberal regimes had flirted with indirect rule and democratic representation; the Fascists had resorted to military repression and extermination. With the last vestiges of organized rebellion crushed by the time Balbo took office, the Italians once again sought reconciliation with the Libyans and promised to rule with a firm but benevolent paternalism.

The Fascist goal now became a curious "separate but equal" policy, officially described as "parallel" development in cultural matters and structural coordination within the framework of the state. Islam's cultural traditions were much too old and deeply rooted to make assimilation possible. The alternative was to allow the Libyans to retain their own speech, religion, personal law, customs, and manners. However, their tribal structure was to disappear, to be replaced by economic and political institutions similar to those of Italian nationals. As Balbo told the Volta Congress in 1938:

The image of the *cabila* or tribe wandering in the desert at the orders of its chief, according to the ancient traditions dating back to the great migrations and the barbarian invasions, will be no more than a distant memory in the new Libyan provinces.[9]

In theory as well as in practice, of course, the Italians were to remain supreme in the colony. In their legal status, for instance, the Libyans in 1939, were relegated to second-class citizenship—much to Balbo's fury and dismay. The RDL 9 January 1939 no. 70 created a "special Italian citizenship" (*cittadinanza italiana speciale*).[10] The new category fulfilled Mussolini's 1937 pledge to reward Libyans who had participated in the Ethiopian campaign. The special citizenship was meant to create an elite leadership sympathetic to the Italians. Any Libyan who planned to rise to the top of the indigenous military or civic organizations had to qualify for and acquire the new rank. The requisites were minimal.[11] However, with the creation of the special citizenship Libyans were barred from acquiring metropolitan citizenship (*citta-*

dinanza metropolitana), a privilege they had enjoyed since 1911, although few had availed themselves of it.

In practice, many anomalous situations developed. With the special citizenship, for instance, Libyans who qualified were referred to in official telegrams, proclamations, and the press as "italiani mussulmani" or "Moslem Italians."[12] The expression would have sounded awkward under any circumstances. The phrase rang even more disagreeably and confusedly in the climate of racism and anti-Semitism within Italy, and in East Africa it produced rumbles of discontent among Somali and Eritrean soldiers who had also fought loyally in Ethiopia, but who had received no such special recognition.

To foreign observers the Italians seemed unduly severe in demanding formal public respect from the Libyans, even in the remotest oases.[13] Yet there was also much informal fraternization. Italian laborers worked side by side with Libyans, and Italian officials treated Libyan notables with a friendliness and equality that surprised some visitors. There was little discrimination in the use of public facilities. Libyans were free to stay at any hotel, ride first class on public transportation, and even share brothels with Italians—if the Libyan could afford these opportunities. In the field of agriculture and colonization—a major sector of the economy—Libyans were eligible for the same benefits as Italians. The RD 3 April 1937, no. 896, published just a few weeks after Mussolini's visit, extended the De Bono legislation to the indigenous peoples. Libyans became eligible to receive concessions from the colonial domain. Zones for Libyan agricultural development were established, and Libyans could apply for government subsidies to support any agricultural reclaimation work they performed.

The crowning piece of legislation in the plan to create a *quarta sponda* was the decree of 9 January 1939 which legally created the "fourth shore."[14] The four northern provinces of Libya—Tripoli, Misurata, Benghazi, and Derna—became an integral part of the Kingdom of Italy.[15] The colonists could now emigrate without leaving the *madre patria*. The dream of colonialists and patriotic Italians since unification had been fulfilled.

The Sailing of the *Ventimila*

Balbo announced his long-term program for intensive colonization in May 1938. The first sailing was scheduled for 28 October 1938, to mark the sixteenth anniversary of the March on Rome. In a little less than six months, the colonization companies were to prepare for an immigration that would more than triple the number of colonist families under their care, from about 700 at the time of the 1937 agricultural census to

2,500 at the end of 1938. The labor needed to build the new projects provided welcome temporary jobs for 5,000 men who emigrated from Italy and another 4,650 who were hired in Libya.[16] However, the bulk of the 33,000-man labor force was Libyan.

While this vast work force built the roads, aqueducts, villages, and homes for the colonists, a selection committee toured Italy to recruit the families.[17] The committee consisted of a chief inspector and a four-man delegation from the CMCI. They were assisted by a representative of the Libyan colonial administration and a representative of the Fascist Federation of Tripoli. The committee traveled throughout Italy for three months reviewing applications that were submitted through the local civic authorities.

The colorful and spectacular sailing of the *Ventimila* reflected Balbo's talents as a leader and superb organizer. From his days as the *ras* of Ferrara, he had learned to lead with "a certain youthful sprightliness" (*una certa giovanile gaiezza*), whether the expedition was a raid on a Socialist stronghold or a mass demonstration for more public works employment.[18] Yet, under Balbo, zest, enthusiasm, and camaraderie were never allowed to overshadow a concern for discipline and detail.[19] Whether he was leading the mass flights which gave him his fame as an air ace or arranging to honor the Duce on a visit to Libya, Balbo organized with a concern for the smallest details.[20]

The *Ventimila*, part country carnival and part military parade, reflected Balbo's style of leadership. Careful organization began with the leaflet of instructions which each colonist family received before departure. Written in the familiar *tu* form, the leaflet began:

You who have had the good fortune to be chosen, together with your family, to go to live in a new home and work a new farm in Libya must now prepare yourself for departure.[21]

Each colonist was to wear his best clothes, preferably his Fascist uniform or the uniform of the Fascist organization to which he belonged.

The colonists were instructed to take a minimum of baggage. For the voyage they were to pack their clothes, toilet articles, and sleeping blankets; for their new homes in Libya they needed only clothing, bed and table linen, mattresses, crockery and kitchen utensils, sewing machines, and bicycles. Everything else awaited them in the colony.

The actual departure took place in a gay and festive atmosphere. The parade and carnival aspects of the expedition were important to allay any fears and anxieties the colonists might have about leaving their homes. Everything was arranged to make the families feel important.

The *Ventimila:* Governor Italo Balbo meets with wives and children of the colonist families in 1938. From *Libia,* December 1938

The *Ventimila*: one of the families that participated in the mass emigration of 1938, pictured in front of the tent which housed them in transit. From *Libia*, December 1938.

Officials in charge of the emigration stressed that the regime would care for the colonists, and that in sailing for Libya the families were not leaving Italy. The celebrations began the day before the sailing, scheduled for 28 October. Each village organized its own special farewell. At San Dona di Piave, northeast of Venice, for instance, an ox was roasted whole. Speeches by the local *federale* reminded the emigrants that the Duce would never forsake them and exhorted the families never to forget that they were Italians, members "of the nation which gave civilization to the world." Late in the afternoon of 27 October, with bands playing and the local Fascist hierarchy much in view, the colonists from the North began their journey. Streamers and banners with slogans like "We are the Duce's *rurali*" and "We, Fascist peasants, will always march wherever the Duce orders us to go" decorated the special trains. Chants of "Duce, Duce" and snatches of the Fascist anthem "Giovinezza" alternated with the benedictions of the local priests as the trains left for Genoa.

At the port, nine vessels were ready to embark 1,430 of the 1,800 families. Balbo had planned to parade the colonists on foot through the streets of Genoa, but rain spoiled the arrangements. To get the colonists on board as quickly as possible, Balbo turned the parade into a triumphal drive as the Genoese volunteered their taxis, buses, and private cars. Balbo personally supervised the operation from a little blue sports car.

For the colonists, it was a great day of "extraordinary happenings." They enjoyed showers of biscuits and candy, and they marveled at the crowds "as great on the right as on the left." Newspapermen besieged them for interviews. The colonists reminisced about their military experiences and the struggles in the old life they were leaving. They voiced their hopes for the future and their faith in the Duce.

Fertility was another favorite topic of discussion. Fathers and mothers of ten children found themselves instant celebrities. Newspapers estimated that already in the "fruitful wombs" of the colonists' wives as many as nine hundred new lives were stirring. The birth of a boy on the train provided an excellent omen for the future. Once aboard ship, with Balbo as godfather, the baby was christened Italo Vittorio Benito to honor Balbo, the king, and the Duce. Before the convoy left Genoa, three more of the spare cradles which Balbo had thoughtfully provided were occupied.

The colonists from the *Mezzogiorno* embarked at Naples on six ships. The entire convoy formed off the coast of Naples and passed in review before the Duce. Then, escorted by eight destroyers, the ships sailed for Tripoli, where they arrived 2 November. As the colonists found out, the carnival was far from ended. As one colonist wrote later,

If you could have seen it—all the sirens whistling, all the ships whistling, the artillery fired their cannons. . . if the world had ended you wouldn't have heard a thing.

The following day the families were free to roam the city. They generally marveled at the "extraordinary things, not to be believed if we had not seen them," but one skeptic also commented, "Tripoli is a very beautiful city—I wouldn't have believed it." In the evening there were fireworks in the Piazza del Castello and a speech by Balbo. Then came the main event, the unveiling of an equestrian statue of the Duce—"our great DUCE on a horse," as one colonist put it. On 4 November the families left by truck for their new homes. Those who were bound for Cyrenaica sailed for Benghazi, where they once again enjoyed a celebration and the inexhaustible shower of biscuits, candy, salami, and jams that greeted them everywhere. After an overnight stay in a tent encampment, minutely arranged by the army under Balbo's supervision, the colonists rode in truck convoys to their new homes on the Gebel. Many colonists shared the elation of one who wrote:

You can't know what joy we experienced when we saw our houses, which looked like little palaces; and as far as the land: ah! how much better it looks than that of Regalbuto, because we found it just ready for sowing.

Reaction to the *Ventimila*

High on the list of benefits the regime hoped to reap from the emigration of the *Ventimila* was national and international publicity. The Fascist press, of course, played up the colonization effort as yet another of the regime's marvelous achievements. For "old Libya hands" (*vecchi Libici*) like Luigi Bongiovanni, an exgovernor of Cyrenaica, the *Ventimila* came as a fulfillment of their fondest hopes.[22] Bongiovanni predicted that the parched and desolate steppe he remembered from the conquest would soon yield rich harvests; the "indigenous peoples who had shown such decided hostility and incomprehension" when the Italians first arrived would now live in harmony with the masses of peaceful colonists. For those with long and nostalgic memories, like the historian Gioacchino Volpe, the *Ventimila* suggested "in miniature an entire people on the move, just as at the time of the mass emigrations" at the end of the nineteenth century.[23] As Volpe remarked proudly, "how things had changed" from those depressing days when the government considered emigrants as little more than a source of remittances from abroad. The same theme—a vindication of the emigrants that De Amicis knew, those emigrants who left Italy cursing and crying—was celebrated in verse. "No one cries anymore," exulted a work entitled "Chorus of Italian Peasants in Libya," for

> The sea is ours;
> We cross it as if it were a piazza;
> And where we land
> We still find Italy.[24]

The regime arranged numerous ways to publicize the colonization. Many foreign journalists accompanied the *Ventimila;* others visited the villages early in 1939. Delegates to an international congress of agricultural experts held in Tripoli in 1939 enjoyed Balbo's lavish hospitality and were invited to visit the colonization projects.[25]

Most visitors returned with enthusiastic impressions. They praised the organization and discipline of the *Ventimila* expedition, and they were impressed with the careful planning and the lavishness of the colonization projects. Balbo's masterly organization of the *Ventimila* "worked with a smoothness of which I thought the Italians were incapable," an English observer remarked.[26] While touring the projects, the New York *Herald Tribune* correspondent found a Ferrarese family complaining vigorously about an organizational flaw—a smoky chimney in their new house in Cyrenaica. Yet his overall impression was one of superb organization that managed to avoid "cold mechanical efficiency."[27] In his view, the emigration of the *Ventimila* was "paternalism at its best." An American agricultural expert was astonished at the speed with which the villages had been constructed, as though "a fairy wand" had been waved across the desert and vast regions were suddenly transformed into thriving agricultural areas.[28] Other visitors remarked on the lavishness of the villages and the colonists' new homes, a standard "well above the lot of the average Italian rural worker."[29] "Never before have pioneers in a new land found colonization so de luxe as in Italian controlled North Africa," remarked another visitor.[30]

Balbo, always the charmer before journalists, received excellent reviews. An English correspondent described him as being a man who "disdains flattery," yet possessed "inexhaustible energy and a talent for giving and receiving friendship."[31] Balbo's talents and charisma rubbed off on his staff, according to many visitors. They contrasted Balbo's men with the bureaucrats and officials in Italy and concluded, "Fascism really does seem to produce a better man for the colonies than it does for Italy."[32] A frequent remark was that Balbo's dynamic leadership would make the difference between success and failure for the colonization projects.[33] Ironically, the *Ventimila*—and especially Balbo—enjoyed too much success for the Duce's taste. Ciano noted in his diary that "the Duce was annoyed at the trumpeting made by Balbo over the sending of colonists to Libya." In the future, the emigration was to take place quietly.[34]

Of particular interest to visitors from the democracies, troubled with domestic unemployment, social dislocation, and overpopulation, was the way totalitarian Italy handled these social problems.[35] The method and discipline of the Italian land settlements in Libya, and their stress on the family rather than the individual as the unit of colonization, seemed more fruitful and efficient than the "haphazard colonization" and free enterprise that characterized the development of the British Empire and North America. Moore was not at all certain that the Italian methods would work in England, for "families in industrial England are neither so large nor so amenable to state-shepherding as Italian peasant families." Nevertheless, for Moore and others the Italian example was one to be watched:

At a time when so many thousands of unwanted or excess Europeans, faced with a parasitic or homeless existence, have become an unsettling and disquieting element of our daily life, the Italian technique of overseas settlement...offers us much to learn.[36]

Despite the genuine admiration for these projects as a possible answer to internal social problems, observers did not neglect the long-term political implications of the mass migrations. Visitors wondered what new directions Fascism's apparent dynamism and discipline would take. Where would Mussolini move next—toward Egypt or Tunisia?[37] Nor were Europeans the only ones concerned. The Arab nations were alarmed at the mass emigration, as Ciano noted in his diary. Demonstrations took place in Baghdad:

they think that this nucleus of Italians will break the Arabic preponderance in the Mediterranean. They are right; such is our objective.[38]

The French quickly seized on the mass emigration as an effective anti-Italian propaganda theme to broadcast among the Arabs of North Africa and Syria. The French resident general in Tunis noted with satisfaction in 1939 that thanks to the French propaganda the "Moslems of Tunisia were now complaining of the fate of their coreligionists in Tripolitania who were under Italian rule."[39]

Nor were visitors blind to the enormous technical problems the Italians faced if the projects were to be a success. Often the criticisms echoed Salvemini's warnings of the dangers of an "artificial colonization." As a Belgian observer wondered, what would happen to these projects, so admirable in their planning, if state subsidies were withheld?[40] What would happen to the colonists in case of war or financial crisis? Many wondered about the fate of the Libyans who had been displaced from their grazing and farm lands and now appeared "sullen and restive and only submissive because forced to be so."[41] Many difficult environmental problems loomed. Some wondered about the salt content in the water used for the irrigated farms. Others raised the possibility of eventual shortages of good agricultural land. Still others questioned the efficacy of the marketing system controlled by the colonization companies. Balbo himself referred to the dangers of the system's growing bureaucracy.[42] He also apparently faced—or at least he anticipated—internal objections to the costs of the colonization and to possible competition between Libyan and metropolitan agricultural products.[43]

Despite these problems, Balbo went ahead in 1939 with his plans for a second annual mass migration.[44] This time the colonization companies were to develop about sixty thousand hectares into 1,350 new farms for the colonist families and 100 new farms for the Moslem colonization program. The preparations for the second wave of colonists provided work for 4,500 laborers imported from Italy. The actual sailing, however, partly because of the adverse political repercussions in the Moslem world and partly because of the Duce's humors, was muted. Only 10,000 colonists emigrated on 28 October 1939. This time there was no spectacle in Tripoli. The colonists bound for Cyrenaica broke off from the main convoy without landing in Tripolitania. If the colonists in 1939 received a bit less fanfare, they certainly did not complain. They sent home glowing reports of being "treated like royalty" and exulted in the showers of treats that marked their trip.[45] Like the group in 1938, they felt that they were on their way to the "land of Bengodi."

7

Intensive Colonization: The Perspective of the Colonist Families

For nearly three decades, Italians had argued over Libya's value as a colony. Was it merely one of the largest among the "collection of deserts" that composed Italy's African empire? Or was Libya truly a potential "land of Bengodi"—the fabulous country described in Boccaccio's *Decameron*? The Duce was determined to show up the scoffers. Under the program of intensive colonization, the regime launched a massive effort to transform Libya into the long-sought paradise for Italy's immigrant masses.

For the colonist families who emigrated to Libya under the programs of intensive colonization, the colony came close to being such a land. Libya presented opportunites that most of the families had only dreamed about. Whole farms and villages were constructed for them, complete with all the supplies and facilities they would need for their new lives. With a benevolent and paternal hand, the colonization companies furnished the families with tools, seeds, livestock, machinery, financing, and technical advice. Most important of all to the families was the promise that with patience and diligence the prize of land and independence could be theirs.

As the colonists soon learned, the Duce's Bengodi also had its imperfections. The climate could be brutal. Droughts and insects destroyed the crops. In return for financial and technical help, the colonization companies demanded discipline and sacrifice. Worse still, from the colonist's view, were the problems created by a sluggish bureaucracy and mistakes in planning. Nevertheless, if the Duce had not ultimately betrayed the families by blundering into war, many of the colonists might have succeeded in their long-term aspirations for land and independence.

The agricultural experts and the Libyans—the two other major groups involved with the colonization projects—saw the colonization from a less rosy perspective. Their views will be discussed in the next two chapters. This chapter describes the locale and structure of the ECL and INFPS villages and discusses the colonists' perspective on the land of Bengodi.

The Projects in Tripolitania

From the rolling hills of the Gebel to the monotonous coastal plain of the Jeffara the settlement projects in Tripolitania were scattered over a wide variety of locales. To the casual visitor, none looked very promising for colonization. "The astonishing thing about this land to the uninstructed observer is that it can be made to foster any kind of vegetation at all," commented a visitor on a tour of semi-irrigated farms south of Tripoli.[1] However, as he noted, with hard work and great patience the Italians had laid out neat farms and villages. Olives and almond trees, "dwarfish but vigorous," and green fodder crops were sprouting among the dunes and steppe.

Tripolitania's extremes of climate and temperature and the area's lack of surface water have been described in an earlier chapter. For the colonization—especially the intensive phase—to succeed under such conditions, the Italians had to find underground water resources.

Until the De Bono era, the Italians, busy with problems of establishing the domain and the region's military security, did not explore extensively for water.[2] The concessions were expected to rely primarily on dry farming and on the same sources the Libyans used. Along the coast, the concessioners utilized the phreatic layer which could be found at a depth ranging from 6 to 22 meters. Between Tripoli and Tagiura (Tajura) alone, this source fed an estimated eight thousand wells. The concessioners complained that the water was often brackish and that the capacity of the wells was limited. Farther inland, the first phreatic layer could be found only fifty to eighty meters below the surface. Thus these concessioners relied on a few natural springs and on rainwater they accumulated in storage tanks, some of which dated from Roman times.

To increase these limited water resources, the Italians began to explore more intensively, and in 1926 they found a second—and sometimes even a third and a fourth—phreatic layer at depths ranging from twenty to forty meters below the surface. These layers proved to be particularly abundant in the triangular area formed by Sabratha, Azizia, and Tagiura. The yields averaged forty to sixty cubic meters per hour, but sometimes went as high as two hundred to three hundred cubic meters per hour. The quality of the water depended on the locale. In general it proved to be slightly alkaline, with varying

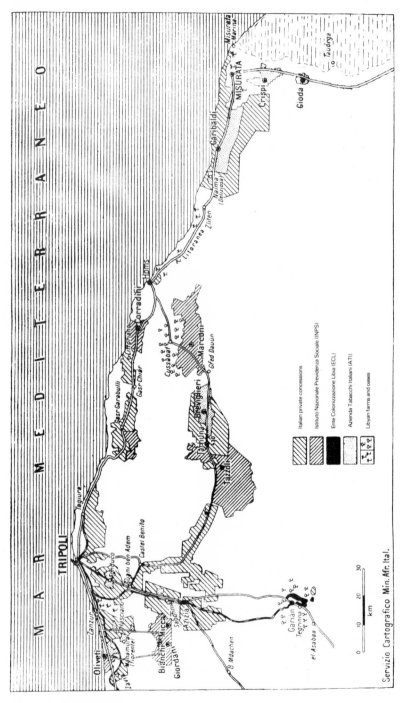

Map 3. Location of colonization company projects and of private concessions in Tripolitania (1940). Adapted from Istituto Agricolo Coloniale, *La colonizzazione agricola della Tripolitania* (Rome, 1947).

degrees of hardness and saltiness. To develop this second layer required expensive drilling and pumping equipment. The government, through the De Bono laws, offered subsidies to encourage exploration and development. The government also gradually introduced an electric power network so that the concessioners could replace their gasoline-powered pumps with electric motors. Nevertheless, the cost of pumping the water always remained high.

To prepare for intensive colonization, the Italians explored for artesian wells. They found an artesian layer near Tripoli and at Bir Tummina, at depths ranging from 135 to 400 meters. Under the direction of Professor Ardito Desio, a geologist from the University of Milan, between 1936 and 1940 the water exploration program—which also included keeping an eye out for oil-bearing strata—proceeded at a feverish pace.[3] By 1940 twenty-eight drilling engines were at work, compared with only two during the period 1934–36; and by 1940 the Italians had drilled 20,100 meters a year in contrast to 550 meters annually for the 1934–36 period.[4] As of March 1940, sixty-six wells had been drilled and seventeen more were being developed. Of the sixty-six wells completed, fifty-five had given good results.[5]

With the discovery of these underground water resources, the Italian agricultural technicians planned for three basic types of farms to deal with the varieties of Tripolitania's agrological conditions: irrigated, semi-irrigated, and dry.[6]

The 470 irrigated farms of the Crispi-Gioda settlements, all operated by the ECL, depended on the artesian waters found in 1936. The farms were located on ten thousand hectares along the Misurata-Tauroga road, an area in which the rainfall ranged between 100 and 150 millimeters annually. Although the artesian water could be used for agricultural purposes, it had a high mineral content, and a rain-fed auxiliary irrigation system had to be devised to rinse out the mineral deposits. The irrigation system was made up of about 700 kilometers of canals and pipelines and included some seventy catch basins and reservoirs. The ten-hectare plots were planted with olive trees, interspersed with fodder crops, wheat, or barley, some experimental cotton plants, and garden vegetables. The farms were designed so that only two hectares would rely on regular irrigation. The rest could survive on the moisture from rainfall. Each farm was furnished with six head of cattle and a work mule, which the agricultural technicians estimated would furnish enough manure for the irrigated crops.

The semi-irrigated farms totaled 826. The ECL operated Oliveti, with 49 farms, Fonduco (Fonduk el-Togar), with 27 farms, and Azizia, with 30 farms. The INFPS operated Bianchi, with 167 farms, Oliveti, with 71 farms, Hascian, with 19 farms, Giordani, with 193 farms, Micca, with 148 farms, Corradini, with 64 farms, and Castelverde (Gasr Garabulli), with 58 farms. These farms were in areas in which phreatic water was relatively abundant and close to the surface at depths varying from twelve to twenty-five meters. The lots varied in size from twenty-two to twenty-five hectares and were primarily dedicated to vineyards, olives, and almonds. However, five hectares were reserved for irrigated crops, including citrus fruit trees, and fodder crops to support the livestock. Each lot had a well with a catch basin and an electric pump. The electricity for Bianchi, Giordani, and Micca was furnished by a power station at Bianchi. Each farm had a canal network for water distribution. The length of the canal systems at Oliveti and Giordani alone totaled some four hundred kilometers. In addition, when necessary the colonist families distributed water by ox-drawn water carts. To defend the farms at Bianchi, Giordani, and Micca from winds and shifting dunes, the Italians initiated an extensive network of tamarisk windbreaks and settled the dunes by planting elephant grass.

The dry farms totaled 478. The ECL operated 168 at Breviglieri, east of Tarhuna, at an altitude of four hundred to five hundred meters. The area rainfall totaled 250–275 millimeters annually. The locale was picturesque. Each white concrete home had its own view, and each farm had its distinguishing contours and landmarks. At Breviglieri, the farms comprised about 50 hectares. Half of the land was planted with olives, almonds, and vineyards; the rest went into fruit trees, India figs, and grain. The houses were sixty to eighty meters from each other and grouped in clumps of four to six around the water sources. Where no water was found, the lots had to be fed by a twenty-five-kilometer aqueduct. At Breviglieri, the farms were limited to four head of cattle and a mule.

The INFPS dry farms were located at Tazzoli, where 179 farms were created, and at Marconi, south of Qussabat, in the Gasr Daun zone of the Gsea Valley, where 131 farms were established. These farms varied in size from thirty-five to fifty hectares. At Tazzoli, where there was an opportunity to cultivate grain, the farms were as large as one hundred hectares. The types of crops were similar to those at Breviglieri.

The ECL's 318-farm settlement of Garibaldi, between Zliten and Misurata, was to have been partially irrigated with artesian wells. However, only one well had been drilled by the time the war broke out, and the colonists were forced to operate their thirty-hectare plots as dry farms.

To house the families, the colonization company's technicians designed a single-story family dwelling, usually with three rooms, a kitchen, and an annexed *fonduco*, or courtyard, enclosed by a solid wall.[7] The design was not unusual in Southern Italy, Sardinia, or other parts of North Africa. In the courtyard the colonists sheltered their livestock, tools, and forage. The solid wall provided a good defense against the winds and against thefts and permitted easy surveillance of the livestock.

In Tripolitania alone, the Italians built 1,752 of these structures in 1938 and 1939: 845 for the ECL and 907 for the INFPS. The houses varied somewhat in size and accessories, depending on when they were built and where they were situated. As the accessories became more elaborate—the coastal settlements near Tripoli, for instance, were equipped with indoor running water, showers, and electricity—the costs mounted. Inflation, high transportation costs, and the Duce's autarkic economic policies all contributed to the rising expenses. The houses built at Bianchi in 1938, for instance, were valued at seventy-five thousand lire, double the cost of the first houses built in 1936 for thirty-six thousand lire.

To serve the colonist's civic and social needs, the government built rural centers (*centri rurali*).[8] Six were constructed in 1938 (Bianchi, Giordani, Oliveti, Breviglieri, Crispi, and Gioda) and an additional four in 1939 (Micca, Tazzoli, Corradini, and Garibaldi). In these villages, the colonists found such facilities as a church, a post office, a café, a commissary, a haberdasher, the town hall, a police station, a hospital or medical center, and schools. The rural centers also included a marketplace, craftsmen's shops, and the offices and storage facilities of the colonization companies. If the distances were too great for the colonists to reach the major centers, the families found the essential services in smaller villages or hamlets (*borgate*).

The Projects in Cyrenaica

The bleak and rugged Gebel Akhdar—the main focus of the Italian colonization effort in Cyrenaica—belonged to a different world from the dunes and rolling hills of Tripolitania. In a landscape of rocky hills and thickets, against a skyline of wild olives and stunted trees, some of the colonists' villages took on a certain picturesqueness and grandeur. Looking at the village of D'Annunzio, one visitor remarked that it stood above the road "with the sheer militancy of a Spanish convent."[9] In this wild and isolated setting, the Italians managed to coax olives, almonds, and vineyards out of the red earth. Particularly memorable to the Italians, accustomed to the patchwork fields of their native peninsula, was the expanse of the wheat fields of Cyrenaica.[10]

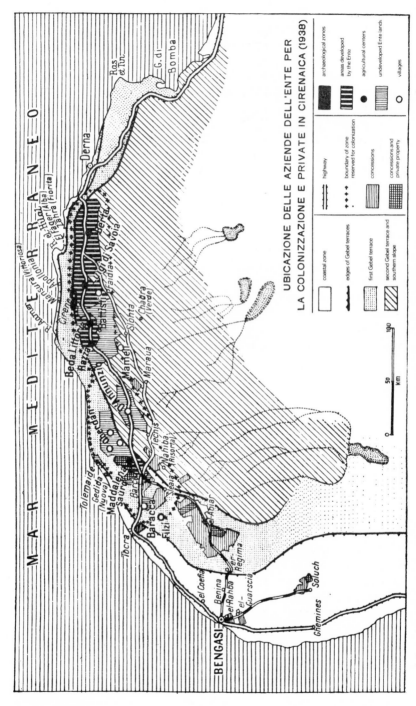

Map 4. Location of Ente farms and private concessions in Cyrenaica (1938). Adapted from Istituto Agricolo Coloniale, *La colonizzazione della Cirenaica* (Rome, 1947).

The natural environment of Cyrenaica's Gebel Akhdar proved to be comparatively less troublesome than that of Tripolitania.[11] Unlike Tripolitania, with its extremes of climate and wide variations in water resources, Cyrenaica's Gebel presented relatively uniform conditions. Once the brush and thickets had been cleared and the rocks and stones blasted away, the Italians reached pockets of good earth. Despite the many hills and gorges in the area, there was little need for terracing or drainage work.

The chief problem, from the planner's point of view, was organization. The challenge was to settle large numbers of colonists on vast and isolated tracts of land in a relatively short time. In a matter of seven years between 1933 and 1940, the ECL established thirteen farming districts with a total of 1,760 farms on tracts totaling 62,901 hectares. The pace of settlement was uneven and makes the total achievement even more remarkable. The first four villages of Beda Littoria, Luigi di Savoia, Luigi Razza, and Giovanni Berta were built among the juniper, lentisk, and cypress of the Gebel in 1933–34, and about three hundred families were settled. With the mass emigrations of 1938–39, the number of families swelled almost sevenfold to more than twenty-two hundred, including the families of the ECL personnel.

In general, since the conditions were relatively uniform on the Gebel Akhdar, the colonists planted crops which did not differ much from those in Tripolitania. At least a third to a half of each farm on the Gebel Akhdar was planted with olives, almond trees, and vineyards. The rest went to forage, cereals, fruit trees, and a small garden of fruits and vegetables for the colonist family's personal use. The livestock usually included six cows or oxen, a mule, and a pig.

The size of the farms averaged thirty-five hectares. However, depending on the locale, the families worked plots ranging from fifteen to fifty hectares. The first families had been given small farms which averaged fifteen to twenty hectares. These, however, were gradually enlarged. As in Tripolitania, some families were given exceptionally large lots for the development of their orchards and groves. The plan was that in the future, when the trees were mature, the plot would be divided with a new family, or perhaps with the colonist's eldest son when he was ready to farm on his own.

During the early days of the colonization, the farms were laid out in irregular fashion to experiment with different locales and to compensate for or eliminate unproductive areas. The intensive phase of colonization eliminated these experiments. For the *Ventimila* and the successive immigration in 1939, the farms were laid out with great uniformity. The placement of the colonists' houses also changed. As

security increased on the Gebel, the houses were no longer grouped
together for protection. Under intensive colonization, the houses were
isolated and situated in the center of each plot.

As in Tripolitania, the colonists' houses became progressively more
comfortable, elaborate, and expensive.[12] Originally, the technical experts had debated whether to build temporary or permanent dwellings.
If the houses were to be permanent, the planners considered whether
the structures should be completed or only partially finished when the
families moved in. The decision was made to build permanent and
complete houses. The first batch of 298 houses was built in 1933–34.
Each structure was designed to accommodate two separate families. The
families were to share certain common facilities such as cisterns and
ovens. Each family had two rooms, a kitchen, and a shed for their
livestock. As the technical experts themselves admitted, these houses,
built with a rigid concern for economy, were "modest buildings and
rather limited."[13]

Two later models were considerably larger and more comfortable.
The houses were single-family dwellings with three rooms and a
kitchen. The accessories, such as the stable, storehouse, and storage
shed, became increasingly elaborate. About 50 houses of the second
model were built in 1935–36. For the mass colonization, 1,414 houses of
a third model with enlarged rooms were built.

With the improvement in design also went an improvement in the
quality of construction. However, the costs, too, mounted steadily, from
thirty-seven thousand lire for the first type of house to sixty thousand
lire for the second, to more than one hundred thousand lire for the
third. The increased costs reflected the improved materials and the
high costs of transporting these materials to the isolation of the Gebel.

As in Tripolitania, the government built rural centers or hamlets
(*borgate*) to serve the colonist families' civic needs. These villages also
served as marketing and storage centers for the colonists' products.

Although the water problems of the Gebel Akhdar were somewhat
less severe than in Tripolitania, the Italians planned to build a vast
aqueduct which was designed to support an eventual population of
sixty thousand colonists.[14] The main system, when complete, was to
have been about 190 kilometers in length, with branches stretching out
for another 50 kilometers. The aqueduct was to transport water from
the spring at Ain-Mara near Derna to the plateau, a rise of about 300
meters. A reservoir was to be built at Zawiya Tert, about 36 kilometers
west of Ain-Mara. From there the water would be distributed to the
colonist villages through a system of tanks and reservoirs that stretched
the length of the Gebel. The cost of the project was estimated at 70

million lire. Construction on the aqueduct began in May 1939. By December 1940, when building stopped because of the war, all but 40 kilometers had been completed. In the meantime, the colonists had to rely on rainwater and on a truck convoy that brought water daily from Barce or Derna.

How much did the Italians spend on this elaborate colonization structure? Some estimates of the aggregate Italian investment in Libyan agriculture are given in chapter 10. For the eighteen hundred farms of the *Ventimila* alone in 1938, including the entire infrastructure of roads, houses, water services, and villages, total costs were officially estimated at 20 million prewar American dollars.[15] The costs per farm ranged from $6,750 for Breviglieri to $9,250 for the Cyrenaican farms in the Gebel Akhdar.

To evaluate these costs is extremely difficult. To make comparisons on an economic basis is largely academic. The regime did not really care about expenses. The agricultural experts estimated that the average costs of developing the demographic farms in Cyrenaica was about ten thousand lire per hectare, in contrast to the four thousand to eight thousand lire average per hectare, depending on the locale, for private colonization.[16] The comparison has little meaning, for the private concessions had not achieved the political and social goals the Fascist regime desired: the creation of an intensive network of small independent farmers.

The agricultural experts who advised Balbo had to account for the spiraling costs of the colonization programs.[17] In February 1938, six months before the sailing of the *Ventimila*, Maugini reported to Balbo that the estimated costs of the new farms to be built would be about one hundred seventy thousand lire, an increase of about forty thousand lire over the farms which had been constructed in the past. He blamed this increase on the particular economic conditions of the moment, in which there was a shortage of labor and building materials. But the costs were also higher because of the need to build the elaborate infrastructure for the colonists: the roads, the aqueducts, the rural centers. He also claimed that the ECL would have to buy additional farm machinery. In December 1938, in preparation for the emigration of 1939, Balbo received another memorandum from his advisers with the estimate that the farms would cost at least one hundred ninety thousand lire. The increased costs were attributed to higher wages for the crash construction programs, the costs of clearing a large number of farms on the Gebel Akhdar, and the need for elaborate water systems in the Tripolitanian projects.

The technical experts defended these rising costs partly on economic grounds. They pointed out that these figures represented an initial investment. Such start-up costs were bound to be high because the Italians had to invest heavily in the colony's infrastructure. As the colonization proceeded, the unit costs would undoubtedly decline. On the other hand, no one could predict the amount of future investments and subsidies that would be needed until the farms became independent. These future investments would depend on such imponderables as the skills of the colonist families, weather, and market conditions.

Ultimately, however, the technical experts defended the costs of the colonization on noneconomic grounds. "Such high costs may raise doubts about the advisability of carrying out the programs," Balbo's technical advisers remarked. They concluded that the expenses were worthwhile because "the development of land with the goal of settling it immediately is the only way to prepare a future prosperity for Libya, a way that resolves political and social problems as well as economic ones." Some foreign observers, too, concluded that judging the investment according to an economic yardstick was not very meaningful. The Italians were paying for the satisfaction of creating a fourth shore. As Moore concluded, "From a strictly commercial standpoint, the investment in the colonization may be an unremunerative expenditure, but it does not appear to be an unduly extravagant sum to spend on so cherished a dream."[18]

The Colonist's Perspective: Work and Discipline

As one visiting journalist observed, the colonists were "very simple people, and they were obviously much more prosperous and much more secure than they would have been in Italy."[19] To a large extent this accounts for the satisfaction which many of the colonists expressed with their lot at the time and for the memories of Libya which they still cherish today.

The colonists' delight in their newly found prosperity shines through in their letters home—especially in letters that were published for obvious propaganda purposes. To friends, relatives, and Fascist party officials, the families enjoyed cataloging the groceries, the furniture, the details of the house and land they found upon their arrival. A colonist from Chieti abbreviated his list in a letter to the secretary of his local *Fascio*:

- We are at the village of Beda Littoria. In few words: Plenty to eat. Twenty five hectares of land. A new house, big and solid. New furniture.[20]

A woman from the province of Venezia, who made the trip to Libya

Aerial view of the village center at Oliveti (Tripolitania) against a background of olive trees. From *Tripolitania: Some Photographic Representations of Italy's Actions* (Florence: Istituto Agricolo Coloniale, 1946).

Fourth Shore: A Libyan seems unmoved at the news that he is now living on Italy's *quarta sponda*. The proclamation before him, issued in 1939, explains that the "old colony" has disappeared. In its place is Libya, the nineteenth region of Italy. From *Libia*, January 1939.

alone with her eight children, was impressed by the number of beds in her home:

We have ten beds now [sic] it doesn't seem true because when I think of when I was at home we slept five in a bed.[21]

A colonist from Udine, added at the end of his inventory that in his village, "there is electric light, even for the toilet."[22]

The promise of land and independence was another source of hope and satisfaction. As a colonist from the village of Mameli wrote, he did not expect to get rich. He hoped merely that "in a day not too far distant" he would "have bread for my sons without too much trouble and without being bawled out by others."[23]

The colonists, however, could not take their prosperity for granted. To reach the ultimate goal of land and independence, the families were expected to work hard. In theory, at least, the discipline and regulation in their lives is impressive. The Fascists liked to boast about an "army of *rurali*," and the image is appropriate. From the day he left his native village in the company of an escort until the day he earned his farm, the colonist and his family lived as if they had signed up for a twenty- or thirty-year period of quasi-military service. The battle for Libya was to be won through a highly coordinated attack led by the colonization companies and the government. For better or for worse the colonist and his family provided the masses of infantry whose main task was to follow orders and provide labor.

Upon their arrival, the families were assigned to their houses and farms. In general, the assignments were made by lot, but the process was not purely random.[24] The ECL in Cyrenaica, for instance, tried to match the topography of the farms with the regional origin of the families. The hilliest plots were assigned to families from Calabria and the Abruzzi, who were accustomed to such terrain. The company also took regional origins into account in planning for social cohesion and harmony among the families. At first the companies assigned neighboring farms to families from the same regions, assuming that common habits and traditions would help keep peace. In practice, the company found that families from different regions squabbled and quarreled less—often because they could not understand each other's dialects.

After about a week of orientation following their arrival, the families were expected to begin meeting their work schedule.[25] Oxen, horses, hand tools, appropriate carts and harnesses, seeds, and cuttings were all provided. The company also arranged for communal use of heavy agricultural machinery like threshers and harvesters. When additional hired labor was needed for the harvest or for planting vineyards or for blasting rocks, the company provided it.

A record of the goods and services furnished to the colonist was kept in his account book, or *libretto colonico*. The booklet consisted of three parts: the debits and credits he accumulated over the course of a year; the cumulative annual balance which would determine the moment when he would become an independent landowner; and, finally, the account of his livestock.

The company official most directly in touch with the colonist families and the one most responsible for supervising and disciplining them in their day-to-day activities was the *capo zona*.[26] For this critical task, the companies recruited technical experts with advanced degrees or diplomas in agriculture and with practical experience in climates analogous to that of Libya. With the help of his immediate staff, which might include an assistant, an accountant, and a clerk in charge of the storehouse, the *capo zona* administered a zone which included about 250 farms.

The *capo zona*'s main task was to supervise and evaluate the development of each farm. Inevitably, however, he found that his tasks took him far beyond the technical problems of developing a farm. He became involved in all aspects of the colonists' lives. He kept the peace between quarreling families; he policed those who were too fond of wine; he prodded the slackers. In administering discipline to the recalcitrant families, he was authorized first to warn them, then to fine them by withholding part of their monthly salary, and finally to propose that the family be repatriated.

The relationship between colonist and colonization company was formally regulated by contract.[27] In general, under the pact the state provided the land and capital; the colonist supplied the labor to develop the land into working farms. The colonization companies drew up the development plans, provided supervision and technical advice to the colonists, dispensed the necessary capital, and recovered the state's investment from the colonist when the land was in production.

The contracts usually consisted of three basic parts: (1) an initial transformation relationship in which the colonist and the colonization company did the preliminary work to develop the farm into a productive enterprise; (2) a productive phase in which the farm began to yield; and (3) a phase of redemption in which the colonist, now working a productive farm, made long-term arrangements with the company to pay off his debts and receive full title to the land.[28]

Although the principles behind the contract remained fairly constant, specific clauses varied widely according to the types of farms in each district and according to the policies of the colonization companies. The INFPS, for instance, considered its settlements in Libya as only one of many projects in the field of social insurance and unemployment. Accordingly, the organization limited its responsibility to management, coordination, and administration of the colonists' farms and expected to recover its investment over a thirty-year period. The ECL's sole concern, on the other hand, was colonization in Libya. Initially—until the period of intensive settlement—the company was free to indulge in speculative enterprises connected with colonization and agricultural development. For this reason, the company was willing to shoulder a greater responsibility in developing the colonists' farms. The contracts developed before the legislation on intensive colonization reflected these different approaches.

Under the INFPS contract, the colonist was obligated from the beginning of the agreement.[29] He assumed all the responsibility for agricultural development and all the financial risks. The cost of the farm was computed from the first day of settlement. The colonist's debt consisted of the cost of the land, the company's cost of transformation (roads, houses, wells, power network), and an anticipated monthly salary for the family that lasted for a five-year period—the length of the transformation phase. To this debt the company added a 5 percent interest charge for technical and administrative services. The colonist's debt was to be repaid over a twenty-five-year period. The time when the colonist would receive title to his farm and initiate the redemption phase of the contract was not specified. The only stipulation was that his debts to the company had to be cleared. The colonist was responsible for selling his products, although the company would perform this service for him. The contract could be broken in cases of circumstances beyond the colonist's control. Any indemnity for the work he had done depended on the conditions that led to breaking the contract.

Under the ECL contracts, the company shouldered far more of the responsibility. The price of the farm was determined after the first two years of development during which the colonist family worked as salaried labor. At the end of this transformation phase, the family had the option to continue with the contract or to leave the farm. This option presented advantages to both sides. If the colonist wished to leave he had lost nothing, since he had received an equitable salary. For the company, the option provided a convenient way of eliminating families that were not considered suitable for the work. If the colonist chose to continue, he then entered the five-to-ten-year productive phase as a sharecropper. The colonist's share of the profits was credited to his account against the debts he owed for the total cost of the farm and any additional financial assistance provided by the company. During the sharecropping phase, the company received all the produce of the farm and marketed it. At the end of the productive phase, the colonist received the farm as private property and arrangements were made for him to pay off the rest of his debt to the company over a period of about twenty-five years. To ensure repayment of its investment, the company often acquired a mortgage on the farm.

The contracts that were developed for the phase of intensive colonization beginning in 1937 were variations on the conditions described above.[30] In general the financial obligations on the colonist and companies were eased and the government took up the burden. The period of amortization was lengthened to thirty-five or forty years; the interest rate on the colonist's debt and the company's charge for administrative expenses were reduced; the colonist's debt to the company was interest-free for the first five to eight years and then set at 2 percent thereafter; the government's contribution toward reclamation was set at 30 percent and then at 33 percent; the colonist was to receive title to his property at the end of the eighteenth year.

For the colonists, the contracts were never much of a burden. In the first place, the contracts were constantly being revised with the changes in government policies. The pacts developed under the 1928 laws were amended for the intensive colonization of 1938. In turn, by the time the war broke out an entirely new system of agreements was under study. In general, the contracts tended to become increasingly complex, detailed, and uniform—but also more generous toward the colonist families.[31] Despite this trend, as the contracts proliferated colonists and colonization companies became embroiled in endless conflicts and disputes.

A political factor also helped protect the colonist families from fulfilling their obligations under the contracts. The regime feared the adverse publicity which disgruntled or repatriated families might generate. For this reason the companies seldom enforced the contracts with much severity. For instance, during the sharecropping phase the colonists usually found ways to conceal part of their production from the company. They sold the illegal portion on the open market, pocketed the profit, and cheerfully allowed their debts with the company to mount up. The war favored these abuses. As the contracts were more and more openly violated, the companies tried to draw up new ones that might be more easily and realistically enforced. Yet even as the experts worked to devise these new contracts, they were skeptical that the families would ever be forced to fulfill their obligations.[32]

The Colonist's Perspective: Social and Civic Life

The colonist's social and civic life was completely provided for by the state through the colonization companies.[33] The colonist paid no taxes. He received free medical care and free education for his children. Although the colonist's life generally seems to have been a healthy one, a doctor, a nurse, and a midwife were available in the rural center.[34] Six to eight elementary school teachers, depending on the size of the community, taught the colonists' children. School attendance was compulsory from six to twelve years. So peaceful and so well regulated did the colonist's life appear that one visiting foreign journalist compared the families to well-bred cattle, "generally sleek and well fed, but totally devoid of any initiative."[35]

The colonists enjoyed a modest social life at the rural centers. Sundays and holidays generally meant going to mass and then spending a few hours at the *Dopolavoro*, the state-sponsored recreation and cultural organization. At the *Dopolavoro* the men listened to the radio, drank a little wine or played cards or *bocce*, much as they would have done at the cafés in their native villages. The young men and the girls danced. From time to time touring companies presented operatic programs and variety shows.[36] Fascist holidays such as the *Festa del Lavoro* (21 April) were celebrated with the inauguration of a new movie house, dancing, singing, and excursions. Hunting for small game like pigeons, partridges, quail, and rabbits was another favorite recreation for the men. In some villages the men received military instruction. Other festivals centered around rare visits by the Duce and the king and Balbo's more frequent appearances.[37]

But the land of Bengodi was not without its problems for the colonist families. Inevitably there were blunders in planning and organization. A 1939 report describes how the colonists at the INFPS semi-irrigated villages of Bianchi, Micca, and Giordani struggled to develop their farms without adequate electricity for their irrigation system.[38] The power station at Bianchi was not sufficient for all three villages. Hence the power was distributed in turn according to such factors as the degree of development of the farms, the rainfall, and the time of year. The colonists could rely on electricity only twice a week, or at best perhaps every other day, sometimes for no more than two hours.

Another problem was a sluggish bureaucracy which distributed necessary tools and supplies only after long delays—or which delivered materials and livestock that were inadequate or inappropriate. Military horses that were unsuitable as draft animals; fertilizers in short supply or not available; rubber tires for the colonists' carts—a vehicle essential both for personal transportation and for hauling materials—out of stock; long delays in repairing damaged equipment or faulty buildings: these are only a partial list of the families' frustrations.

The contracts too were an eternal source of dispute. A May 1936 letter signed by Balbo and directed to the Foreign and Colonial ministries illustrates the colonists' complaints.[39] The families claimed that their monthly salaries were inadequate for families of eight to fifteen members. Another dispute was over a clause that the colonists could be paid in kind with goods from the company's commissary. The clause was intended to be to the colonists' advantage, but in practice the families complained that commissary prices were higher than in the open market and that many necessary goods were not available. Still another source of contention was the division of the harvest between the colonists and the colonization companies.

To discuss their problems and to air their grievances, the heads of each family met periodically with the *capo zona*.[40] In general, he was expected to agree with the majority decision expressed at the meeting, except in cases when the authority of his superiors was required. The *capo zona* often could be sympathetic to the complaints of the families. An angry letter from the *capo zona* at the village of Razza in Cyrenaica, for instance, complained about shortages and inequities in his district, especially about the lack of facilities for social life on the Gebel Akhdar.[41] The *Dopolavoro*, the center of social life, had no funds. Thus there was no light in the building and it wasn't even possible to listen to the radio. He complained that hunting "for one reason or another" had been prohibited in the district for years, and the colonists couldn't even enjoy the mobile movie service as the military did. "Country folks have few pretentions," he concluded, "but those few must be satisfied . . . not even country people can live for years and years on bread and water alone."

If the *capo zona* could not resolve a problem, the colonists theoretically could carry their complaints to higher echelons through a committee of their representatives chosen by the *capo zona*. However, company officials in the higher ranks were instructed to be suspicious of the colonists' complaints on the grounds that in most cases the families were merely trying to milk extra benefits from the company. Palloni recalled that he almost never met with representatives of the colonists, although he often visited the villages informally.[42]

In addition to their struggles with human institutions, the colonists had to battle against nature. To some extent the families were cushioned from the full rigors of frontier life by the facilities and services provided for them. Nevertheless, there was little the company could do against bad weather, drought, or marauding insects. Perhaps even more demoralizing, particularly to those families of good will, was the frustration of being assigned a "bad" farm. Inevitably, even in the most promising districts, some plots were less favorably situated than others. Since the farms were usually assigned by lot, purely by chance one family might battle excessive wind exposure, rocky soil, lack of rainfall, or a hundred other problems while their more fortunate neighbors flourished. Only experience could reveal a farm's potential.

Both visitors and company officials paid tribute to the dedication and hard work of the best families. On some of the farms in Tripolitania in which serious water problems developed—such as in the village of Marconi—the colonists hauled water in their carts from as far away as twenty-five or twenty-eight kilometers to irrigate their crops.[43] A foreign journalist, visiting the farms at Crispi, was amazed to find the colonists working on their hands and knees, "picking the pathetic grain only nine inches high, a pathetic little fur on the sand." The sight impressed him like a "Pauline illumination":

I realized . . . that here I had come to a crossroads in the history of Europe and Africa. I have travelled throughout the southern continent, but I have never seen the white man, without native labor, down on his hands and knees squeezing the grain out of the soil.[44]

Despite these hardships, many of the excolonists who returned to Italy after the war remember their life in Libya with pleasure and nostalgia. They reminisce about a society that was more open and trusting than that of Italy today. They speak of a sense of community and comradeship, of a bond of *italianità* far stronger than they ever felt in metropolitan Italy. "In Libya we used to work together; here it's the same old story: we seem to be at each other's throats," an excolonist from Cyrenaica recalled wistfully.[45]

For many Libya is a happy memory associated with their youth and with one of the great opportunities of their lives. A garrulous old Sicilian, who had devoted his best years to his *podere* on the Gebel, summed up this attitude. Certainly life was hard on the farms, cultivating such a rough, windswept land in which "the water was our sweat," he reminisced.

But we were happy. . . . At that time I was young. . . . I was full of energy, full of ideas.[46]

Nevertheless, he recalls that even at the time he had felt an undercurrent of uneasiness, doubts about how long his good fortune would last.

I knew that the land was not ours. . . . I told myself that I wasn't the real owner. But it was my life, my trees and my vineyard. . . . It's very hard to abandon one's life all of a sudden for nothing.[47]

Yet with the defeat of the Italian army in Cyrenaica he was evacuated with the rest of the colonists. After the war he was one of the few Italians to return to Cyrenaica. There was no question of reviving his farm. On the Gebel, for the Italians "there is nothing left. Even the dogs are dead."[48]

The excolonists living in Italy today, their memories mellowed by more than three decades, look back on Libya with a touch of *mal d'Afrique*, the famous romantic nostalgia for Africa which is said to grip anyone who has lived there. Nevertheless, even if they were allowed to return, few of the colonists would seriously think of going back. The colonization is an episode of their youth—an opportunity that blossomed and then wilted abruptly. For most of the former colonists, Libya is "so many chapters of a dear book which one day the hand of destiny brutally slammed shut."[49]

Yet in these nostalgic memories the surviving colonists tend to gloss over the full range of their behavior. The Fascists liked to present the families as simple and hard-working, contented with the rural life a benevolent regime had provided for them. "They are like children; one has to think of so many things for them," one of the agricultural technicians was quoted as saying in 1933.[50] In practice, of course, the families were often not so simple-minded. As Maugini warned from the beginning, many families regarded the colonization primarily as an opportunity to milk subsidies and benefits from the government and the colonization companies. When these opportunities ended, the families preferred to seek their fortunes elsewhere, either by drifting to the cities or by returning to Italy. No one was more aware of these problems than the agricultural technicians.

8

Intensive Colonization:
The Perspective of the
Technical Experts

The Technical Expert's View: A Professional Critique

As wards of the state, showered with benefits beyond their dreams, the colonist families generally took a benevolent view of the colonization. The project technical directors and supervisors and the other technical experts who furnished advice to the colonization companies and to the Ministry of Italian Africa took a more critical view. Most of the technical directors and supervisors had been trained at the Istituto Agricolo Coloniale in Florence, one of the leading centers for the study of tropical and subtropical agriculture in Italy.[1] Since one of the chief technical advisors for the colonization projects, Professor Armando Maugini, was a member of the faculty and later director of the institute, it was natural that he recommended many of his former students for positions in the colonies. These young men were the ones responsible for the day-to-day operations of the projects. For them the colonization presented both an enormous challenge and an enormous frustration.

The challenge lay in making the desert bloom, in creating successful farms where once there had been only bleak steppe, in establishing a tradition of prosperous sedentary agriculture in a country which for centuries had lived at a subsistence level.[2] Even with the most careful planning, the technical experts anticipated years of experimentation and hard work which might lead to results quite different from what they had expected. Their problems were compounded by the ultimate goal of the projects: the social task of creating independent small landowners. Thus the technical directors faced the dual challenge of reclaiming men as well as land.

The technical expert's frustration came with the political atmosphere in which the colonization developed. The politicians had only one interest: to populate Libya rapidly. In the face of this directive, the qualities so dear and important to a scientist or technician—time, order, method—had to give way. Yet speed brought more and more maladies: the proliferation of conflicting contracts; the lack of time to absorb growing amounts of information about the environment; the increasingly haphazard selection of the colonist families. As one expert summarized the conflict, "too often action had to precede thought."[3]

The conflict between the political directives and the technical imperatives of the colonization emerges clearly in the technicians' reports, especially those reports written during and immediately after the war. By that time, the technicians had had nearly a decade of experience with which to evaluate the projects. As might be expected, they dwell at length on the many technical mistakes which had been made. They complain of unsatisfactory or unrealistic locales for the farms;[4] of false economy in the restricted sizes of certain plots;[5] of an administrative system that was too cumbersome.[6] Most of these problems were expected, and with time and experience the technicians were confident that they could be overcome.

Far more perplexing and disturbing were the social and political goals of the colonization. The task of the colonization companies was to transform a mass of immigrants from varying backgrounds and with a wide variety of agricultural skills into independent small farmers. The problem went beyond providing the families with the technical skills necessary for their success. The colonization companies also had to instill certain habits of mind: self-discipline, thrift, independence. As the experts commented frequently, the technical problems of the colonization were far easier to resolve than the human ones.

One major drawback in the colonist families was their lack of agricultural skills. Despite the regime's propaganda about the many innate virtues of the Italian peasantry, the colonists could furnish little more than their labor. Even the quality of their labor was "much more modest" than had been anticipated.[7] Many of the best technical results, particularly during the initial phases of transformation, were achieved directly by the companies' using heavy machinery and temporary labor.[8]

Far more damaging than the lack of technical skills was the colonist families' attitude toward the settlement program. Ideally, the colonists viewed the company's financial aid and technical direction as a temporary expedient along the road to independence. In practice, as one report concluded in 1947, "the colonist tried to take as much as he could while giving up as little as possible" to the companies.[9] The companies could not say that they had not been warned, for in 1933, in his blueprint for the Cyrenaican colonization company, Maugini had commented that the "man of the fields" possessed a "very keen scent" for benefits and subsidies. He added:

and this Ente which is born and operates in a political atmosphere, arouses in the peasant's mind—perhaps from the very first day—the hope of milking lots of money [from the company] without ever returning it.[10]

Some of the technical supervisors blamed the families' attitudes in part on the carnival spirit that Balbo had fostered during the mass migrations of 1938 and 1939. One agricultural expert remarked in 1945:

It doesn't take much to realize how the festive atmosphere in which the colonists found themselves from the day of their embarkation, and which continued for several weeks, encouraged a Bengodi mentality in sharp contrast to the hard and serious tasks which lay ahead. It certainly has not been easy to lead these people back to reality; only in the last two years has this damaging mentality finally been overcome.[11]

Balbo's grandiose style may have had something to do with encouraging these attitudes. Yet even without the initial carnival atmosphere, the colonist families probably would have wheedled and complained just as much. The more they were showered with benefits, the more they demanded. "If you give a man 100 lire, he will soon demand 110," Palloni commented.[12] The president of the ECL described the process as he personally observed it in a letter to Maugini in 1940:

Naturally, now that the colonists find themselves well off, they begin to complain, since this—as you taught me—is a fundamental law of the colonist's psychology.[13]

The colonists, through various administrative and political organs, were pressuring the ECL for more shoes and clothes, he complained. Yet he had gone to mass on Sundays at several of the villages and had observed that, at least to his way of thinking, the colonists, "especially the young people, are excessively well dressed."

Another eventual distraction, regardless of how well the colonists were treated on the farms, would have been the lure of the cities. No figures are available on the number of colonists who abandoned their farms for Tripoli or Benghazi, but most probably the colonists were not in Libya long enough for the problem to develop, at least before the war. Certainly, the technicians' reports show little concern.

The colonization companies, however, anticipated problems in the future.[14] A 1939 INFPS report outlined a program of technical education, frequent meetings between colonists and company officials, and prizes for those colonists who best carried out the company's directives. It was hoped that through education and incentives the colonist would remain absorbed in developing his farm. The educational program in particular was important, according to the report, to train incoming families and also to combat "the otherwise inevitable exodus of the colonists' children toward the urban centers" in the future.[15]

For the long run, the technical advisors and the colonization companies had no illusions that they would be able to stop the rural-urban flow entirely. But neither did they anticipate a major exodus. They thought in terms of their metropolitan experiences. Fascist Italy never knew the massive movement to the cities which developed during the postwar period, and the regime took strenuous measures to prevent any such migration. Thus the technical experts reasoned that during the first years of the colonization—which were also the early stages of Libya's development—there would be little industry to attract and absorb the colonists. The thirty-hectare farms were large enough to provide for a family's needs for about a generation. As the family grew and expanded, the future would take care of itself. The technical experts anticipated that a certain natural selection would take place among the colonists. The successful ones would eventually buy out the weaker ones. In the meantime, the colonization would have achieved its purpose: a generation would have become solidly rooted in the Libyan countryside.

The colonists' attitudes toward their contracts provides a concrete illustration of the Bengodi mentality. In general, the colonists were not concerned with working for the long-term transformation of their farms, for this meant focusing their energies on their trees. They preferred to work on the short-term crops that would yield a quick profit. Despite the company's attempts to supervise and control the farms' production, especially during the sharecropping phase of the contracts, many of the colonists soon developed "official" and "unofficial" accounts of their production.[16] Unofficially, the colonists sold as much of their crops as they could on the open market, often for substantial profits, especially during the crisis brought on by the war. The profits the colonist enjoyed soon influenced his attitudes toward the farm and the colonization company. He began to think of the farm as his own, although he had not come near to paying off his debts to the company. He paid less and less attention to his official account with the company. While his debts mounted, he complained about his financial "difficulties" and demanded more loans and subsidies.

There were two ways to combat the Bengodi mentality. The first was to insist that the families be more carefully selected in Italy. The second was more stringent discipline once the families arrived in the colony. Because of overriding political considerations, neither of these remedies proved very effective.

The Problem of Discipline

If the "carrot" of ultimate land ownership and independence was not enough to prevent the colonist families from developing a Bengodi mentality, then the technicians favored discipline, discipline, and more discipline. In his 1933 report outlining the operations of the future Ente Cirenaica, Maugini commented that if the colonists complained that they were getting harsh treatment, this was a good sign. He urged future administrators to "have the courage to throw complaining letters from the colonists into the wastebasket."[17] He concluded that:

Poor countries can be developed according to the Ente's goals only by imposing hardships; this truth must be kept in mind in every act by the Ente.[18]

This authoritarian philosophy of harsh discipline and close supervision, although it was probably not consciously based on Fascist ideals, harmonized well with the regime's credos. Mussolini always dreamed of forging a new, tough Italian people, ready to "Believe, Obey, Fight!" In practice, among the colonists in Libya as well as among the Duce's followers in Italy, neither the discipline nor the new tempered and hardened Italian ever emerged. As the technicians soon learned, once the colonists had immigrated to Libya discipline and sanctions were difficult to impose. Troublesome families could be eliminated, but the process involved "an enormous loss of time and money and it is a serious disturbance to the villages which are in formation."[19]

One of the chief obstacles to effective discipline was the bureaucracy. Authority over the colonist families was divided between the colonization companies and a network of local organizations ranging from the Fascist party to the state labor organizations to the colonial administration. This "meddling of the civil, political, and labor organs" encouraged the colonists to oppose the company's discipline, the technicians complained.[20] Before any harsh sanctions or discipline could be imposed, the company had to wait for the opinion of "this or that office." The colonists quickly learned how to play one organization off against another to the family's advantage.[21]

A second problem in enforcing discipline was that for political reasons the ultimate sanction of repatriation was rarely used. The authorities feared that unsuccessful or disgruntled families would spread derogatory information about the colonization once they were home—as no doubt they would have. A Maugini memorandum to Marshall Graziani in August 1933 comments that nine workers had to be sent home. Maugini wanted the Commission for Internal Migration and Colonization to instruct the prefect of Bari to do what he could "most of all to try to avoid or to neutralize any eventual derogatory propaganda which might be spread by the repatriated."[22]

As the technical advisors pointed out, repatriation was not always an effective threat. Some families welcomed a chance to go home. The disgruntled and discouraged wanted to leave at any cost. There were also those who had done well and wanted to leave. Company officials either suspected or observed that a surprising number of families had property in Italy, kept bank accounts in Tripoli, and sent savings home.[23] If the company gave them the choice of working harder or returning home, the families—particularly those who had been in Libya for some time—gladly accepted the opportunity for a free passage to Italy.

The Problem of Selection

The difficulties with discipline were symptomatic of a still more fundamental problem: the selection of the colonists. If the selection had been done more carefully and consistently, many problems with the colonist families would never have arisen in the first place.

To insure stability, the regime recruited families rather than individuals for the settlement projects. The ideal recruits for the colonization companies consisted of a family of eight members working as a unit under the direction of the father, who acted as a kind of foreman.[24] Ideally, the father was a bit over forty. He had at least three male children of about seventeen. Smaller families meant an inadequate labor force to develop the farm. Larger families posed a series of problems. The houses needed to be enlarged to accommodate them. The more enterprising families demanded more land and sometimes quarreled among themselves—or faked quarrels—to pressure the company into allotting another *podere*.[25] In larger families with several able-bodied males, the men were prone to migrate to the cities or to look for work outside the farm. Large families with younger children could not generate enough labor to earn an adequate paycheck during the salaried phase of the contract.

For a maximum of harmony, the companies preferred a strong father to provide discipline and leadership and the closest of kinship ties to prevent squabbling. The father's duty was to execute the company's orders and to keep the family labor unit intact. He had to be strong enough to prevent his sons from drifting into temporary high-paying construction jobs or to prevent his daughters from seeking work as domestics—or worse—in the city. It was particularly important that he groom the eldest son as the natural leader and successor to the *podere*. Through experience the companies found that the ideal kinship ties were parents and children, a family working for the future of the children. Invariably a family work force that included nephews, daughters-in-law, or stepchildren led to squabbles over succession to the land.

The relation between a family's regional origins and its success in Libya was a subject of much speculation and dispute among the technicians. Maugini favored Southerners from the Puglie and Sicily, "people who aren't even aware of their suffering because they are accustomed to it from the day of their birth."[26] In his view, the ghibli, the droughts, and the rocky soil in Libya would be no novelty to them, and they would have some experience with the tree cultures that would be so necessary to success. For Maugini the Sicilian emigrants to Tunisia had demonstrated what Southerners could do. Maugini was less optimistic about Northerners. If they had to be chosen, he preferred that they come from the rugged mountain areas rather than the Po Valley. Colonists from the great northern plain would have trouble adjusting to the Libyan climate, he felt.

The few available studies tend to confirm Maugini's ideas. Minnucci, for instance, looking over five years of experience in Cyrenaica (1934–39), complained that too often the Northerners did not show the industrious, disciplined habits necessary for success in Libya.[27] The Venetians who composed 50 percent of his sample of 1,707 families (13,206 individuals) were good at raising livestock, but they drank too much and saved too little, and their women were too loose. The Emiliani, who made up 10.8 percent of the sample, also drank too much, lived beyond their means, and drifted away from the *poderi* to work as *braccianti*. The Lombards (5.65 percent of the sample) enjoyed too much good living and good eating at the expense of their savings. Worst of all were Balbo's own Ferraresi, who proved to be "eternal malcontents" who "refused discipline." The best elements in the sample were frugal, hard-working, disciplined families from Benevento and Macerata. Minnucci also had high praise for other Southerners, especially families from the Abruzzi, the Puglie, and Sicily. Other technicians confirm Minnucci's observations. The *capo zona* in the village of Razza, for instance, reported that the Sicilians were seldom among the "excessive devotees of Bacchus" and had to be urged— particularly during their first years—to spend more money on food for the family.[28] The families from the Emilia, Lombardy, and the Veneto, on the other hand, accustomed to a higher living standard, proved to be much less frugal. Yet the technicians often pointed out that regional origins were never a certain indicator of a family's aptitudes.[29]

The technicians were resigned to working with families who were considerably less than ideal. What they resented most was that their task became increasingly difficult with the gradual decline in the standards of selection, especially under the policy of intensive colonization.

One factor in the decline of selection standards was the sheer number of applicants. Before the mass colonization of 1938–39 the number of families to be selected was small. The total number of families that emigrated to Africa under the CMCI's auspices, during the entire period 1930–37 was 1,920.[30] Yet in 1938 alone nearly 1,800 families emigrated with the *Ventimila*. With the intensive colonization there was far less opportunity for careful screening.

There was no dearth of applicants. In 1938, for instance, 6,000 families were actually examined by the selection committee before it made a final choice of 1,800 families. However, many more than 6,000 families had applied and had been judged unsuitable without even being examined.[31] In 1939, after the publicity that surrounded the 1938 migration, it was reported that some 40,000 families applied. Of these, 1,465 families, or about one out of every 27, were finally chosen.[32]

The appeal of the projects is clear. The families did not need their arms twisted to see the opportunities for land and subsidies the government was offering.[33] Since the vast majority of the colonists came from the North, they were familiar with the reclamation projects in the Po Valley. Those peasants from the *mezzogiorno* who were not hopelessly isolated or forgotten by the regime had heard of what the Duce had accomplished in the Pontine Marshes.[34] If the regime could produce such marvels at home, the peasants had faith that it could do the same in Libya. Most important of all, for those who applied, Libya, despite its hardships and unknowns, could only be an improvement over their current precarious situation. In most cases, the families had nothing to lose by emigrating.

What criteria were applied in selecting the families? As Maugini had warned in 1928, one of the perils of state colonization was that the emigrants were selected for reasons other than their potential as colonists.[35] Many foreign observers at the time of the mass migrations also wondered if selection was based on a family's political reliability. Certainly a good war record and a history of Fascist party activity was helpful in being chosen for the colonization projects. Yet it seems likely that official allegiance to Fascism or an active career in the party played only a small part in the selection.[36] Far more important was the size and composition of the family; the health of its members; their attitudes and morality; their professional background and experience. In some cases families were chosen even if the members were not politically active. In exceptional cases, according to an official publication, the family could be accepted even if the father was not a member of the Fascist party, as long as the rest of the family belonged to appropriate Fascist youth or women's organizations.

Thus politics did not enter into the selection process in a formal way. However, political considerations undoubtedly influenced the selection process in a more subtle way. For the prefect or the *federale* or other local officials, the colonization provided a splendid opportunity to eliminate undesirables from their jurisdictions. Because of the large numbers of applicants for the projects, the official selection committees could not screen all the families directly. The committees relied on the recommendations of the local civic officials without bothering to investigate further into a family's background.[37] Inevitably, then, the colonization companies had to deal with malcontents and troublemakers as well as incompetents.

The regional origins of the colonists suggest another way in which politics may have influenced the choice of families. With the intensive colonization of 1938 and 1939, the regional origins of the colonists changed from the Puglie, Calabria and the Abruzzi to the unemployed and *braccianti* of the Po Valley, and especially the Veneto.[38] Intensive colonization never realized the old dream of Libya as an outlet for the Southern peasantry. In 1938, 1,433, or nearly 80 percent, of the 1,798 families came from the North. In 1939, 913 of the 1,358 families, or about 66 percent, were from the North. The Veneto, especially the areas around Padova, Venice, Rovigo, and Treviso, furnished the largest numbers of families during both migrations. In 1938 the Veneto contributed 1,032 or, 57 percent, of the families; in 1939, 853 families, or 62 percent, came from the Veneto. These were areas where unemployment was high and where the peasants were familiar with the problems of reclamation. They were also areas that were traditionally restless and prone to socialism. Thus the emigration clearly served as a safety valve to eliminate unemployment and also to quell potential political dissidents.

The reports of local Fascist party officials to the party secretary in Rome illustrate the poverty, unemployment, and potential turbulence in these areas during the years of intensive emigration to Libya.[39] A report of 10 January 1937 from Padova comments that the "population is quiet only because of fear" and warns that "one day hunger may overcome fear and unpleasant incidents may occur." A few days earlier, the report continues, some peasants had been arrested for singing "subversive songs." Two weeks later the same official spoke of the continued high unemployment rate in the province and noted that "tens of thousands" of workers and peasants were seeking to emigrate to the empire. A party official from Treviso, in June 1939, described similar circumstances. Local unemployment was worse than in the past, most of the major public works projects had been completed, and every day crowds of unemployed gathered around government hiring halls and party offices, with an "impatience and restlessness that cannot be further ignored."

There is no way to estimate how many of these dissident elements emigrated to Libya. The number of repatriations from Libya might provide a clue, but no aggregate figures are available. Minnucci estimated that of the approximately 2,000 families for which he was responsible in Cyrenaica over a five-year period, not many more than 20 were repatriated.[40] An INFPS offical report for the mass migration of 1938 listed only 11 repatriations for various reasons out of a total of 489 families.[41]

TABLE 2. ORIGINS OF THE COLONIST FAMILIES OF THE 1938 MASS MIGRATION

Province and District	Number of Families	Province and District	Number of Families
Venice:		*Abruzzo:*	
Padova	223	Aquila	39
Rovigo	228	Chieti	23
Trento	5	Pescara	22
Treviso	100	Teramo	8
Udine	45	*Puglie:*	
Venice	211	Bari	57
Verona	101	Foggia	30
Vicenza	119	Lecce	13
Lombardy:		*Calabria*	
Bergamo	13	Catanzaro	28
Brescia	25	Cosenza	16
Mantova	51	Reggio Calabria	15
Emilia:		*Sicily:*	
Bologna	27	Agrigento	13
Ferrara	135	Caltanisetta	17
Forlì	21	Catania	19
Modena	57	Enna	16
Parma	11	Messina	8
Reggio Emilia	61	Ragusa	23
		Syracuse	20

Source: Governo Generale della Libia, *Prima migrazione di masse per la colonizzazione demografica* 17(Tripoli: P. Maggi, 1939): 7–8.

However, these figures do not mean that the colonists were well selected or that they made a successful adjustment to the Libyan projects. From the scattered bits of evidence available, it is clear that individual projects sometimes faced serious problems with families that proved unsatisfactory. A letter to the Duce from the president of the INFPS about the development of Bir Terrina in 1936, for instance, admits that of the twenty-six heads of families on trial, fourteen had requested repatriation or were eliminated for bad work.[42] A report on the village of Razza in 1939 complained that six out of nine of the new families who had emigrated in 1939 had to be repatriated and another had asked to leave.[43]

TABLE 3. ORIGINS OF THE COLONIST FAMILIES OF THE 1939 MASS MIGRATION

Province and District	Number of Families	Province and District	Number of Families
Venice:		*Abruzzi:*	
Padova	203	Aquila	47
Treviso	193	Campobasso	34
Venezia	166	Chieti	26
Udine	102	Pescara	21
Vicenza	83	Teramo	7
Verona	81	*Lazio:*	
Trento	7	Frosinone	23
Belluno	18	*Sicily:*	
Lombardy:		Palermo	29
Mantova	32	Ragusa	27
Brescia	25	Messina	22
Emilia:		Syracuse	21
Modena	2	Caltanisetta	19
Piedmont:		Catania	15
Cuneo	1	Agrigento	13
Campania:		Enna	13
Benevento	48	Trapani	10
Avellino	41	*Calabria:*	
Napoli	28	Catanzaro	1

SOURCE: *L'Azione Coloniale,* 26 October 1939.

Thus, from the technical expert's perspective, probably the major flaw in the program was the poor selection of colonists, especially during the intensive phase of colonization. Rejects, social misfits, troublemakers, and incompetents made up a good share of the colonist families who emigrated to Libya under the colonization programs. Unfortunately no records are available that would allow a reconstruction of the colonists' social origins. The reports of the agricultural experts, however, are unequivocal in their complaints. As Marassi commented, for some of the colonist families emigration was a way of life.[44] They had worked in France or Germany or the United States, most often not in agriculture. Others were dissatisfied with their jobs as craftsmen or artisans at home and hoped to find an easy new life in the colony. Finally, there was the tiny minority who were excellent farmers and who emigrated because they saw a real future for themselves in the colony. Even those who came from agricultural backgrounds—and the vast majority undoubtedly did—were not always suitable. The technicians certainly would have preferred peasants with some experience as independent farmers, colonists with a bit of capital of their own. If this group had to be excluded for political reasons, the technical experts wanted colonists who at least had experience as sharecroppers. Instead, the vast majority were simply day laborers.

The technicians had no choice except to work with them. Some project leaders looked back to the days before the intensive colonization when a three-month trial period was a standard clause in the ECL contracts. During this initial phase, the head of the family was employed as a salaried worker. In addition to his political background, the composition of his family, and his education, the company's technical experts noted the candidate's working skills.[45] Could he drive a tractor, manage a team of oxen, plant vineyards, care for livestock? They also observed his character and temperament. How well did he take orders? How much of his wages did he manage to save during each fifteen-day salary period? At the end of the three month's trial, if the potential colonist liked the work and if the company felt he would be successful, the worker was invited to send for his family. If a trial period had remained in effect as it was in Breviglieri in 1936, "we would have made gardens out of the agricultural centers, as was done, moreover, with the sixty farms at Breviglieri, and much time and money would have been saved," lamented a technical expert in 1947.[46]

The technicians found a certain pride and satisfaction in their accomplishments. Despite the many obstacles they faced, including the war, they had taken a giant step toward creating a modern, flourishing system of agriculture for Libya. Moreover, they had done everything in a remarkably short period of time. "For better or for worse, everything that was done was accomplished in a matter of seven or eight years," Palloni remarked about his work in Cyrenaica.[47]

Despite these accomplishments, two sources of frustration remained to haunt the technical advisors. The first was the problem of political interference in their work. The technicians could never quite reconcile themselves to the political impulse which had initially stimulated the ambitious Italian effort. For the technicians, political interference in the projects did little more than introduce "new and often insuperable difficulties" in a process that was already sufficiently complex and arduous.[48] A second source of frustration was the attitude of the Libyans. For political—but also for humanitarian—reasons the technical experts planned to integrate the Libyans into the new Italian agricultural system, a system they were confident would eliminate the age-old cycles of poverty and misery which had plagued the indigenous peoples. To the frustration of the technicians the Libyans greeted the new ways with diffidence and hostility.

9

Intensive Colonization:
The Perspective of the Libyans

As the Italian colonists settled down to work their farms, what was to be the fate of the indigenous peoples? The colonists created a growing population pressure on resources which for centuries had yielded a bare living at best. For both peoples to survive without a major upheaval, the Italians had to reach some kind of accommodation with the Libyans.

The vast majority of the indigenous peoples squeezed their livelihood from a subsistence-level agriculture concentrated in an area that comprised less than 3 percent of the colony's vast territory. About 90 percent of the Libyans, who totaled about 800,000, lived in an area of 44,600 square kilometers which was suitable for agriculture.[1] Only about 15 percent of the work force was engaged in manufacturing— mostly handicrafts and food processing—and less than 5 percent worked in trade. Thus more than 75 percent of the indigenous population, including all the major ethnic groups except the Jews, relied on agriculture.[2]

The arrival of the colonists in 1938–39 meant that the Italians would compete far more directly with the Libyans for the area's limited agricultural resources. Until the mass migrations, the majority of the Italian population was engaged in civil service and manufacturing, with only 15 percent working in agriculture.[3] By about 1940, with the influx of colonists, the portion of the Italian labor force working in agriculture had risen to perhaps as high as 40 percent.

Nor was the competition from the colonists likely to diminish in the future. Within the agricultural zone, the Italian population was growing faster than the Libyan. During the last four years of colonization activity, the Italian population in every district of Northern Tripolitania except Sabratha and Zuara expanded at a more rapid rate than did the indigenous population.[4] The Italian increase was due primarily to the mass immigrations. But there are also indications that the prolific colonist families reproduced more rapidly than the Libyans.[5]

The problem of dealing with the indigenous peoples included many complicated economic and political overtones. There could be no question of wholesale deportations of Libyans from the agricultural zone. Such policies might rekindle old animosities to the point of open warfare. More likely, any massive displacement would induce the Libyans to migrate toward the cities, where they might form a socially and politically dangerous proletariat. Furthermore, the Libyans were needed in the countryside. The Italians relied on their labor to help develop the colonists' farms and the private concessions. Although indigenous agriculture provided only a meager subsistence living, whatever the Libyans produced helped relieve the tax burden on the Italians.

To keep the Libyans in the countryside and at the same time to develop the colonization was no simple task. The Italian settlements threatened to disrupt the tightly integrated system of oasis gardens, dry farming, and pastoral enterprises which made up the indigenous forms of agriculture. Once their traditional existence was disturbed, the Libyans became far more vulnerable to the higher wages and excitement of the cities.

Ideally, by means of settlement schemes, loans, subsidies, technical help, and jobs—the same opportunities offered to metropolitan colonists—the Italians hoped to incorporate the indigenous peoples into a new and more productive agricultural system. Italian technical experts were convinced that given enough time their programs would work. Whether or not their optimism was justified can never be fully answered. The war intervened and political factors disrupted the programs. The best that can be done is to describe the Italian plans and the initial Libyan reactions to them.

The State of Indigenous Agriculture

To the Libyans, the invasion of Italian colonists meant not only new population pressures on meager resources but also the introduction of a form of agriculture which threatened their traditional ways.[6] For most Libyans, agriculture meant first of all livestock. All over the colony, from the most arid areas to those that were most intensively cultivated, the Libyans pastured sheep, goats, cattle, and camels. A typical herd numbered two hundred fifty to three hundred head but might run even larger. The grazing areas were privately owned or rented, or were perhaps the common property of a *cabila*. The owners of oases or dry farms—as well as nomads—took an interest in raising livestock. The sedentary farmers often hired a shepherd to look after the flocks which were pastured on land near the farms or oases.

The large numbers of nomadic peoples, especially prevalent in Cyrenaica, supplemented their activities as shepherds by practicing "shifting cultivation."[7] As they followed their herds along the coastal plains of Tripolitania and in the Cyrenaican Gebel and in the Sirtica, the nomadic Libyans sowed scattered patches of grain in selected wadi beds and basins near the migratory tracks. To insure some harvest from this technique, the seeds were sown over as wide an area as possible during the autumn rains. Between planting and harvest time the Libyan tended his flocks, worked on a temporary job, or perhaps simply loafed. At harvest time, if the spring rains had been sufficient, he and his family returned to gather the crop.

The *sania* (plural: *suàni*), or irrigated oasis garden, constituted one of the major sedentary agricultural enterprises. A postwar estimate concluded that oasis gardens covered as many as fifty thousand hectares in Tripolitania and three thousand hectares in Cyrenaica (including the Fezzan). The date palm, which furnished Libyans with food, drink, livestock fodder, and eventually firewood, flourished in the oases. On tiny irrigated plots ranging from a few hundred square meters to perhaps two hectares, the Libyans also cultivated citrus fruits, vegetables, dates, pomegranates, and cereals. The water was drawn from local wells by animal power, often cattle or camels. The unit production from these gardens could be quite high, but the plots were so tiny that the cultivator absorbed everything for his personal use. If he had any surplus, he marketed it in nearby cities or villages. The oasis gardens were most widely developed in Tripolitania and often drew favorable comments from the Italians. By contrast, those around Benghazi, estimated at 2,500 in 1937, were not nearly so flourishing.[8] Yet, even in Tripolitania, during this period these gardens seemed to be on the decline. As the Italian agricultural technicians repeatedly observed, the faster the colony developed, the more the Libyans abandoned the oases for new opportunities to work in the nearby cities or on Italian private concessions.

The *genàn* (plural: *genanàt*), or dry farm, whose mainstays were olives and figs, was another type of sedentary enterprise particularly common on the Tripolitanian Gebel in the areas of Msellata and Garian. The olives often reached monumental proportions—sometimes larger than in the best areas in Italy. The Italians also found olive groves in Cyrenaica containing trees that dated back to classical times. However, because of neglect the trees had grown wild and unproductive. As the Italian technical experts lamented, the Libyans did little or nothing to improve the olives or to protect them from disease.[9] Irrigation often amounted to no more than digging a hole around the tree's base and letting the rainwater collect. The farmer on the *genàn* often supplemented his olives with patches of wheat or barley and the products of his livestock.

As the Italian agricultural experts pointed out, the oasis gardens, the dry farms on the Gebel, and the pastoral activities and "shifting cultivation" of the steppe were all closely linked. Italian technicians readily acknowledged the rationality and balance of the total scheme and admired the ingenious way in which it made use of even the most marginal resources.[10]

At best, however, as the Italian technicians pointed out, the traditional techniques provided only a subsistence living. Indigenous agriculture yielded no more than three head of livestock and 1.5 quintals of major crops per capita.[11] Even this meager subsistence was constantly threatened by drought. In 1936 Tripolitania's flocks of sheep were reduced from 1.5 million head to three hundred thousand head, despite Italian efforts to save them. Moreover, the indigenous system of agriculture was static. By themselves the Libyans were unlikely to break the precarious cycle of their existence, a member of Franchetti's mission to Tripolitania had observed, and even with the stimulus of outside investments and new techniques the Libyans would be slow to change their ways.[12]

Italian Plans for Indigenous Agriculture: Loans and Subsidies

To woo the Libyans away from their traditional existence and to better integrate them into the new agricultural order on which the colonization was based, the Italians offered a number of programs and incentives. Libyan entrepreneurs who participated in the Italian programs for agricultural development were eligible for land, subsidies, and tax advantages. Indigenous families who wished to take up sedentary farming but lacked financial resources could join Italian-designed "demographic villages" which paralleled the communities for Italian colonists. Finally, the Libyans were expected to benefit from the new jobs that would develop in the growing agricultural sector.

To a certain extent, of course, the Italians conceived these programs for propaganda purposes. The lands and subsidies were intended to quiet disgruntled Libyans whose lands were preempted for the colonization schemes. Since the opportunities for the indigenous peoples were virtually the same as those for the Italian colonists, the Libyans could not even complain that they were being discriminated against. However, the programs for the Libyans were also intended to have substance. Any increase in the productivity of the indigenous agri-culture would decrease the financial burdens of the Italians. Sedentary farmers presented fewer political and police problems than restless nomads. Finally, the technicians in charge of the programs displayed a certain missionary zeal. For the sake of Italy's reputation as "an old colonizing people" and for the sake of their own professional integrity, the agricultural experts wanted the programs to succeed. They were certain that the new systems would lead to the "general improvement and the material and moral elevation of the indigenous peoples."[13]

The Italians offered the Libyans virtually the same financial and technical assistance that was available to the metropolitan colonists.[14] First of all, the Libyans could apply, under RD 3 April 1937 no. 896, for land from the public domain. Until 1937 lands had been reserved for the Italians only. Each family could receive up to fifteen hectares. As of 1939 in Tripolitania, about twenty requests for these concessions were granted, fifteen in the area of Sabratha and a few others near Gasr Garabulli.

Second, both new concessioners and established proprietors were eligible for subsidies to help develop their lands under the 1928 laws. The program was hampered by two regulations.[15] One was that the minimum area to be developed must total at least four hectares (this was later changed to two hectares), which meant that many of the owners of the small oases—the group the Italians wanted to preserve—were not eligible. A second obstacle was that the applicant had to show title to his land. In practice, because of the extreme subdivisions of the plots and the nature of the Moslem inheritance system, this rule was often difficult to fulfill.

Despite these obstacles, the Italians claimed that the program of subsidies was received with great enthusiasm in Tripolitania. During the first year of 1938–39, the Italians were proud to announce that 86 out of 109 applicants in the province of Tripoli alone received financial aid valued at 1.2 million lire.[16] The subsidies were granted for development or improvement of 140 wells, 60 houses, 400 hectares of irrigated land, 600 hectares of land under dry farming, and 70 hectares for reforestation. At the end of 1942, the government had approved a total of 220 plans, for total subsidies of 2.5 million lire.

The Libyans could also take advantage of various Italian programs which made available farm machinery, seeds, technical assistance, centers for improved livestock breeding, development of wells, and reforestation. In times of special hardship, such as the drought of 1935–36, the Italian government intervened with emergency measures.

Balbo saved much of the livestock of Tripolitania by having it shipped to Cyrenaican pastures. The following year, to compensate for their bad harvest, the Libyans were exempt from taxes on their livestock and cereal crops.

Italian Plans for Indigenous Agriculture: The Demographic Villages

Another aspect of the Italian program for indigenous agriculture was the series of Libyan villages which paralleled the settlements for metropolitan colonists.[17] Each Libyan colonist family was given a small plot of land, a farmhouse, tools, and supplies. Nearby, a small village or center—complete with café, marketplace, schools, and mosque—provided for the colonist's communal needs. In addition to villages for sedentary agriculture, the Italians had also planned at least two "pastoral villages" for Cyrenaica. These centers, situated south of the Gebel Akhdar, were intended to serve the nomads displaced by the Italian colonists. In these "pastoral villages" the Italians planned to provide extra fodder and water and the medical services and market facilities useful to the nomads in caring for their livestock.

The Libyan villages made good propaganda. The official notes for newsmen covering the mass emigration of 1939 dealt at length with the plans and progress made on the indigenous settlements.[18] Balbo found them useful during a diplomatic mission to Cairo in May 1939, for King Farouk expressed much interest in their development.[19]

The Italians, however, insisted that the villages had more than publicity value. They were necessary for "economic equilibrium," especially in Cyrenaica.[20] Significantly, six of the eight projected villages were planned for Cyrenaica to ease the problems created by the displacement of the bedouins from the Gebel Akhdar.

The program as a whole never progressed far beyond the blueprint stage before the war broke out.[21] The first two villages for sedentary agriculture in Cyrenaica, known to the Italians as Alba and Fiorita, were occupied in 1938. They were laid out over an area of about forty hectares each along the coast near Marsa el Hilal. Each settlement was to have been irrigated with water from a nearby wadi. Alba was to have consisted of ten farms of about four hectares each, and Fiorita was planned for twenty-two farms of about two hectares each. In 1940 the village of Gedida (Nuova), situated near Tolemaide, was divided into fifty farms of ten hectares each; some houses were built, but the settlement was never occupied. In Tripolitania, a settlement known as Mahamura, with one hundred farms of about four hectares each, was begun near Zavia. Another project, Naima, in the province of Misurata west of the Italian village of Garibaldi, was planned with a goal of eighty farms of about five hectares each. Naima, however, was never occupied.

In their reports, Italian agricultural experts showed little enthusiasm for these projects. They complained about the poor and restricted locales of the settlements and the often haphazard selection of the colonists. To collect ex-farmers, shepherds, and unemployed day laborers and settle them in the villages was "a waste of time and money," one technician remarked as early as 1939.[22] Particularly foolish was the practice of shifting farmers from their oases into the new villages, he argued. This merely encouraged the abandonment of the oases and loosened the farmer's ties to his land. By 1943, he labeled the experiments in Tripolitania as "total failures" and concluded that the entire concept was a "false model."[23]

Just as the Libyan villages were modeled after their Italian counterparts, so they also displayed the same technical, administrative, and morale problems. The village of Mahamura in Tripolitania, which had been settled with one hundred families in 1939, provides an example.[24] After two years of activity, the catalog of troubles in the agricultural experts' reports reads remarkably like those that developed in the Italian settlements. As always there were frustrating technical problems: Mahamura suffered from shifting sand dunes and from wells that persistently caved in and had to be restored.

The chief difficulty, however, was the mentality of the colonists. The families for Mahamura had been chosen with some care. Only about one-third of the families who had applied for the project were actually accepted. Despite this selection, the Libyan colonists behaved no differently from their Italian counterparts. They fought any curtailment of their advances and subsidies, even when they were prospering; they ignored the Ente's orders; they showed much carelessness and technical incompetence. As the technical experts complained, instead of expressing gratitude or appreciation to the Ente, the colonists voiced only "continual signs of discontent" and made demands on the Ente which were "in most cases exaggerated and absurd."[25] Despite these troubles, in 1947 Mahamura was still in operation with a population of ninety families, or a total of about eight hundred inhabitants.

If the Libyans of Tripolitania showed little interest in the demographic villages, the Cyrenaicans showed even less. The chief examples of sedentary agriculture in Cyrenaica were the oasis gardens around Benghazi, worked by the descendants of slaves and Berbers, whom the bedouins regarded with contempt.[26] Thus the bedouins described the demographic villages as no more than "throwing dust in our eyes" while the Italians helped themselves to the best grazing lands on the Gebel.[27] By their own admission, the Italians "found no little difficulty" in recruiting enough families for the villages.[28] Once their period as salaried laborers ended, those families who participated showed little interest or skills in developing their farms. Just how alien the Cyrenaicans felt in the settlements is illustrated by their living habits. According to Italian reports, the Libyans ignored the farmhouses as living quarters and used them as stables for the livestock. The colonists preferred to camp in the courtyards.[29] By 1947 only Fiorita, which was reported to have twenty-eight families living there, was still functioning.

Libyan Opposition in Cyrenaica: The Conflict Over the Gebel

In Tripolitania, the indigenous peoples showed little opposition to the Italian colonization. The land settlement schemes displaced few Libyans, and the Italians provided alternative opportunities for work on private concessions, public works projects, and in the cities.[30]

The Cyrenaicans offered far more resistance. Although only 15,000 colonists settled in the area—compared with 24,000 in Tripolitania— their presence was more deeply felt.[31] The ratio of Libyans (152,000) to Italians (38,000) in Cyrenaica was about 4 to 1, compared with 8 to 1 in Tripolitania. The Cyrenaicans were largely nomadic—the Italians estimated that 75 percent of the population lived in tents—and resentful of the invading sedentary farmers who appropriated good pasture lands.

The Cyrenaicans also retained bitter memories of the long years of colonial warfare. They had fought the Italians far longer and had suffered far more cruelly than the peoples of Tripolitania. The war in Cyrenaica had ended in 1932 with an estimated twelve thousand exiles in Egypt and as many as fifty-five thousand—perhaps nearly half the remaining population—in five detention camps.[32] To rebuild the area's shattered economy and to encourage the return of the exiles, the colonial government sponsored a number of relief measures. These included public works projects, government-sponsored cereal farming, and subsidies to help the Cyrenaicans rebuild their herds which were decimated during the war. Despite these conciliatory gestures, the Cyrenaicans did not easily forget the Italian repression.

The most bitterly contested area proved to be the Gebel Akhdar. The settlement of Italian colonists meant the displacement of the bedouins from their traditional grazing areas. The Italian technical experts had planned a number of ways to compensate the bedouins for the loss of these lands.[33] New zones on the northern slopes of the plateau were reserved for the bedouins. Access corridors were marked so that these lands could be reached without disturbing the colonist farms. Once the zone reserved for Italian colonists was clearly defined, the technical experts recommended that the rest of Cyrenaica be redivided among the tribes according to their size and needs. The government was to revive and rebuild wells and cisterns and to dig new ones if necessary. In 1939, the government gave the Libyans a monopoly over pastoral activities—a concession which cost the Italians very little, since their colonists were sedentary. For those Libyans who wished to forsake their nomadic ways, the Italians hoped either to absorb them as salaried laborers on colonist farms or to settle them in villages, as in Tripolitania.

In practice, this plan for coexistence never worked very well.[34] The block of colonist farms deprived the bedouins of some of their best sowing and grazing lands and water resources. The colonist farms also interrupted the traditional migratory paths and the continuity of territory controlled by the various tribes. The result was that the wells and cisterns in these regions decayed, since no one felt responsible for them anymore.

Nor, despite the repeated pleas of the technical experts, did the government effectively control the movements of the bedouins. Bureaucratic warnings and regulations failed to impress the nomadic peoples with the need to observe "complete respect for [private] property."[35] When colonists or Ente officials demanded action to keep the nomads and their herds away from the farms, the response was usually bureaucratic vacillation, or at best "temporary and compromise solutions," Maugini complained.[36]

Sometimes the colonial administration's ineffectiveness in controlling the nomad's movements was due to bureaucratic bungling or inertia. At other times, however, local officials took no action because they had their own vested interests to protect.[37] The invading herds, although nominally registered in the name of the shepherd, really belonged to some enterprising Italian official. In other cases, when patrols of Libyan police were sent out, the enforcement was often minimal because the offenders were tribesmen or kinsmen of the patrol members.

The experiences of the *capo zona* at the village of Razza illustrate the conflict between colonist and bedouin. The problems at Razza were particularly acute because the locale, with its scattered patches of woods and thickets, favored the return of the bedouins and their flocks.[38] The nomads began reappearing as early as 1936 at the time of the Ethiopian War, the *capo zona* recorded. When he protested to the authorities, he was told that since Libyan units were fighting with the

Italians in Ethiopia, "the political situation demanded comprehension" on the part of the colonists. Later complaints, the *capo zona* claimed, were dismissed with charges that he was stirring up the colonists against the Libyans.

By 1940, with the outbreak of World War II, the bedouins returned permanently, and he observed them nonchalantly breaking down the remaining young olive and almond trees to make sticks and staffs. The war also encouraged a resumption of overt violence. Sporadic Libyan raids against the villages resulted in looting, destruction, and occasional murders.[39]

Shortly before the final collapse of Italian rule in Cyrenaica during the war, a number of Italian agricultural experts concluded that coexistence with nomads on the Gebel would not be possible. They recommended that the Libyans be completely excluded from the region and resettled in areas to the south. The harassed *capo zona* for the village of Razza demanded that the colonization areas be fenced off in the same way that the Libyan-Egyptian frontier had been sealed off at the time of the Sanusi war. If the financial means could be found to make war, he declared, then they should also be found to "guarantee the works of peace and particularly the peace between natives and colonists."[40]

All in all, the Libyans showed little enthusiasm for the Italian programs to develop indigenous agriculture. Certainly the indigenous peoples were happy to receive grants and subsidies during periods of emergency. Perhaps the financial aid spurred a few Libyan entrepreneurs to imitate Italian farming methods. However, even in Tripolitania, where the traditions of sedentary agriculture were most developed, the Italian programs seem to have had little effect. There is no evidence in Tripolitania that the Libyan sedentary agricultural area expanded or that their agricultural production increased appreciably as a result of Italian financial, technical, or marketing incentives.[41]

Significantly, the technical experts eagerly cited even the most isolated examples of Libyans who took advantage of the Italian agricultural program in any way.[42] In general, as the Italian agricultural experts remarked, perhaps with a note of bitterness, the Libyans preferred to abandon the "hard and uncertain life of the farmer" in favor of opportunities in the cities where they could find a "comfortable fixed salary" working for the Italians.[43]

The Italians and the Libyan Labor Force

Although the Libyans showed little interest in Italian efforts to improve indigenous agriculture, they were attracted by the new jobs created as the colony developed. The Libyans found opportunities in public works projects, in the army, on Italian private agricultural concessions, and in the colonist villages.

In practice, Libya's development, including the agricultural colonization, depended heavily on indigenous labor. The notion of building up the colony by making use almost exclusively of Italy's own labor resources never materialized, for metropolitan workers never proved sufficiently cheap or abundant. Thus Libya developed through a process of association, much in the way the Bertolini Commission had favored in 1913.

For their public works projects, for instance, the Italians relied far more on Libyan labor than on imported metropolitan workers. The public works projects for the mass emigrations in 1938 occupied 23,000 Libyans out of a 33,000-man labor force.[44] The INFPS village construction in 1938 required a total of 412,479 work days—"a demonstration of the not indifferent contribution of the institute to the battle against unemployment," an official report boasted.[45] Yet of this total the Libyans furnished 245,875, or about 60 percent of the work days.

The agricultural effort, too, relied heavily on indigenous labor. In Tripolitania, for instance, the number of Libyans hired varied from area to area, but in every locality except Tripoli and Garian far more Libyan than Italian laborers were used. The 1937 census showed that Libyan workers totaled about 3,500, nearly three times the number of Italian laborers (1,096).[46] The Libyan laborers totaled nearly half of the combined Italian population (managers, technicians, foremen, colonists, and laborers) of 8,997. The census figure included only those Libyan workers who could be considered fixed or permanent on the demographic farms and concessions. In practice, large numbers of Libyans were also hired as temporary labor. In Cyrenaica, for instance, about 900 Libyan laborers were included in the 1937 census. Nevertheless, during peak seasons the Ente Cirenaica sometimes hired as many as 2,000 temporary workers.

The Libyans did a variety of tasks on the Italian agricultural enterprises. Their jobs ranged from driving tractors to pruning trees and clearing new land. The colonization companies often hired Libyans as watchmen or stableboys, and especially as shepherds. In 1935, for instance, 41 of the 65 Libyans on the Ente Cirenaica's payroll worked with livestock.[47]

The attraction of Italian employment is clear enough: the Italians offered relatively high salaries which increased steadily as the years went by. In periods of crisis, they skyrocketed. In 1935, for instance, a Libyan could earn four to seven lire a day as a salaried laborer, depending on the work and his qualifications.[48] During the war, he could get twelve to eighteen lire a day working in the demographic villages. However, few were interested in such work when they could earn thirty-five to fifty lire a day working on roads. Both on the private concessions and on the colonization projects, Libyans and Italians also developed remunerations based on sharecropping, payments in kind, and rights to pasture land. The colonists at the village of Garibaldi, for instance, relied on Libyans to help harvest their grain and forage crops.[49] The forage crops were divided in half; the division of the grain crops depended on the yield per hectare. In addition, the Libyans were allowed to pasture their flocks on colonist land at certain times and to plant small plots of their own there.

The need for Libyan labor had a number of serious drawbacks from the Italian point of view. The Italians often complained about the quality of the labor. An Italian observer remarked that if the indigenous worker earned comparatively low wages and sometimes got half the salary of an Italian, the Libyan also did half the work.[50] An Italian technical expert commented that if the Libyan seemed to work from sunup to sundown, he didn't work with any great diligence—even for a Libyan employer—and he often took time out for tea breaks.[51]

The supply of labor also proved to be a problem. During critical periods of labor shortages, the Italians were sometimes willing to offer bonuses of fifty to one hundred lire to attract laborers.[52] Yet this strategy could also backfire. Although the Libyans responded with enthusiasm to the bonus, they seldom worked steadily. Like many other peoples in a preindustrial society, the Libyans were often content to work just long enough to fulfill their immediate needs. They seldom thought of long-term savings.[53] After a few days of work, they abandoned their jobs. Sometimes the Italians experimented with cutting wages in hopes that the Libyans would have to work steadily for a longer period. The lower wages usually made little difference. The Libyan accepted his lowered living standard with a certain fatality and worked neither longer nor harder. From these experiences the Italians soon developed the stereotype of the Arab as "lazy" or "unwilling to work."

The demand for indigenous labor also created a migration pattern that disturbed the Italians. They saw the gradual abandonment of the countryside for the relatively secure and high-paying jobs in the cities. Such a movement, they feared, could have only pernicious effects. First of all, these migrations would accentuate labor shortages in the countryside. Second, the Italians anticipated that the movement would lead to the formation of a restless urban proletariat. Since Fascism was intent on preventing rural-urban migration at home, there was no reason why such a movement should be tolerated in the colonies. Yet one observer, writing in 1935, remarked that the colonial government "does not seem to be sufficiently concerned with this harmful situation" and concluded that government intervention was "urgently needed."[54] Thus, one of the chief reasons for Italian interest in developing indigenous agriculture was to try to control the rural-urban migration.

Over the long term, Italian fears appear to have been justified. Certain rural areas have suffered population losses from migration to the cities and the result has been a reduction in the cultivated areas.[55] In the Fezzan, for instance, the numbers of workers in the date palmeries decreased from about ten thousand in 1936 to only about two thousand in 1960. The loss of labor through migration, and the reduced efficiency of the remaining labor force, which is often composed of the very old and the very young, has meant a reduction in the cultivated area. According to Italian statistics, there were 2.6 million hectares under all types of cultivation in Tripolitania in 1925. By contrast, the 1960 agricultural census recorded only 1.7 million hectares in arable and permanent crops (including fallow land).

The main goal of the migration seems to have been the city of Tripoli, which increased its population more than sevenfold from an estimated 29,761 in 1911 to 212,577 in 1964. The mechanics and dynamics of this population movement and the impact of the Italian agricultural colonization is only now being explored. The preliminary evidence suggests that the migration in Tripolitania was not a result of any massive or forceful displacement of the Libyans from their lands. These areas were thinly populated, and the Libyans had traditionally used them for pastoral activities and cereal cultivation. Nor is there evidence that the Libyans were attracted extensively to the locales of the Italian colonization. Tripoli, on the other hand, had a long history of being a focus for temporary migration from all parts of Libya. As the Italians developed the city, the wages and excitement of the capital attracted more and more migrants on a permanent basis.

By the time the war broke out, the Italian program to integrate the indigenous peoples into the new agricultural programs had scarcely begun. The Duce, noting the hostility of the Libyans during his last trip to the colony in 1942, concluded peevishly that "the Balbo policy failed completely and the only good thing he did was to build Balbia."[56] Not only was such a verdict premature, but it is difficult to see what else Balbo—or any other administrator—might have done. To some extent the Libyans rejected the Italian agricultural schemes on political grounds. The programs were promoted by foreign invaders and conquerors. Yet the opposition was far more deeply rooted: the Italian programs represented an attack on a way of life that had persisted for centuries. The indigenous peoples would have opposed the new ways no matter what the politics of the innovators.

The independent postwar Libyan governments soon learned this lesson. In recent years, in an effort to stem the migration from the countryside to the cities and to lessen Libya's dependence on food imports, the government has attempted to revive a number of the former Italian agricultural projects.[57] Among the villages in Tripolitania which the Libyan government redeveloped are Naima and Mahamura, Garibaldi, Gioda, and Crispi. In Cyrenaica, the Libyan government launched a major program to refurbish the ex-Italian villages on the Gebel. The Libyan government, however, seems to have had little better success with these settlements than the Italian colonial regime did.

In Cyrenaica, for instance, studies made in 1964-66 indicated that the sixteen thousand colonists settled on the revived ex-Ente farms, which totaled slightly more than one thousand eight hundred, were making very slow progress toward the ideal of independence and self-sufficiency. Surveys revealed that the majority of colonists relied on nonagricultural activities, especially government jobs, for at least 36 percent of their income. Among agricultural activities, the most important was animal husbandry. The continued reliance on pastoral activities helped explain why only 58 percent of the farmhouses were regularly occupied. Many of the colonists remained seminomadic. Like their Italian predecessors, the Libyan agricultural experts have concluded that planning, subsidies, and technical help are no guarantee of success: "a settler is not a synonym of farmer."[58] The Libyan colonists, like the Italians, require "continuous educational assistance and advice" in order to develop the "new outlooks" which characterize a skilled, independent farmer. For Italian agricultural experts, these comments have a familiar ring.

III. The End of the Fourth Shore

10
The War and the Peace

The Situation in 1940

The Italian dream of creating a fourth shore in Libya reached its peak in 1940. The war prevented any further settlement and seriously disrupted the programs for agricultural development. With the Axis defeat, the story of the colonization trails off into a long epilogue. Although the war entirely destroyed the Italian settlements in Cyrenaica, Tripolitania remained the home of an Italian community of nearly fifty thousand during the early postwar years. The demographic villages and private concessions employed between a third and a quarter of the Italians remaining in Libya. For nearly thirty years the colonists defended their creations as best they could. But they were no longer masters of Libya, and without Italian political control the colonization rested on treacherous foundations. The definitive end to the fading dream of a fourth shore came with the expulsion of permanent Italian residents from Libya in the summer of 1970.

The phase of intensive settlement had given an impressive impulse to the Italian colonization effort by 1940. In a little more than four years, the Italian population in Libya had nearly doubled from the sixty-four thousand registered in the April 1936 census to more than one hundred ten thousand persons at the beginning of 1940.[1] The increase was due in large part to the immigration of the agricultural colonists. In relation to the colony's population as a whole, the Italians in 1940 made up nearly 12 percent, a figure comparable to the European population at its peak in Algeria.[2]

As a demographic outlet designed to attract large numbers of Italian immigrants, Libya was an abject failure. After three decades of settlement programs, including the extraordinary measures of state colonization, one hundred ten thousand Italians in Libya constituted a community about as large as the Italian colony in Tunisia.[3] As a solution to Italy's demographic pressures, Libya's contribution was infinitesimal. The average annual natural increase in the Italian metropolitan population between 1935 and 1940 totaled about four hundred thousand.[4]

Within Libya, however, the influx of colonists meant that the Italians were well on their way to fulfilling the old dream of a fourth shore based on immigrant families tilling the soil. The colonist families constituted the social and economic backbone of Libya's Italian population.[5] In Tripolitania, where the bulk of the Italian community was concentrated, the twenty-four thousand colonists made up just under a third of the total Italian population of seventy thousand. In thinly populated Cyrenaica, the fifteen thousand colonists constituted nearly half the Italian population in the region.

If the war had not intervened, what would have been the future of the colonization? In theory, there was no shortage of land. In Tripolitania, the colonization companies had developed about 68 percent of their lands; in Cyrenaica, the ECL had developed about 60 percent of its land. Balbo, the eternal optimist and enthusiast, looked forward to extending settlement beyond the agricultural zone of the colony's northern shore. He often returned from his flights over the colony excited about the future potential of bits of greenery he had seen deep in the desert.[6]

Even if the agricultural zone had not been extended beyond the lands already in concession, the more optimistic technical experts claimed that the settlement could have been far more intensive. In Tripolitania alone, depending on the intensity of cultivation and the methods used, one technician calculated that the rural population of about 15,000 Libyans and twenty-four thousand Italians could have been increased as much as 2.5 times to a total of nearly one hundred thousand persons when the lands were fully developed.[7]

Others, however, were less sanguine. Palloni and Maugini were skeptical about finding additional zones suitable for colonization.[8] In some cases, as for instance with the village of Gioda, south of Misurata, the colonization had been overextended with disastrous results.[9] The theoretical calculations which indicated that Tripolitania could be settled even more intensively were no more than guesses based on limited experience. Given the high birthrate among the colonist families, the demographic projects at least may have already reached saturation by 1940.[10]

A second major problem was productivity. As the Italians developed the agricultural zone, could they have increased its production sufficiently to support both Italians and Libyans at an acceptable standard of living? There is, of course, no way of predicting how successful the farms would have been in the long run. In 1940, the vast majority of the farms were still in the earliest stages of development. Even the oldest ECL farms in Cyrenaica had been in operation only half a dozen years.

The sketchy data available on production contain some positive signs for the long run. Through intensive development, the Italians estimated that in Tripolitania where once twenty to thirty hectares per person were needed to support the population, by 1946 only two to three hectares were necessary.[11] The districts of Micca, Giordani, and Bianchi, for instance, which supported perhaps five hundred persons and two thousand sheep before the Italian development, now supported three thousand persons and ten thousand sheep. Sowed land in the area had expanded from fifteen hundred hectares to five thousand hectares. The harvests from olives, almonds, vineyards, and fruit trees in Tripolitania also increased enormously over the decade 1940-50 as the trees gradually came into production. In Cyrenaica, the *capo zona* at Razza commented on the improved return on cereals from initial yields of four to seven times seed.[12] With continual work and the use of fertilizers, the yield averaged eight to ten times seed, with maximums of fourteen to fifteen times seed.

The future of the colonization depended on the development of the vast numbers of almonds, olives, fruit trees, and vineyards the Italians planted. By 1940, in Tripolitania plantings totaled 2,226,510 olives, 1,646,949 almonds, 36,826,505 grapevines, 93,380 fruit trees, and 1,032,223 trees for reforestation and miscellaneous uses.[13] In Tripolitania, except for the fruit trees, the vast majority of the plantings had been carried out on private farms. The comparable figures for Cyrenaica were 196,813 olives, 208,727 almonds, 3,277,841 grapevines, 176,030 fruit trees, and 96,470 plants dedicated to reforestation and miscellaneous uses.[14] In Cyrenaica the ECL projects had planted nearly four times as many trees and vineyards as the private farms. Once the trees and vineyards matured, agricultural experts estimated that the production would be enough to feed Libya's growing population and provide a sizable surplus for export.[15]

The Italians also anticipated that as the colonization developed, the industries based on the processing of agricultural products would also grow.[16] By 1940 there were an estimated 426 such plants in Tripolitania, with facilities for manufacturing or processing tobacco, flour, noodles, canned fruits and vegetables, olive oil, alcohol, beer, animal hides and esparto grass. Cyrenaica in 1940 was much less developed, for only 58 such establishments were listed. One of the most important industries related to the colonist villages was wine making. A plant for manufacturing and storing wine was built at Beda Littoria in 1937 and produced five thousand to six thousand hectoliters during the period 1938-40. Two other such facilities were planned for the villages of Luigi di Savoia and Giovanni Berta.

In the meantime, as the farms developed, Libya was far from self-sufficient. As of 1938, her trade balance showed imports of 882 million lire against exports of only 109 million.[17] Italy had a monopoly of trade, furnishing 91 percent of the imports and absorbing about 90 percent of the exports, which primarily included agricultural products such as wheat, hides, wool, sponges, alfa and esparto grass, dates, and tobacco. The imports mainly included manufactured goods and canned foodstuffs, but also comprised such items as olive oil, wine, and cereals—the very items Libya was expected to produce.[18]

The Costs of Colonization

Libya's future was dependent on an enormous and continuous investment that Italy could scarcely afford. With the conquest of Ethiopia completed, the Fascist regime turned to the task of developing the new empire, as the vast increase in the colonial budget indicates. The budget for 1937-38 totaled 1,614 million lire, about 12.5 percent of the total state budget and nearly quadruple the amount for the previous year.[19] The budget for 1938-39 of 1,795 million topped the previous year by 11 percent.

How did the Italians meet the enormous jump in their imperial expenditures? The colonies contributed only a small fraction of the expenses. In 1937-38 colonial revenues amounted to 432 million, or about 27 percent of the total budget. In 1938-39 the amount rose to 562 million, or about 31 percent of the budget. The rest had to be made up through special taxes levied at home and through a steadily declining standard of living for the majority of Italians.[20]

Libya reflects the sudden, intensive outpouring of investment. Nearly half (960 million lire) of the estimated total investment in the colony (1.8 billion lire) during the thirty-year Italian occupation was made during the years 1937-42.[21] Agriculture and colonization enjoyed top priority. The colonization projects and the development of agriculture absorbed about 654 million lire or roughly two-thirds of the expenditures made during this period of intensive investment.

Despite this impressive financial commitment during the last years of Italian rule, the investment in Libya seems relatively modest compared to the 68 billion lire lavished on East Africa during the period 1937–41. The sums devoted to agriculture and colonization in Libya also appear to be relatively modest compared with investments in the domestic showpiece of colonization, the Pontine Marshes. The total public and private investment in Libyan agriculture up to 1940 has been estimated at between six hundred and seven hundred million lire each for Tripolitania and Cyrenaica.[22] Thus, during the nearly three decades of Italian colonization the investments totaled somewhere between 1.2 and 1.4 billion lire. During the decade 1925–36 the Pontine Marshes alone absorbed a staggering investment of at least 1 billion lire.[23]

The chief investor in Libyan agriculture was always the state, which provided up to 75 percent of the funds,[24] in the form of subsidies, prizes and direct contributions. Thus it is not suprising—given the political goals of the colonization—that the demographic projects absorbed the great bulk of agricultural investment. In Cyrenaica alone, for instance, one estimate, based on the average cost of development per hectare, shows that by 1940, 605 million lire out of a total investment of 718 million went to the colonization projects.[25] Private colonization absorbed the remaining 112 million. The larger investment in demographic colonization was due not only to the larger tracts of land assigned for the projects but also to the higher unit costs of the demographic farms.[26]

These spiraling costs, as Balbo's advisers explained, were due in part to the crash nature of the projects and to the enormous initial investments needed in a country that had no infrastructure.[27] The costs were also high, however, because the colonists were in no hurry to cut themselves off from their subsidies. Theoretically, the farms should have produced enough to fulfill the families' needs, pay off the debt to the colonization company, and eventually offer a surplus. One report concluded that by 1942 the average annual income from the oldest farms in Cyrenaica, after the costs of operation and the family's food and clothing needs were taken into account, ranged from six thousand lire on "mediocre" farms to eighteen thousand lire on "good" farms.[28] The estimates for Breviglieri, Azizia, Oliveti, and Fonduco ranged between eighty-eight hundred lire and sixteen thousand lire.

No figures are available, however, to show what progress the families made in paying off their debts. The reports of the *capi zona* indicated that the families and the companies waged eternal battles over the agricultural contracts.[29] The uniform clauses of the contracts did not correspond to the fluctuations in what the different farms could actually produce. The colonists, too, showed wide variations in their capabilities and interests. The temptations of the war-inflated market led them to sell their produce on the sly, thus making it impossible for the companies to decide when the colonist had gone beyond the salaried stage of tenancy. Even during a good harvest year, company officials complained that very few of the colonists made any effort to pay off their mortgages or any of the advances which they had received in money or in kind.

To remedy some of these problems and to bring the colonization into conformity with Fascist concepts of the corporate state and economy, new legislation was drawn up in 1942.[30] Agricultural development and colonization in Libya was declared to be in the "public interest" and subject to approval and control by the state. The state claimed rights to all lands where production was not maximized. The legislation outlined complementary sectors of Libyan and Italian colonization. There were indications that Libyans might be resettled to develop fully pastoral activities on lands that were not used for Italian settlement.

The constant revision of the contracts and the pressures on the colonists to make payments on their debts provided some semblance of control over the expenses of colonization. Yet these controls were largely academic. The settlement administrators and the colonist families knew that the regime was determined to have the colonization succeed—if necessary, to buy that success. Government funds would always be available to support the colonization. If for some reason government funds dried up, Balbo was prepared to appeal directly to the people through a campaign of public subscriptions.[31] He was confident—and some of his advisors privately concurred—that the public would support the *quarta sponda* with enthusiasm.

The Impact of the War

Under conditions of peace, the colonization might have survived, perhaps even flourished. The war insured the demise of the fourth shore. For years the Fascists—imitating the slogans of the Nationalists at the time of the Libyan conquest—had clamored for Italy to free herself from her Mediterranean "prison." In June 1940, with France and Britain apparently on the verge of defeat, Mussolini launched his war to make Italy master of her "own sea." The result was tragic. The Duce had squandered the nation's military resources in Ethiopia and Spain.[32] To compensate for Italy's lack of military preparedness, Mussolini counted on a quick, cheap victory. The Allies, however, gradually rallied from their initial defeats of 1940, and eventually turned North Africa into a major battleground. For nearly two years the Allies and the Axis fought a series of seesaw engagements across Egypt and Libya. Balbo, who had lobbied violently against the German alliance and the war, never lived to see the full impact of the conflict on his colony.[33]

Historically, when a conqueror swept across North Africa, Cyrenaica and Tripolitania had often undergone different experiences. World War II was no exception.[34] In Cyrenaica, the colonization was totally destroyed and the area came entirely under control of the British and their Sanusi allies. The Egyptian piaster became the currency and justice was based on proclamations of the British Military Administration (BMA). In Tripolitania, the colonization survived largely intact and an Italian community of fifty thousand remained at the end of the war. Even under British administration, the lira was used as currency and the Italian penal code regulated legal matters.

The three successive campaigns which raged back and forth across Cyrenaica in 1941–42 completely destroyed the Italian colonization. The demographic villages in the Gebel were especially hard hit during the first two-month British occupation in the spring of 1941.[35] The colonists suffered eighteen dead and seventeen wounded from events connected with the hostilities and the occupation. Fascist propaganda made the most of the incidents of robbery, rape, and outright murder, both by the occupying troops and by Libyans.[36] Still more demoralizing was the return of the nomads with their herds, which now grazed openly in the colonists' fields. Another major blow to the agricultural effort was the demolition of public utilities, wells, windmills, and pumps by the retreating British army.

Under the brief Italian reoccupation, the colonists never recovered their morale.[37] Optimistic agricultural experts considered the occupation experience as a selection process. Those colonists who did not have the determination to succeed were eliminated. But the colonist population dropped by half, from 8,426 at the end of 1941 to 4,163 in the spring of 1942. The second British occupation delivered a final crushing blow to the settlements on the Gebel. The colonists suffered forty-two dead and twenty-six wounded and another round of rapes, murders, and robberies. Many of their homes had become uninhabitable; the families had lost most of their household necessities; their agricultural machinery was destroyed or requisitioned, and the livestock was lost. Even the oldest and most experienced colonist families, those who left their houses under direct threat from armed Libyans, no longer had the courage to return to their isolated farms.

Under these conditions the remaining Italians in Cyrenaica were evacuated in November and December of 1942, shortly before the third and final British occupation. The majority of the agricultural colonists were resettled in Tripolitania.[38] About 500 families joined the farms of the two colonization companies and about 300 families found work in the cities. Thus, of the Ente's 916 families who left Cyrenaica in 1942, only about 100 returned to Italy. By early 1943, the thirty thousand

Italians who had been living in Cyrenaica were reduced to a handful.[39] Most of those remaining belonged to religious orders.

With the evacuation of Cyrenaica, the colonization decayed rapidly. The British Military Administration operated Razza, Beda Littoria, Savoia, and Berta, the four oldest ECL villages on the Gebel, under a plan known as the "Hill Farms Scheme."[40] Libyan colonists, working under the advice and supervision of a British officer, harvested a grape crop and produced wine at Beda Littoria in the summer of 1943. On the Barce Plain, the British cultivated about four thousand hectares of land formerly operated by private concessions. During July and August of 1943, these lands produced wheat and barley crops.

By 1947, however, the agricultural settlements had deteriorated badly. An Italian visitor estimated that 60 percent of the olives and almond trees had been destroyed, although the vineyards had fared a little better.[41] The colonists' houses were a "disheartening spectacle of ruin and decay." All of the twelve villages that had been founded were abandoned except for their service centers. These had been turned to various uses: Oberdan had become the site of a training school for Sanusi police; the infirmary at D'Annunzio had been transformed into a stable for police horses. A few of the farms at Razza were being developed by Libyan day laborers who had worked for the Italians.

Compared with Cyrenaica, the colonization in Tripolitania suffered relatively little. For the most part, the demographic projects remained occupied. Throughout the war, the ECL managed to keep about 80 percent of the 1,032 farms settled in 1939 operating under colonist families.[42] In February 1947 the Ente farms were being worked by 840 families, or 4,079 persons. The INFPS had filled 904 out of 1,031 farms for a total of 4,997 persons, according to a survey made 30 April 1947.

The direct war damage was light. No major military engagements wasted Tripolitania. However, irrigated farming practically collapsed, since the water projects remained incomplete and the retreating Germans destroyed water pumps, power stations, and irrigation ditches. A shortage of agricultural equipment developed when the Germans took many of the trucks and tractors with them to Tunisia. The systematic slaughter of livestock for meat to feed the German military reduced the herds to one-third of their prewar total.[43] Some farmland was converted to airfields and other military needs.[44]

More harmful to the colonization than the physical damage was the interruption in the long-term programs for developing the farms.[45] Families could no longer work as a unit: the men had been called up for military service and the youngest children had been evacuated. The colonists, always more interested in short-term profits than in long-term reclamation goals, gladly produced food for urban centers and military needs. They enjoyed good harvests in 1944, 1945, and 1946, and there was a high demand for their produce.[46] Under these conditions the colonists neglected the almond and olive trees and the vineyards which were vital to the long-term success of their farms. The colonization companies could do little to enforce discipline and proceed with their programs.

For the duration of the war, the colonization companies, including ATI, came under the BMA's Department of Agriculture. The development and scale of the programs impressed the British, and they expressed much admiration for the work that had been done. Major R. L. Robb, director of agriculture for the BMA, for instance, praised the technical conception of the colonization as "magnificent" and added that the detailed organization was "of a very high order indeed."[47] However, as one Italian observer remarked, the social and political concepts that lay behind the projects remained perplexing and alien to the British authorities: "It's a question of mentality. That demographic colonization could be possible, necessary, useful, is beyond the comprehension of the majority."[48]

In accordance with international law, the British placed the colonization projects on a "care and maintenance" basis. Although such a policy was legally correct, some Italians were bitter at its political implications.[49] By discouraging further development of the colonization, the British were obviously undermining the basis of the Italian community in Libya. The Italian agricultural experts, however, were not entirely displeased. Without subsidies and political interference, they foresaw a natural selection process. Those colonists and private concessioners who had been content to idle along with the help of state subsidies would be eliminated. When the colonists and concessioners could no longer be "content with today and had to think about tomorrow"—during that period "real colonization was done," one expert concluded during a postwar visit.[50] Food shortages would also force colonists to produce or starve.

With subsidies curtailed and discipline difficult to enforce, the companies decided to encourage independence among the colonists by transferring ownership of the farms to the families as quickly as possible.[51] They hoped that the transfer would still preserve the goals of demographic colonization and the stability of the colony's agricultural economy. The colonization companies were ordered to divide their farms into "advanced" and "retarded" according to whether or not the unit was close to self-sufficiency. A total of 108 farms, all of them occupied before the first mass migrations, qualified for transfer. By the end of October 1942 the colonists received them on the condition that they pay the price of the farms established at the time of sale. In effect, the contracts meant that the colonist entered the third or "redemption" phase of the old contract prematurely. An additional 249 "promise of transfer" contracts were signed in 1942 with colonists whose properties were in Cyrenaica. These contracts were similar to the "conditional transfers." They were designed to indicate the company's good faith in wanting to convey the property to the colonist. The contract promised to complete the shift within a year after the end of hostilities when all the necessary technical-legal data had become available. A new system of contracts was also devised for farms that were not transferred.

The conditional transfer of the farms and the war crisis infused some of the colonists with a new enthusiasm and interest in their work. In general, the colonists had shared a "company" mentality: they "worked for the Ente." If the harvest was good "the Ente profited," and if the harvest was poor "the Ente lost."[52] Under the new contracts the *capo zona* at Fonduco reported that some of the Sicilian women, who by custom would not have worked in the fields "for all the gold in the world," now labored side by side with their husbands.[53]

Faced with food shortages, the colonists also produced more. In the village of Garibaldi, the harvest of 1945 totaled eight thousand quintals of cereals and that of 1946 ten thousand quintals.[54] In 1947, because of the drought, production dropped to five thousand quintals. During the sharecropping phase of the contract, the colonists had never harvested more than four thousand quintals. The *capo zona* also noted that the colonists extended the areas planted in vineyards and took much better care of their livestock.

Nevertheless, the "company mentality" died hard. In various forms, the system of subsidies and inducements persisted throughout the war. The colonists often had to be prodded, coaxed, or even threatened to assume responsibility for the farms. At the village of Crispi, for instance, the *capo zona* induced 202 of the 275 families to accept the new contracts.[55] The remaining families continued in their status as sharecroppers. As such, they received a special food subsidy (*assegno alimentare*). The majority of families, who under the new contracts were not eligible for this special treatment, immediately wanted to revert to their old status. To keep the peace, the *capo zona* was forced to reduce the food subsidy to the sharecroppers.

From a general survey of the farms which he made during a 1947 visit to Tripolitania, a colonial ministry official concluded that the ECL farms—in contrast to the INFPS settlements—had developed best so far and would fare best in the future.[56] He attributed the superior development of the Ente farms to the organization's better planning, superior technical experience, and better control over the colonist families. He also cited differences in the philosophies of the two organizations. In his view, the ECL had practiced a policy of genuine reclamation and development; the INFPS had pursued too much of a policy of exploitation.[57] The Ente farms had used tree culture as the backbone of their development program whereas the INFPS had used the trees as a finishing touch. Fantoli concluded that the differences in approach between the two organizations explained the impression of "squalor" and partial abandonment in the villages of Marconi and Tazzoli.

Among the other villages he visited, Fantoli was most impressed with Corradini and Breviglieri.[58] Corradini, with 64 families, or 271 inhabitants, had lost only an eighth of its families, and the olives and vineyards were doing well because of the area's favorable soil and climate. Breviglieri had a population of 1,088 colonists, and none of its 168 farms had been abandoned, despite water shortages in the region. Other villages—such as Oliveti, Hascian, and Bianchi—had not lost any families during the war and had actually increased in population as families were reunited. Nevertheless, these villages faced severe physical handicaps. Giordani and Micca's 360 original farms, for instance, were occupied. But the severe drought of 1947, the high temperatures, and the gradual return of nomadic Libyans with their flocks had led to many requests for repatriation.

The drought of 1947 marked the end of the wartime boom and the colonists' temporary prosperity. With the end of the war, the local markets had been contracting. Large military expenditures had ceased since 1944 as the garrisons were reduced. Export trade with Italy was at a standstill. The drought compounded these troubles. The rain-fed crops failed, and the expense of water for irrigated crops ran up the colonists' electric bills to figures that they could not afford.[59] Only Crispi had an olive crop, and the harvest met barely a third of the settlement's oil requirements. Tigrinna's tobacco crop failed completely. At Garian the laborers were forced onto a diet of reduced rations.

Despite the hardships of the war and the drought in 1947, the Italian colonists and the private concessioners still retained a substantial stake in Tripolitania's future. The colonists and the private concessioners numbered 15,000, or slightly under one-third of the total Italian community of 49,536.[60] The Italians retained their position as the largest minority in Libya.

The entire Italian community, however, showed signs of wavering morale.[61] As former enemies, the Italians could not expect support from the British; as fallen conquerors, they got little sympathy from the Libyans. Since the Italian government was in no position to provide support or guidance, and such a basic means of communication as an airmail letter took ten to fifteen days to arrive—if it arrived at all— the Italian community felt spiritually and physically isolated from their homeland. Remarking on the large number of irksome and humiliating formalities that the BMA imposed, a visitor in 1947 observed that for the Italians Tripolitania was a kind of physical and spiritual "concentration camp." In reaction to their plight, many in the Italian community turned to a kind of "sentimental Fascism," made up more of "regrets than of firm plans or goals for the future."[62] Most of all, everyone felt that Italy owed him something. "Everyone has a moral bill—when he doesn't also have a physical one—to present to the *madrepatria*," Fantoli remarked.[63]

The physical signs of hard times and low morale were apparent in all facets of the Italian community's life: long soup lines at noon in front of charity and welfare organizations in Tripoli; men and women begging in the streets; Italian children, dirty and barefoot, roaming the streets with Arab playmates; the marriages of forty-five Italian women who converted to Islam and "more or less legally" married Libyans; the large number of *faux ménages* in the demographic villages while women waited for their men to return.

Perhaps the most important factor in maintaining the Italian community's morale was the steady flow of refugees to Tripolitania.[64] Some families were expecting the return of three or even four young men, most of whom were living in Italy in conditions of misery and unemployment. For the most part, however, the returning colonists were women and children. Practically, this meant adding unproductive members to the family. Nevertheless, the morale factor outweighed economic considerations. As the 1947 BMA report remarked about the return of refugees to Garian:

The arrival of wives and children from Italy reunited families and caused great joy. Little of politics is heard from those colonists. They of necessity work hard on their concessions to earn a simple living and hope that by some means their future will be assured.[65]

The repatriation began as early as 1943, following the allied occupation of Sicily and Southern Italy. During the war the number of returning colonists was relatively small because of the risks of secretly crossing the Mediterranean in a small boat. By early 1946, however, the stream had become an organized traffic. The boats left Syracuse at daylight with up to 250 passengers. By nightfall they were close enough to the coast of Tripolitania so that the refugees could land in small boats. The larger ships tried to be out of sight of land by daybreak. No two landings were made at the same spot.

The BMA, partly for political reasons, viewed the repatriating Italians with little enthusiasm. The unemployment rate among Italians was large enough without adding the refugees. Furthermore, the returning Italians excited the local Libyan population. Wild rumors circulated and one Arab party attempted a countrywide protest strike for a day. In June 1946 the BMA finally insisted on an agreement by which repatriation had to be done on a head-for-head basis. Among the categories of acceptable refugees, the BMA favored agriculturalists. About seventeen thousand persons were exchanged under the head-for-head plan during a four-year period. The refugees returned either at their own expense or with the help of the Ministry of Italian Africa, which chartered vessels specifically for repatriation.

As so often in the past, the key to the colonization's future lay not with the efforts of the colonists, but with the power politics of the Mediterranean. The private concessions and especially the demographic projects were based on faith in the future of an Italian community in Libya. With the Fascist defeat, the entire colonization structure threatened to topple. Neither colonists nor private concessioners were willing to fully commit their energies to their work when they had no idea who would finally govern Libya.

The Postwar Debate over Italian Colonies and Libya's Future

The United Nations General Assembly resolution of 21 November 1949 created a united and independent Libya. Until the United Nations action, Italy had hopes of retaining its former colony—or if that failed, at least of gaining a trusteeship over all or part of the territory. The British had made promises to their Sanusi allies that Cyrenaica would not be returned to Italian control; but they were silent about the future of Tripolitania.[66] Meanwhile, at Potsdam the Big Three had decided to relegate the problem of the Italian colonies to the newly created Council of Foreign Ministers. Certainly there was nothing in the United Nations charter which precluded the Italians from possession of or at least trusteeship over their former colonies. Article 77 said only that the international trusteeship system may be applied to "territories which may be detached from enemy states."[67]

Postwar popular opinion in Italy showed a revival of interest in the colonies. Major colonial congresses were held in 1946 and in 1947.[68]

Newspapers and magazines defending Italy's rights to her former African territories sprang up. As Salvemini, the old anticolonialist, remarked dryly, "The pleasure of collecting deserts and sinking money in them has already been too costly for Italy."[69] Nevertheless, he concluded that "if the old Italian colonies were taken away from Italy and given to someone else, Italians of all parties would consider this an unpardonable injustice." Other public figures and intellectuals such as Count Sforza argued that their country should behave no differently from the other imperial nations: Italy should give up her colonies to international control only if other powers would do the same.

The Italian government outlined its official position in a letter from Prime Minister De Gasperi to American Secretary of State Byrnes. Before Mussolini's invasion of Ethiopia, De Gasperi wrote, democratic Italy had never considered colonies "as a tool for imperialism but rather as a means for absorbing Italy's surplus manpower."[70] Postwar Italy viewed colonies in the same way as had pre-Fascist Italy. While trusteeship was not incompatible "in principle" with Italian interests,

such a collective method hardly corresponds to the peculiar necessities of the Italian colonies, owing to the difference between the Italian colonial conception and praxis founded on emigration and the Anglo Saxon system mainly based on raw materials and markets.[71]

Thus Italy had hopes of retaining sovereignty over the pre-Fascist colonies of Eritrea, Somalia, and Libya. In the specific case of Libya, De Gasperi wrote:

We gather that while no objections are raised against Italian sovereignty in Tripolitania, strategic guarantees are being sought in Cyrenaica in order to afford full security to the bordering countries and to the international sea routes.[72]

De Gasperi hoped that these "strategic areas" could be created in Tobruk and the Marmarica. Once these conditions were established, he hoped that the Gebel Akhdar would remain open to Italy for agricultural emigration and colonization.

Within the context of postwar international politics, Italy's pleas for emigration outlets and her distinctions between democratic and Fascist regimes carried little weight. The victorious allies, now Cold War adversaries, groped their way to a new power balance in the Mediterranean.[73] For the British and French, slipping in the Eastern Mediterranean before Zionist and Pan-Arab movements, Libya appeared useful as a counterweight. For the Russians, eager to establish a new sphere of influence, Libya offered a springboard. Both sides remembered the strategic value of Libya and the Horn of Africa as bases for long-range bombers.

In the Cold War struggle, Italy soon found her traditional balancing role between two great power blocs. The currents of diplomacy shifted so rapidly that Italy's position quickly became an anomaly. At the Foreign Ministers Conference of 1946 in Paris she had renounced all claims to her colonies. This position was enforced by the terms of the Italian Peace Treaty of 1947. At the same time that she renounced claims to the colonies, Italy pursued a vigorous campaign for trustee-ship—a campaign often aided by the very powers that had forced her to renounce the colonies in the first place.

Since the Big Four could not agree on a final disposition of the former Italian territories, the Italian Peace Treaty provided that a decision should be postponed for a year. In the meantime the Council of Foreign Ministers sent a commission to investigate the colonies and prepare recommendations for the council.

The commission spent seven months (November 1947 to May 1948) on their investigation.[74] Their inquiry in Libya during the spring of 1948 lasted for forty days in Tripolitania, twenty-five days in Cyre-naica, and ten days in the Fezzan. Through their interviews and observations, the commission concluded that the Libyans generally opposed the return of Italian rule. However, in Tripolitania the population and the local political parties indicated that they were not opposed to the presence of the Italian colonists.

The Four-Power Commission also heard the sentiments of the Italian community in Libya through the testimony of its political pressure groups. These groups covered all shades of the political spectrum.[75] The Italian Representative Committee, which claimed a membership of fifteen thousand and according to the BMA represented 90 percent of the Italian community in Libya, favored Italian trusteeship over Libya. In a letter to the Four-Power Commission, Admiral Carlo Emanuele Fenzi, one of the Representative Committee's leaders, complained bitterly of the plight of the Italians under the BMA. He accused the British of destroying everything the Italians had created in the colony. With special reference to the demographic settlements, the letter claimed that the projects had degenerated to the point that livestock now occupied the colonists' houses while the Libyan shepherds slept outdoors. The Representative Committee's chief rival, the Italian Association for the Progress of Libya, was composed mainly of Italian left-wing intellectuals, who favored Italian trusteeship only if Libyan independence could not be assured.

Refugee groups in Italy also testified before the Four-Power Comission. These organizations generally expressed a strong desire to return to Libya as soon as possible, preferably a Libya under Italian tutelage. Such was the position of the Libyan Refugees' Association (*Associazione Profughi della Libia*), which claimed a membership of 9,078 families, or 40,744 persons.[76] The association spoke of "cooperation" and "reconstruction," of returning to Libya to rebuild the country—not to make it "Italian." The association favored limiting the return of Italians to those who had some type of property and could serve as employers rather than laborers.

Other refugee groups argued that the Italian presence in the former colony was indispensable if Libya was to continue her development. Without Italian agricultural skills the country would quickly relapse into desert. All spokesmen for the refugees stressed a spirit of mutual cooperation for the sake of rebuilding Libya. When the country became independent, the colonists said, they hoped to stay on and share in the fruits of economic development.

The commission concluded with recommendations that Libya be placed under the trusteeship of one or two of the Big Four.[77] However, there was no agreement as to when the trusteeship should begin or who the powers should be. The Soviet Union, which had formerly sought trusteeship for itself, now favored Italian trusteeship for the whole country. Britain and the United States favored British trusteeship for Cyrenaica and postponing for a year a decision on Tripolitania and the Fezzan. France favored postponing for a year a decision on all three territories.

The Council of Foreign Ministers, meeting in Paris on 13 September 1948 to consider the commission's report, deadlocked once again. The Soviet Union now abandoned her support for Italy in favor of a collective trusteeship in Libya. The other three powers, which at one time or another had favored the collective solution, rejected the Soviet proposal. With no solution in sight, the Big Four, according to the terms of the Italian Peace Treaty, referred the problem to the United Nations.

Before the question reached the General Assembly, one last compromise solution on trusteeship was proposed. British Foreign Minister Bevin and Italian Foreign Minister Sforza reached an agreement by which Italy would retain a trusteeship over Tripolitania, Britain over Cyrenaica, and France over the Fezzan. Libya would be reestablished as an independent state in ten years if the General Assembly agreed. Italian trusteeship over Tripolitania was to begin in 1951 upon termination of the British Military Administration. The plan was defeated before the General Assembly by the Arab-Asian and Soviet blocs. The only solution that remained was a united, independent Libya. This was the plan that was finally adopted under the resolution of 21 November 1949.

The Italo-Libyan Accords of 1956 and the Fate of the Colonists

The United Nations decision in favor of Libyan independence still left the thorny question of the rights of the Italian minority. The 1947 peace treaty with Italy had guaranteed Italian property rights.[78] Yet any final disposition of this matter depended on resolving the question of ultimate sovereignty over Libya. Adrian Pelt, the United Nations commissioner to Libya, stressed the importance of the Italian agricultural holdings, especially in Tripolitania, as the territory's most valuable economic asset. He urged that action should be taken before the farms were dispersed or ruined:

The Italian farms, both private concessions and parastatal settlements, represent a remarkable feat of pioneering and land reclamation, which, chiefly owing to the comparatively long period of immaturity of the olive tree, has only recently begun to demonstrate its full productive value. . . . They are, however, the greatest economic asset of the territory, an asset which can easily be lost if constant care to prevent erosion and other deterioration is not maintained.[79]

The United Nations acted on the matter in a resolution of 15 December 1950, which laid down guidelines for the settlement but left the details to be worked out in a bilateral accord between Italy and Libya.

The main points in the guidelines were: (1) the Libyan government was to receive immediately all landed property that belonged to the Italian state, including public property, inalienable property, and ungranted property under the authority of the ECL and INFPS. (2) Rights to all landed property lawfully acquired by Italian nationals were to be respected. This would include freedom to dispose of property and remove funds from Libya duty-free. (3) All contracts held by colonists and private concessioners would be respected. (4) The farms would be transferred to colonists as private property and the colonization companies would be liquidated.[80]

The negotiations toward the accord were broken off several times and dragged on for nearly six years.[81] The principal points of contention were Libyan claims for war damages from Italy and disagreements over distinctions between private and public property. The Italians maintained that war damages were not an issue since Libya was legally part of Italy during the war. On the issue of public property, the Italians claimed that the problem had been settled when the BMA turned over all public property to the Libyan government.

In 1956 the two sides reached agreement.[82] The Italians offered a sum for war damages on condition that the money be used for Libyan reconstruction and for furthering trade between the two countries. On the question of the agricultural colonists, the treaty provided that the Libyan government would guarantee Italian property rights, except for special restrictions in Cyrenaica. Article 10 of the treaty dealt with the demographic projects. The staffs of the ECL and the INFPS were to complete the development and amortization of the farms by February 1960. The funds, estimated at 2.5 billion lire, were furnished by the Italian government.

The work of the colonization companies was completed well before the February 1960 deadline. In the spring of 1959, the colonization companies could look back at the results of two decades of labor in Tripolitania, often under difficult and extraordinary circumstances. They had succeeded in developing 40,401 hectares; they had been forced to abandon 54,950 hectares, of which part was wasteland. They had begun with 2,098 families, or about 10,500 persons, in 1938 and had finally settled 1,272 families, or 5,100 persons, by the 1960 deadline.[83]

The agreements had done little more than temporarily salvage a group of deteriorating farming communities populated by disgruntled and disillusioned colonists. In a 1953 report, Maugini described the colonists as a "mass of more or less unhappy, undisciplined, occasionally rebellious people."[84] The majority of them, Maugini wrote, claimed that "the government had forced them to come to Libya," and for their sufferings and troubles they blamed the government and demanded compensation. During the long negotiations, the colonists continued to receive subsidies to insure that they would eventually attain full ownership of their farms. The colonization companies, badly understaffed, furnished technical support. Yet a decade of political uncertainty had sapped the families' morale and there was little in their surroundings to revive their faith in the future.

Even with the continuous help of the colonization companies, the condition of the farms was such that the colonists faced hard times. All the projects badly needed repairs, completion of their capital improvements, and new plantings of trees.[85] Most of the farms were underpopulated, and service facilities were minimal. The colonists who remained regrouped to form contiguous blocks of farms. On the peripheral areas of the settlements, Libyans occupied the abandoned houses and allowed their herds and flocks to graze freely, often at the expense of the young trees. The colonists generally operated their farms on a subsistence level, often in open participation with Libyans.

TABLE 4. PEASANT COLONIZATION IN TRIPOLITANIA (1938/39 to 1958/59)

District	Area in Hectares			Lots	
	Initial Phase (1938–39)	Final Phase (1958–59)	Abandoned	Created	Occupied
INFPS					
Irrigated:					
Bianchi	6,121.5	5,259.1	826.3	168	149
Giordani	5,207.7	4,473.1	734.5	194	169
Micca	4,823.7	3,169.4	1,653.6	148	122
Oliveti	1,393.6	1,370.3	23.2	74	74
Hascian	356.1	356.1	...	19	19
Dry:					
Tarhuna	13,707.3	1,103.4	12,603.8	179	19
Marconi	8,282.8	65.9	8,216.9	131	1
Corradini	2,973.6	2,086.7	886.9	64	39
Castelverde	2,577.3	62.9	2,514.4	58	2
Subtotal	45,443.6	17,946.9	27,459.6	1,035	594
ECL					
Irrigated:					
Crispi	9,140.5	3,822.4	5,318.1	370	237
Gioda	2,288.8	24.0	2,264.8	100	2
Azizia	5,570.5	1,043.8	4,526.7	30	22
Oliveti	1,657.0	1,657.0	...	50	50
Dry:					
Garibaldi	15,869.8	6,720.8	9,148.9	318	175
Breviglieri	14,146.6	8,244.4	5,902.2	168	165
Fonduk el Togar	1,235.8	942.2	293.5	27	27
Subtotal	49,909.0	22,454.6	27,454.2	1,063	678
Total	95,352.6	40,401.5	54,913.8	2,098	1,272

NOTE: Abandoned land includes steppe land as well as abandoned lots.
SOURCE: Attilio Rompietti, "La colonizzazione contadina in Tripolitania," *Rivista di Agricoltura Subtropicale e Tropicale,* 55 (January–March 1961): 27.

In general, Maugini's report of 1953 indicated that the ECL farms fared better than those of the INFPS.[86] The ECL's three original projects (Fonduco, Azizia, and Oliveti) were fully developed into privately owned farms only in need of minor repairs. Breviglieri's original nucleus of farms was also in good condition. Conditions in the Misurata area were less satisfactory. Three-quarters of Gioda had been abandoned and Crispi and Garibaldi were in poor condition. Of the INFPS projects, only Oliveti operated according to the original schemes. The rest of the farms were left to pasturage or sown crops, and the trees were neglected. In the Tarhuna area all except ten of Marconi's farms were less than half developed. The other projects were in a state of decay or had been abandoned.

Their social status as an isolated, alien minority discouraged the colonists.[87] They had little contact with other settlements, with Tripoli, or with Italy. Although the demands of seasonal labor forced the colonists to associate with the Libyans, there was little social fraternization. The colonists were frequently reminded that they had come as aliens and had forcibly taken control of Libyan land.

The legal status of the Italian community emphasized its isolation. Italians were required to exercise a citizenship option by the end of 1962. If the colonists chose to retain their Italian citizenship, they would be forced to sell their farms before 1962. If they applied for Libyan citizenship, they still felt defenseless against future encroachments by the Libyan government. Rumors circulated among the colonists that their lands would be nationalized. Meanwhile, Italians could not export money or property until the end of 1962, and they were subject to a heavy duty for alien registration. The Libyan government's decision to change the date for extending the citizenship option to 31 December 1960 and a ruling to enforce the Arabic language law—which included renaming the demographic settlements—only served to increase tensions in the Italian community.

With these prospects for the future, the gradual exodus of the colonists from the demographic settlements is scarcely surprising. An estimated 4,130 colonists left in 1957.[88] Those who remained completed the reclamation of their farms and then sold them to Libyan nationals. By the end of October 1961, nearly 70 percent of the colonist farms in the settlement projects were sold to Libyans; by 1964, only about 120 colonist families were left in Tripolitania.[89]

For the remaining colonists and private concessioners and for the long-term resident Italian community as a whole, which numbered at least twenty thousand, the coup de grace came in the summer of 1970.[90] On 22 July Colonel Mu'amar al-Qaddafi, the young leader of the coup that had overthrown the monarchy ten months earlier, announced the confiscation of all Jewish and Italian properties.[91] The Italian properties in particular were to be confiscated in compensation for the damages Libya suffered under the colonial rule.[92] Italians were given a three-month deadline in which to account for their possessions and leave the country.

As the Italian government pointed out in protests to the Libyan government and the United Nations, legally and diplomatically as well as morally, the decrees were outrageous. They violated the United Nations resolution of 1950, the Italo-Libyan agreements of 1956, and the Libyan Revolutionary Council's own proclamations of September 1969, all of which defended the property rights of the Italian community. However, the decrees and the xenophobic attacks which accompanied them were not unexpected. During its short life the revolutionary regime had already nationalized a number of foreign holdings and imposed new restrictions on foreigners working in Libya.[93] Between September 1969, the advent of the revolutionary regime, and July 1970, the date of the expulsion decrees, four thousand Italians left Libya.[94]

Those who left as a result of the expropriation decrees were subject to a long and often harassing inventory of their possessions before they were given exit permits.[95]

During the three months between the decrees and the 15 October 1970 expulsion deadline, fourteen thousand Italians returned to Italy.[96] To help these refugees reestablish themselves in their homeland, the Italian government provided legal and financial aid and temporary living accomodations in various camps which had also served refugees returning from Africa immediately after World War II.[97] For many of the last survivors of the "fourth shore," however, Italy was no longer home. As a mechanic from Foggia, who had lived forty-one years abroad, commented, "I am returning to my land, where, unfortunately, I feel myself to be a total stranger. I will have to begin from the beginning."[98]

11

Conclusion

Such was the ultimate fate of the colonization—the backbone of the Italian effort to create a fourth shore in Libya. Politics gave life to the colonization; politics ultimately strangled it. In perspective, there is a baroque quality to the entire undertaking: brilliant but enormously expensive and ultimately empty. Despite all the claims which were made for it, the colonization did little or nothing to help resolve Italy's pressing economic and social problems. At best, perhaps, the building of the *quarta sponda* served as a comforting way to distract the Italian people from their grim lives in a world of dictatorship and economic depression.

To conclude on such a harsh note, however, seems a gratuitous insult to the thousands of Italians who dedicated the best years of their lives to building a fourth shore. For them the decades of Italian administration in Libya were a period of positive, constructive achievement to be remembered with pride. In summing up the Italian experience in Libya, it is only fair to at least review their case.

First of all the *vecchi Libici*, the "old Libya hands," point with pride to the scope of the colonization and the concrete achievements by 1940. Most foreign observers, no matter how politically hostile they were to the Fascist regime, could not hide their admiration for what the Italians had attempted to do. For centuries, until the Italian occupation, a long series of invaders had exploited Libya's meager agricultural resources with no thought for the area's future. As the British Military Administration's chief agricultural officer commented in 1943, the Italians had broken with this precedent: they had made a "bold and courageous attempt...to set a new pattern for Libyan agriculture."[1] Nor did these plans remain merely grand designs. Especially during the last decade of their sovereignty, under the impetus of mounting political pressures, the Italians transformed Libya with amazing speed.

Between 1936 and 1940, the population of agricultural colonists doubled. Roads, farms, schools, hospitals, and aqueducts materialized at a pace that impressed even the Italians. By 1940, the *scatolone di sabbia*, the "big sandbox" as the anticolonialists had derisively labeled the colony, was fast disappearing. The outlines of the fourth shore could be clearly discerned.

Second, colonialists cite Libya as an example of how Italy remained true to her tradition of seeking empire for the sake of her emigrants. Balbo's spectacular fleet of colonists struck a responsive chord in patriotic Italians who remembered the humiliating exodus of emigrants who left cursing their homeland at the end of the nineteenth century. To many Italians, including the nationalist historian Gioacchino Volpe, Balbo's mass emigrations symbolized "how things had changed" from the depressing days when the government considered emigrants as little more than a source of remittances to help balance the national budget.[2]

As a final achievement, many colonialists claim that the indigenous peoples also benefited from the colonization. The Libyans—or so the colonialists argue—were not robbed of their lands: the Italians acquired their properties legally and paid for them. As for the confiscations of the Sanusi lands, these were considered isolated and exceptional measures, fully justified against a minority of "rebels." Moreover, the Italians made the desert flourish: Italian investment and modern agricultural techniques transformed barren steppe into productive farmland, and the colonization created new jobs for the indigenous peoples.

To conclude their case, the defenders of the colonization point to Libya's economic development since she received her independence in 1951. Until the discovery of oil in 1959, as United Nations Commissioner Adrian Pelt commented, the agricultural development initiated by the Italians was the new nation's most valuable asset. Even with the discovery of oil, technical experts urged the Libyan government to continue developing the agricultural sector in order to avoid economic and social imbalances, for the oil boom could not absorb the tide of unskilled workers which flowed from the countryside to the cities.[3] The development of agriculture was also important in reducing the nation's reliance on imported foodstuffs. As part of its plan to stimulate agriculture, the Libyan government rehabilitated some of the former Italian demographic villages. Surely, the colonialists argue, what better evidence could there be that the Italians were not plunderers and exploiters? They were builders, concerned with developing the colony's meager resources for the benefit of both Libyans and Italians.

There is, of course, an element of truth in the claims of the nostalgic colonialists. Foreigners as well as Italians admired the scope and technical achievements of the colonization. Like any other colonial regime, the Italians brought with them a new technology and productive organization which in the long run might have resulted in some material improvement in the lives of the indigenous peoples. But the colonialists completely ignore the material and moral price which Italians as well as Libyans paid for these modest "achievements."

In material terms, for the Italians Libya proved to be an enormously expensive demographic outlet. The colony, of course, never came close to accommodating millions of emigrants, as Corradini had predicted with so much fervor at the time of the Libyan War. In 1940, at the peak of the colonization, and after thirty years under the tricolor, the Italian population numbered about one hundred ten thousand, barely a quarter of an average year's natural increase in the metropolitan population. Balbo's plan to settle one hundred thousand colonists over a five-year period was scarcely equal to one year's normal emigration from Italy. Nor did the colonization in Libya really contribute much to resolving the problems of the *mezzogiorno*. In practice, the intensive colonization offered new homes and new land primarily for the dispossessed of the Veneto and the Po Valley regions.

Although the colonization provided opportunities for a tiny proportion of the Italian population, for the nation as a whole Libya was nothing but an economic burden. The colony never achieved economic self-sufficiency, and it contributed nothing to the Duce's schemes for autarky. On the contrary, Italy paid dearly to support a huge bureaucracy and military establishment in addition to the colonization projects. According to official estimates, the state alone invested some 1.8 billion lire (equal to 150 million prewar dollars) in the development of Libya's infrastructure between 1913 and 1942. Of this, the amount allocated directly to agriculture and reclamation totaled 654.5 million lire, most of which was spent during the period of intensive colonization. Private capital never showed much enthusiasm for investing in Libya's agricultural future. Balbo's intensive colonization could therefore be justified only in terms of social and political goals that went beyond mere economic calculus. To continue the development outlined under the demographic schemes was "physically possible but unlikely unless means can be found to assist the farmer beyond the point of prudent investment," as an FAO expert concluded in 1952.[4] Ultimately, the Italian people themselves shouldered the burden of empire through higher taxes and a lower standard of living.

Finally, as the Italians learned, the price of a fourth shore was a regime which led the nation into political and moral bankruptcy. Fascism appeared to realize the imperial aspirations of the colonialists who had dreamed of empire in the days of the Liberal period. Yet, most likely, the leadership, social structure, and tactics of the Duce's regime would have repelled this earlier generation. Men like Sonnino, Di San Giuliano, and Franchetti might have approved of Fascism's ostensible concern with the emigrants and peasants; they might have applauded the Duce's determination to make Italy respected in international circles. Yet this earlier generation was paternalist and authoritarian in its outlook—not totalitarian. Sonnino, Di San Giuliano, and Franchetti admired classical English Liberalism. Their goal was to awaken the moral and social conscience of the nation's ruling class— not to replace that class with a regime of *piccoli borghesi* or to subject the nation to the whims of a dictator. They would have been outraged at a regime that trampled on the constitution and ignored the king. Corradini, who lived to see the first decade of Fascism, complained bitterly that under the Duce "there is too much talk of Fascism and too little of Italy."[5]

And what of the price the Libyans paid? The claim that the Libyans benefited from the colonization is misleading at best. Certainly the Italians introduced modern agricultural techniques and offered financial aid and technical advice to stimulate indigenous agricultural development. But even if these opportunities had developed beyond the stage of token gestures, economic equality for the Libyans seemed a remote prospect. As the racial laws of 1938 and the "special citizenship" of 1939 indicate, the Italian colonial regime, like other European colonial regimes, had no intentions of granting genuine economic or civic equality to the indigenous peoples. The Italians were too humanitarian—and too dependent on indigenous labor—to think of exterminating the Libyans. Hence the regime planned to integrate them into the Italian scheme of things. Under colonial rule, the Libyans would always have been second-class citizens. As in so many other colonial countries, the Libyans gained the full benefits of the Italian colonization only after independence.

In the end, Italy too benefited from the failure of the fourth shore. She was freed from the staggering financial burden of subsidizing Libyan economic development for years to come. In one of the many ironies of colonialism, in recent years Italy has developed highly profitable trade relations with independent Libya. Perhaps more important for Italy, the failure of the fourth shore symbolized the failure of the nation's imperial schemes. Postwar Italy turned away from autarky and empire to resolve her economic and social problems.

By integration into a larger economy through the Common Market, Italy has found a way to resolve her historic problems of a restricted area and a heavy population. Freed from her obsessions with empire and great power status, Italy has never been more prosperous.

Notes

Chapter 1

1. R. Michels, *L'imperialismo italiano: Studi politico demografici* (Milan, 1914), pp. 178-80.
2. L. Villari, *Italian Foreign Policy under Mussolini* (New York, 1956), p. 71.
3. U.S.Department of State, *Bulletin* 13, 333 (11 November 1945): 764-65.
4. C. Giglio, "Italia e Africa, oggi," *Nuova Antologia*, 463 (January 1955): 11.
5. J. L. Miège, *L'impérialisme colonial italien* (Paris, 1968), pp. 250-51; D. Mack Smith, *Italy: A Modern History* (Ann Arbor, 1959), p. 241.
6. A. Lessona, "Lo stato fascista e l'economia coloniale," in *Scritti e discorsi coloniali* (Milan, 1935), pp. 49-50.
7. Michels, *L'imperialismo italiano*, p. 180.
8. C. Gini, "Il fattore demografico nella politica coloniale," *Gli Annali dell'Africa Italiana* 4 (September 1941): 811; C. M. Cipolla, "Four Centuries of Italian Demographic Development," in *Population in History*, ed. D. V. Glass and D. E. C. Eversley (Chicago, 1965), pp. 576-87; M. Neufeld, *Italy: School for Awakening Countries* (Ithaca, N.Y., 1961), p. 520.
9. S. B. Clough, *The Economic History of Modern Italy* (New York, 1964), appendix table 18, p. 381; Neufeld, *Italy*, p. 521. Cipolla, "Four Centuries," estimates that the net average annual loss through emigration was about four per thousand in 1901-11 and thus may have roughly compensated for the rise in the rate of natural increase during the period of "demographic transition."
10. C. Cipolla, *The Economic History of World Population* (Baltimore, 1962), p. 101.
11. R. Foerster, *The Italian Emigration of Our Times* (Cambridge, 1919); A. Capanna, "Economic Problems and Reconstruction in Italy," *International Labor Review* 62 (June 1951): 607-52; J. S. McDonald, "Italy's Rural Social Structure and Emigration," *Occidente* 22 (September-October 1956): 437-56; M. Rossi-Doria, "Land Tenure System and Class in Southern Italy," *American Historical Review* 64 (October 1958): 46-53.
12. Paradoxically enough, among agricultural experts and social thinkers there was little faith in the possibilities of internal reclamation. With the exception of Stefano Jacini, few believed that areas such as Sicily and the

Agro Pontino could be reclaimed and settled. A. A. Castagno, "The Development of Expansionist Concepts in Italy (1861-96)" (Ph.D. dissertation, Department of Political Science, Columbia University, 1957), pp. 64-68.

13. For shifts and developments in popular attitudes toward emigration during the Liberal period see the detailed analysis in F. Manzotti, *La polemica sull'emigrazione nell'Italia unita (fino alla prima guerra mondiale)* (Milan, 1962); Castagno, "Development of Expansionist Concepts," pp. 73-77; G. Dore, *La democrazia italiana e l'emigrazione in America* (Brescia, 1964), pp. 31-111. Despite widespread discussion of the emigration issue and pressures for some form of restriction, the government's official policies only reluctantly evolved away from laissez-faire. For a summary of major emigration legislation to 1914, see Manzotti, *Polemica*, and V. Briani, *L'emigrazione italiana ieri e oggi* (Rome, 1957), pp. 42-46.

14. Miège, *L'impérialisme colonial italien*, pp. 28-31; Volpe, *L'Italia moderna* (Florence, 1946-52), 1: 163-68; R. Ciasca, *Storia coloniale dell'Italia contemporanea* (Milan, 1938).

15. M. Townsend, *Origins of Modern German Colonialism (1871-1885)* (New York, 1921), pp. 86-99.

16. Volpe, *L'Italia moderna*, 1: 97.

17. Volpe, *L'Italia moderna*, 2: 66-67, 182. Volpe speaks of the South's conservative aspirations, which included "centralization, Triple Alliance, Africa," and says that Southerners "intuited vaguely that their future in large part would depend on overseas activities."

18. Ciasca, *Storia coloniale;* Manzotti, *Polemica*, pp. 58-62, 129-31.

19. Carpi's *Delle colonie e dell'emigrazione italiana all'estero* was the first serious statistical analysis of Italian emigration and proved to be nearly as popular as *De la colonisation chez les peuples modernes*. Like Leroy-Beaulieu's work, Carpi's essay won a major prize, an award from the Society of Political Economy in 1874.

20. Manzotti, *Polemica*, p. 58.

21. Atti Parlamentari: Camera dei Deputati (APCD), *Discussioni*, 19 January 1883, pp. 228-38.

22. On Mancini's "conversion" see Ciasca, *Storia coloniale*, pp. 77-92, 115-16; G. Mondaini, *Manuale di storia e legislazione coloniale* (Rome, 1927), 1: 34-40; C. Zaghi, *P. S. Mancini, l'Africa e il problema del Mediterraneo 1884-85* (Rome, 1955).

23. APCD, *Discussioni*, 17 January 1885, 17 March 1885.

24. This from di San Giuliano, later a foreign minister and an enthusiastic colonialist. APCD, *Discussioni*, 17 March 1885.

25. For the following sketch see especially A. C. Jemolo, *Crispi* (Florence, 1922), pp. 124-33.

26. Quoted in Miège, *L'impérialisme colonial italien*, p. 50.

27. F. Crispi, *Scritti e discorsi politici (1849-1890)* (Torino-Roma, n.d.), p. 738.

28. During his campaign in the early 1930s for more intensive government intervention to promote colonization in Libya, Alessandro Lessona, the colonial undersecretary, praised the Eritrean experiments. See his *Scritti e discorsi coloniali*, pp. 49-50. One of the major technical advisors and directors of the Libyan colonization also analyzed the Eritrean case. A. De Benedictis, "La colonizzazione demografica col metodo praticato dall'Ente per la Colonizzazione della Libia," in Sindacato Nazionale Fascista Tecnici Agricoli, *Agricoltura e Impero* (Rome, 1937). Pre-Fascist and Fascist coloni-

zation programs in Somalia are treated in R. L. Hess, *Italian Colonialism in Somalia* (Chicago, 1966), pp. 111-15, 117-18, 162-68.

29. On the Eritrean colonization, see especially: R. Pankhurst, "Italian Settlement Policy in Eritrea and Its Repercussions," in *Boston University Papers on African History* (Boston University Press, 1964), vol. 1; Romain Rainero, *I primi tentativi di colonizzazione agricola e di popolamento dell'Eritrea* (Milan, 1960).

30. On Franchetti, see Leopoldo Franchetti, *Mezzogiorno e Colonie* (Florence, 1950), for a long biographical introduction by Umberto Zanotti-Bianco, a collaborator and disciple of Franchetti's, and for a collection of Franchetti's major writings. Franchetti became head of the Office for Colonization when it was established in 1891. He also created a series of agricultural experiment stations.

31. Franchetti, "L'avvenire della nostra colonia," *Nuova Antologia,* 140 (April, 1895): 622-23.

32. Ibid., p. 614.

33. *Discorsi parlamentari di Francesco Crispi* (Rome, 1915), 3:488.

34. Quoted in Rainero, *I primi tentativi,* p. 83. For the complete report see *Relazione generale della R. Commissione d'Inchiesta sulla Colonia Eritrea* (Rome, 1891); see also Martini's summary in *Cose affricane* (1897).

35. Quoted in Rainero, *I primi tentativi,* p. 85.

36. For an analysis of Eritrea's development and the reasons for its failures see Pankhurst, *Italian Settlement Policy,* pp. 133-56, and Rainero, *I primi tentativi,* pp. 144-46.

37. Pankhurst, *Italian Settlement Policy,* pp. 155-56.

38. Rainero, *I primi tentativi,* pp. 144-46, stresses the divided leadership as a major factor in the failure of colonization efforts.

39. Quoted In Pankhurst, *Italian Settlement Policy,* p. 150.

40. F. Cataluccio, *Antonino di San Giuliano e la politica estera italiana dal 1900 al 1914* (Florence, 1935); M. L. Salvadori, *Il mito del buongoverno* (Turin, 1963), pp. 62-115.

41. Di San Giuliano's rhetoric is often surprising in its foreshadowing of later Nationalist and Fascist demographic arguments for colonial expansion and "living space." See his "I fini della nostra colonia," *Bollettino della Società Africana d'Italia,* 14 (1895): 17-31.

42. Miège, *L'impérialisme colonial italien,* p. 68. The colonial budget was cut for the year 1898-99 from 17 million lire to 7.6 million lire.

43. For the fortunes of colonialism in Italy after Adowa see Miège, *L'impérialisme colonial italien,* pp. 68-80; Volpe, *L'Italia moderna,* 2:341-83; Ciasca, *Storia coloniale,* pp. 291-309; W. Schieder, "Fattori dell'imperialismo italiano prima del 1914-15," *Storia contemporanea,* 3 (March 1972): 3-36.

44. Miège, *L'impérialisme colonial italien,* pp. 69-70; Volpe, *L'Italia moderna,* 2:353-69.

45. For the development of the Nationalist movement, see especially F. Gaeta, *Nazionalismo italiano* (Naples, 1965); J. A. Thayer, *Italy and the Great War* (Madison, Wisc., 1964), pp. 192-233.

46. L. Federzoni, *A.O. "Il posto al sole"* (Bologna, 1938), p. 66; also on Corradini: P. L. Occhini, *Enrico Corradini e la nuova coscienza coloniale* (Florence, 1925); U. D'Andrea, *Corradini e il nazionalismo* (Rome and Milan, 1928); Volpe, *L'Italia moderna,* 2:360-69.

47. L. Preti, *Impero fascista: Africani ed ebrei* (Milan, 1968).

48. Ciasca, for instance, credits the Nationalists with having revived the idea of demographic colonies which had been "buried in forgotten academic writings and proceedings," Ciasca, *Storia coloniale,* p. 300.
49. Antonio Labriola, a Socialist, favored Italian expansion into Libya for demographic reasons. Arturo Labriola, a syndicalist, expressed admiration for Franchetti's ideas on state colonization and argued that perhaps a colony such as Eritrea could be transformed into a socialist cooperative. Miège, *L'impérialisme colonial italien,* p. 84; Michels, *L'imperialismo italiano,* p. 94; Antonio Labriola, *Scritti vari di filosofia e politica* (Bari, 1906).
50. Quoted in C. Seton-Watson, *Italy from Liberalism to Fascism* (London, 1967), p. 351.
51. For the following see E. Corradini, *Il volere d'Italia* (Naples, 1911), pp. 188–90.
52. E. Corradini, *Discorsi politici 1902–23* (Florence, [1923]), p. 89.

Chapter 2

1. G. Salvemini, *Come siamo andati in Libia* (Florence, 1914), p. xi.
2. R. Ciasca, *Storia coloniale dell'Italia contemporanea* (Milan, 1938), pp. 309–15.
3. R. Mori, "La penetrazione pacifica italiana in Libia dal 1907 al 1911 e il Banco di Roma," *Rivista di Studi Politici Internazionali,* 24 (January–March 1957): 103–18; F. Malgeri, *La guerra libica* (Rome, 1970), pp. 15–36.
4. See the editorial comment in *La Stampa* and a letter to Albertini which fretted about Italy becoming a "maritime Switzerland" cited in M. Pincherle, "La preparazione all'impresa di Libia," *Rassegna Storica del Risorgimento,* 56 (July–September 1969): 463.
5. R. S. Cunsolo, "Libya, Italian Nationalism and the Revolt against Giolitti," *Journal of Modern History,* 37 (June 1965): 192–93, for the divisions among various political parties and groups; also Malgeri, *La guerra libica,* pp. 203–67.
6. G. Pascoli, *Prose,* vol. 1 (Rome: Mondadori, 1946), pp. 557–69. A literal translation of the title would be: "The great proletariat has bestirred itself."
7. B. Croce, *A History of Italy 1871–1915* (Oxford, 1929), pp. 260–62.
8. For Salvemini, one of Giolitti's most outspoken critics, much of the excitement over the Libyan war was also a reaction to the boredom and moral stagnation which permeated Italy after a decade of Giolittian prosperity. Politics had reached a nadir of public contempt and "Sonnino resembled an abandoned railway car on a siding," he wrote. *Come siamo andati in Libia,* pp. xx–xxi.
9. Albertini commented that the humiliation in Egypt and Tunisia and the disaster at Adowa "weighed too heavily on our past for us to allow ourselves a renunciation that would have reduced national feeling to despair and destroyed our prestige in the world." J. L. Miège, *L'impérialisme colonial italien* (Paris, 1968), p. 91.
10. J. A. Thayer, *Italy and the Great War* (Madison, Wisc., 1964), p. 242.
11. G. Giolitti, *Memoirs of My Life,* trans. Edward Storer (London, 1923), pp. 253–54; N. Valeri, *Giolitti* (Turin, 1971). About Libya itself Giolitti remarks in his *Memoirs* that the country was "very much behind the times" since slave markets still persisted in Benghazi and that "such infamies" could not be tolerated "at the very gates of Europe." However, he makes it clear that

the chief reason for the war was that Italy had to put an end to an ambiguous diplomatic situation.

12. The role of the press campaign in preparing public opinion is a subject of much current controversy. At the heart of the debate is the role of the Nationalist press. The Nationalists, as Luigi Federzoni commented in a 1913 electoral speech, claimed that "it was through our propaganda that the will of the nation was able to impose conquest on Libya." (L. Federzoni, *Presagi alla nazione* [Milan, 1924], p. 39.) Pincherle, "La preparazione all'impresa di Libia," argues that the campaign for Tripoli began in the Giolittian papers in November 1910, well before the Nationalists joined in the spring of 1911. Since the Giolittian papers were generally careful to warn of the perils of the Libyan undertaking, their subdued tone may account for the impression that Giolitti was "pushed" by the Nationalists, she concludes. Malgeri, *La guerra libica*, argues that the Giolittian campaign was not a genuine, full-blown effort of the sort that developed later and thus would give more credit to the Nationalists. For a review of the controversy, see Salvatore Bono, "La guerra libica (1911-12): Considerazioni a margine di un recente libro," *Storia Contemporanea*, 3 (March 1972): 65-84.

13. Pincherle, "La preparazione all'impresa di Libia," p. 462. Ferrero's language is suggestive of the "Eurafrica" concept that later became popular in Fascist colonial circles. See chapter 5 below.

14. Pincherle, "La preparazione all'impresa di Libia," p. 473.

15. Boccaccio's *Decameron* refers to the fabulous land of "Bengodi," a mythical country in which the choicest foods were gathered and the inhabitants did nothing except prepare and enjoy them. In this country the vineyards were tied with sausages; and cooks, stationed on top of a mountain of grated parmesan cheese, threw down macaroni and ravioli boiled in the broth of a capon to whoever wanted to enjoy them. S. Battaglia, *Grande dizionario della lingua italiana* (Turin, 1961), 5 vols. "Bengodi" suggests the American folksong "The Big Rock Candy Mountain."

16. Quoted in Malgeri, *La guerra libica*, p. 51.

17. Ibid.

18. G. Piazza, *La terra promessa: Lettere dalla Tripolitania* (Rome, 1911).

19. Ibid., p. 171.

20. Ibid., p. 192.

21. G. Corradini, *L'ora di Tripoli* (Milan, 1911), p. 14.

22. Quoted in Malgeri, *La guerra libica*, pp. 52-53.

23. Ibid.

24. E. Lémonon, "La Libye et l'opinion publique italienne," *Questions Diplomatiques et Coloniales* 36 (July-December 1913): 596-604.

25. M. Mirtil, *Et l'Italie?* (Paris, 1921), p. 105.

26. E. A. Powell, "Tripolitania: Italian White Man's Burden," *American Review of Reviews* 44 (November 1911): 565. See also J. W. Gregory, "Cyrenaica," *Geographical Journal* 47 (May 1916): 338-39.

27. Powell, "Tripolitania," p. 566.

28. Salvemini, *Come siamo andati in Libia*, p. ix.

29. For a summary of the opposition, see Malgeri, *La guerra libica*, pp. 67-96.

30. For the following, see Bono, "La guerra libica," pp. 70-72.

31. Malgeri, *La guerra libica*, p. 70.

32. Ibid., p. 68.

33. Salvemini, *Come siamo andati in Libia,* pp. 289–95.
34. M. Camperio, *Autobiografia di Manfredo Camperio,* ed. S. M. Camperio (Milan, 1917).
35. Ibid., p. 117.
36. A. Medana, "Il vilayet di Tripoli di Barberia nell'anno 1902," *Bollettino del Ministero degli Affari Esteri,* no. 300a (1904), pp. 1043–1196. Medana listed the leading exports as esparto grass, hides, sponges, and ostrich plumes. The chief imports were coffee, tea, sugar, spices, tobacco, cotton thread, and flour. With the exception of 1900, imports and exports had declined proportionally at an average annual rate of 8–10 percent during the period 1899–1902. Two chief items in the trans-Saharan trade, ostrich feathers, which made up 14 percent of Tripoli's total export value, and Sudanese hides, which contributed 8 percent to total export value in 1899, were on the decline. By 1902 the value of both of these items had decreased by half. For Medana, the decline in trans-Saharan trade had begun during the period 1872–81, and he saw no likelihood of a renaissance.
37. L. Einaudi and E. Giretti, "A proposito della Tripolitania: Ottimismo e pessimismo coloniale," *La Riforma Sociale,* 18, vol. 22, 3d ser. (1911), p. 604.
38. G. Mosca, *Italia e Libia* (Milan, 1912), pp. 17–18.
39. R. Michels, *L'imperialismo italiano: Studi politico-demografici* (Milan, 1914), pp. 119–24.
40. Mosca, *Italia e Libia,* p. 21.
41. Einaudi and Giretti, "A proposito della Tripolitania," p. 614.
42. Ibid., p. 604.
43. Salvemini, *Come siamo andati in Libia,* pp. 218–22.
44. Ibid., p. 222.
45. Mosca, *Italia e Libia.,* pp. 24–35.
46. Gregory, "Cyrenaica," pp. 321–45. The JTO sponsored an expedition to Cyrenaica in 1908 to explore the area's possibilities as a population colony for Eastern European Jews, since Palestine was closed as an outlet. In the expedition's report, J. W. Gregory concluded that Cyrenaica was unsuitable for such a project because of the hostility of the Arabs—despite the Turkish government's initial invitation—and because of Cyrenaica's relatively dense population. In 1916, however, Gregory made it clear that the area offered definite possibilities for the Italians, who had been willing to spend millions on the conquest and "should not grudge a few millions for the necessary water-supply works, roads, railways, harbors and afforestation." He also cited Cyrenaica's geographical proximity to Italy, the "sentimental interest" which the Italians had in this old Roman province, and Italy's "overflowing population of peasants who are skilled in the cultivation of the olive," which he felt would be Cyrenaica's most profitable product. Nevertheless, he commented that by 1916 Italians had generally recognized that Cyrenaica was not a colonial paradise and that expenditures on the colony might give "better political than commercial return."
47. Einaudi and Giretti, "A proposito della Tripolitania," pp. 610–13.
48. G. Salvemini, "L'emigrazione transoceanica e l'impresa libica," *L'Unità,* 10 Jan. 1913. Mosca estimated that perhaps Libya could absorb 15,000 to 20,000 Italians after a decade of occupation. In the long run, perhaps the colony could support 200,000 to 300,000 Italians, well under the 500,000 Italians that Tunisia had absorbed in 15 years. Certainly the Libyan emigra-

tion would have no perceptible effect on the flood of migrants to the United States and South America, he concluded. Mosca, *Italia e Libia*, p. 34.

49. Einaudi and Giretti, "A proposito della Tripolitania," p. 613.
50. Salvemini, "L'emigrazione transoceanica."
51. G. Salvemini, "A mosca cieca," *L'Unità*, 6 December 1912.
52. Einaudi and Giretti, "A proposito della Tripolitania," p. 640.
53. Valeri, *Giolitti*, p. 227.
54. Salvemini, *Come siamo andati in Libia*, p. xvi.
55. Bono, "La guerra libica," p. 71.
56. Einaudi and Giretti, "A proposito della Tripolitania," p. 747.
57. Salvemini, *Come siamo andati in Libia*, p. 190.
58. "When the war is finished, then I must prepare to take some money with me and go to beautiful Tripoli, then America will be there and not here, all those who are here are getting ready to go to Tripoli." Quoted in F. Manzotti, *La polemica sull'emigrazione nell'Italia unita (fino alla prima guerra mondiale)* (Milan, 1962), p. 90, n. 2.
59. Quoted in Malgeri, *La guerra libica*, p. 45.
60. Ibid.
61. C. Galli, *Diari e lettere, Tripoli 1911, Trieste 1918* (Florence, 1951), pp. 132–33.
62. Ibid.

Chapter 3

1. G. Mosca, *Italia e Libia* (Milan, 1912), pp. 35–36.
2. Italian versions of the 1911–12 campaigns can be found in Ministero della Guerra, Ufficio Storico del Corpo di Stato Maggiore, *La campagna di Libia* (Rome, 1925), 4 vols. For a convenient summary see G. Mondaini, *Manuale di storia e legislazione coloniale* (Rome, 1927), 1:283–99. For a version from the Libyan view, see E. E. Evans-Pritchard, *The Sanusi of Cyrenaica* (Oxford, 1949), pp. 104–91.
3. The casualties were relatively light: 1,432 battle deaths, 1,948 deaths from sickness (especially from a cholera epidemic), and 4,250 wounded. The financial strain, however, was significant. Official estimates placed the costs at 527 million lire. Diplomatic reports indicated that the war had shaken the Italian stock market, and that French bankers were showing great caution in their loans to Italy. The Italian socialists charged that Italy would soon be bankrupt. W. C. Askew, *Europe and Italy's Acquisition of Libya* (Durham, 1942), pp. 99, 210, 249.
4. Askew, *Europe and Italy's Acquisition of Libya* pp. 64–81, 100–109, 201–4.
5. In ancient times all of North Africa except Egypt was known as Libya. With the destruction of Carthage and the creation of a Roman province known as "Africa," the term "Libya" fell into disuse, although it was generally accepted as an alternative to Tripoli or Barbary. The name "Libya" was revived by Italian scholars, especially F. Minutilli, at the turn of the century, and was officially adopted at the time of the conquest with the RD 5 November 1911. J. Wright, *Libya* (New York, 1969), p. 21; Ministero degli Affari Esteri, Comitato per la Documentazione dell'Opera dell'Italia in Africa, *L'Italia in Africa (Il territorio e le popolazioni)* (Rome, 1955), 1:77. On Libya's geography and climate see: J. Despois, *La colonisation italienne en Libye* (Paris, 1935); Ministero degli Affari Esteri, *L'Italia in Africa* 1:77–110; C. L. Pan, "The Population of Libya," *Population Studies*, 3 (June

1949): 100–102; A. Fantoli, "Elementi preliminari della pluviometria libica," *L'Agricoltura Coloniale,* 33 (January 1939): 1–27.
6. The first two terraces average about 300 millimeters annually; the Barce area and the Gebel Akhdar average 400 millimeters annually, and Cyrene receives 500–600 millimeters. However, the coastal plain south of Benghazi receives less than 200 millimeters and the desert south of the Gebel receives 100–200 millimeters. The frequency of the rainfall is as irregular as in Tripolitania but somewhat less torrential. The highest part of the Gebel receives sixty days of rain a year, Cyrene gets seventy to seventy-five, and elsewhere the rate is about forty days a year. Despois, *La colonisation italienne,* pp. 23–25.
7. Wright, *Libya,* p. 23. In Tripoli the effects seldom last more than three days, but in the Fezzan, where the effects are far more severe, an old saying goes, "If the ghibli blows forty days—God preserve us from evil—the camel becomes pregnant without the intervention of the male."
8. The western Gefara receives about 200 millimeters. Near Tunisia, the annual total drops as low as 75 millimeters. The rains are often torrential. Only the Tripoli area and the eastern half of the Gebel receive more than forty days of rain a year. On the Gefara, the total sometimes drops to twenty-five to thirty days a year. Despois, *La colonisation italienne,* pp. 8–10.
9. Ibid., pp. 11–16.
10. F. Vöchting, "Italienische Siedelung in Libyen," *Jahrbucher für National-oekonomie und Statistik,* 151 (February 1940): 134–35.
11. E. Corradini, "Proletariato, emigrazione, Tripoli," in *Discorsi Politici (1902–1923)* (Florence, 1924), pp. 121–22.
12. Ibid.
13. Homer, *The Odyssey,* 4. 1. 85.
14. Vöchting, "Italienische Siedelung"; J. W. Gregory, "Cyrenaica," *Geographical Journal,* 47 (May 1916): 321–45.
15. Despois, *La colonisation italienne,* pp. 42–43; Evans-Pritchard, *The Sanusi,* p. 46.
16. Vöchting, "Italienische Siedelung," p. 36; Gregory, "Cyrenaica," p. 338. See also the review article: Rhoads Murphey, "The decline of North Africa since the Roman occupation, climatic or human?" *Annals of the Association of American Geographers,* 41 (June 1951): 116–32.
17. The following historical sketch relies on Despois, *La colonisation italienne,* pp. 34–42; M. Khadduri, *Modern Libya* (Baltimore, 1963), pp. 3–10; British Military Administration, *Survey of Land Resources of Tripolitania* (Tripoli, 1945), pp. 61–70; Wright, *Libya,* pp. 27–118.
18. British Military Administration, *Survey of Land Resources,* p. 68.
19. A 1923 census, before the final repression of the Sanusi, totaled 185,400. Despois, *La colonisation italienne,* p. 43. Unlike Palestine, Syria, Iraq, Egypt, and the Maghreb, Cyrenaica lacks any substantial peasantry. This made the population unusually difficult to govern. There was no way to fix them to the soil. See Evans-Pritchard, *The Sanusi,* p. 46.
20. The first Italian census of 1915 showed a population of 569,093. A far more precise one in 1931—after the Italian reconquest—totaled 522,914. Despois, *La colonisation italienne,* p. 43.
21. For the following see Wright, *Libya,* pp. 116–17; A. Medana, "Il vilayet di Tripoli di Barberia nell'anno 1902," *Bollettino del Ministero degli Affari Esteri,* no. 300a (1904), pp. 1043–1196; Comitato per la Documentazione

delle Attività Italiane in Africa, *L'avvaloramento e la colonizzazione*, vol. 3 (Rome, 1971); J. L. Miège, *L'impérialisme colonial italien* (Paris, 1968), p. 89.

22. Istituto Coloniale Italiano, *Atti del Convegno Nazionale Coloniale per il Dopo Guerra delle Colonie* (Rome, 1920), p. 576.

23. G. De Luigi, *Il Mediterraneo nella politica Europea* (Naples [192?]). pp. 433-34.

24. Ibid.

25. Any agricultural enterprises were difficult to initiate because Turkish legislation prohibited land sales to Europeans. Moreover, there were no cadastral surveys to speak of, and the area beyond the city limits was not secure. The Banco di Roma bought some land through local residents and began operations in October 1908. The Italians planted wheat, barley, fruit trees and olive trees, and alfalfa. Although the director admitted that he had begun the experiment with "very little faith" in the region's possibilities, he became quite enthusiastic. The Banco di Roma also invested in various other ventures, including olive oil presses, printing presses, ice plants, and flour mills, and was engaged in the export of esparto grass and sponges. R. Mori, "La penetrazione pacifica italiana in Libia dal 1907 al 1911 e il Banco di Roma," *Rivista di Studi Politici Internazionali* 24 (January-March 1957): 103-18.

26. Among the travelers were F. Minutilli, *La Tripolitania* (Turin, 1912), who argued that "in the hands of intelligent and industrious farmers, who can say what immense resources that region, now largely sterile and abandoned, might offer?" (p. 149). Paolo Vinassa de Regney, a professor of geology at the University of Verona, came to similar conclusions after a trip to Tripolitania in 1902. See his "Osservazioni sui terreni della Tripolitania settentrionale," *Giornale di Geologia Pratica* 1: (1903): 275-91; and "Nella Tripolitania Settentrionale," *Bollettino della Società Geografica Italiana*, 42 nos. 10 and 11 (1905): 762-73, 930-49.

27. "Improvisation, superficiality, confusion and glaring incompetence" marked the government's planning for the new colony, Enrico De Leone concluded. E. De Leone, *La colonizzazione dell'Africa del Nord* (Padua, 1957), 2:374.

28. E. Lémonon, "La Libye et l'opinion publique italienne," *Questions Diplomatiques et Coloniales* 36 (July-December 1913): 602.

29. By *colonia di popolamento*, or "population colony," the Italians meant a colony that would permit extensive settlement by immigrants from the mother country. The Italians planned to dominate economic, social, and political aspects of life in the colony. Eventually the Italian community was expected to grow sufficiently to easily counterbalance the indigenous populations in political power if not in actual numbers. The *colonia di popolamento* was distinguished from the *colonia di sfruttamento* (the equivalent of "plantation colony"), in which settlement was impossible and a tiny minority of Europeans were concerned with the development and exploitation of the area's natural resources.

30. A. Franzoni, *Colonizzazione e proprietà fondiaria in Libia* (Rome, 1912), pp. 14-15.

31. Ibid.

32. L. Einaudi and E. Giretti, "A proposito della Tripolitania: Ottimismo e pessimismo coloniale," *La Riforma Sociale*, anno 18, vol. 22, 3d ser. (1911), pp. 613-14.

33. Franzoni, *Colonizzazione*, pp. 20–21. Franzoni's work was one of the most comprehensive discussions of the colonization problem. He began his work as a theoretical examination of the Ottoman land code, then changed his emphasis to dealing with the concrete problems the Italian colonization would face. He had no illusions about Libyan attitudes toward the invaders and warned throughout his work that Italians must prove themselves masters of the colony through military victory. Since he assumed that hostilities might continue for some time, he favored beginning with a military colonization with centers at Tripoli, Homs, and Benghazi. He estimated that fifty thousand to sixty thousand colonists could be settled during the early stages of development. About a third of these would be subject to military service. Once the colonization was secure, he favored expanding the colonization through private enterprise. Franzoni believed that the best colonists could be found in Sicily, Puglie, and Tunisia, and he also favored trying to attract Italians who had emigrated overseas. Although Franzoni's ideas never became official policy at the time, many of his ideas were implemented by subsequent regimes.

34. E. De Sanctis, *Dalla Canea a Tripoli: Note di viaggio* (Rome, 1912), pp. 212–13.

35. Lémonon, *La Libye*, p. 597.

36. The first commission, appointed by F. S. Nitti, the minister of agriculture, visited the Tripoli area early in 1912. Because military operations were still in progress, their fieldwork was restricted primarily to the Tripoli-Zanzur-Tagiura oases. The Nitti commission was generally pessimistic about any quick revival of agriculture in Tripolitania and warned against developing the area as a population colony. See: Ministero di Agricoltura, Industria e Commercio, *Ricerche e studi agrologici sulla Libia. I. La Zona di Tripoli* (Bergamo, 1912). The second commission, appointed by P. Bertolini, Italy's first minister of colonies, published its findings as: Commissione per lo Studio Agrologico della Tripolitania, *La Tripolitania settentrionale* (Rome, 1913), 2 vols. The third commission, privately sponsored, was under the leadership of Leopoldo Franchetti. Their report was published as: Società Italiana per lo Studio della Libia, *La missione Franchetti in Tripolitania (Il Gebel)* (Florence and Milan, 1914).

37. *La Tripolitania settentrionale*, 1:363.

38. Ibid.

39. Ibid., 1:345.

40. Ibid., 1:421–22.

41. Ibid., 1:430.

42. L. Franchetti, *Mezzogiorno e colonie* (Florence, 1950), p. 425.

43. Ibid., pp. 425–26.

44. For the political and military history of Libya during the first decade of Italian occupation see R. Ciasca, *Storia Coloniale* (Milan, 1938), pp. 360–74, 392–407; Evans-Pritchard, *The Sanusi*, pp. 104–56; O. Gabelli, *La Tripolitania dalla fine della guerra mondiale all'avvento del fascismo* (Airoldi, 1939), 2 vols.

45. For the programs of experimental colonization in Tripolitania, see G. Fowler, "Italian Agricultural Colonization in Tripolitania, Libya" (Ph.D. thesis, Department of Geography, Syracuse University, 1969), chapter 5.

46. Istituto Centrale di Statistica del Regno d'Italia, series 6, vol. 20, *Censimento delle colonie italiane al 1 dicembre 1921* (Rome, 1930), pp. 15–53.

This first official census of Tripolitania showed a total labor force of 16,073 (everyone over the age of ten years). Of this total nearly half (7,905) were in the military or the government bureaucracy. Only 93 were listed as employed in agriculture.

47. A. Maugini, *Sviluppo agricolo e progresso sociale dei paesi tropicali* (Florence, 1966), pp. 210-11, n. 2.

48. See below, chapter 4.

49. *La rinascita della Tripolitania: Memorie e studi sui quattro anni di governo del Conte Giuseppe Volpi di Misurata* (Milan, 1926); R. Ciasca, *Storia coloniale dell'Italia contemporanea* (Milan, 1938), pp. 392-460; De Leone, *La colonizzazione dell'Africa del Nord* (Padua); R. Rapex, *L'affermazione della sovranità italiana in Tripolitania* (Tientsin, 1937). Throughout Volpi's governorship, Tripolitania and Cyrenaica were governed as separate territories with independent governors at the capitals of Benghazi and Tripoli. Such was the original administrative organization created in 1913. In 1929, the administration was consolidated under a single governor with a capital at Tripoli. The two territories merged into the single colony of Libya with the capital at Tripoli in 1934. The final step in the administrative evolution of the colony came in 1939 when the four northern provinces were annexed to the mother country.

50. Rapex, who was one of Volpi's chief aides in Tripolitania, comments that Luigi Federzoni, the first colonial minister under the Fascist regime, was a friend and admirer of Volpi and a staunch advocate of a "hard line" in Tripolitania. The day that Federzoni assumed office, he met with Volpi and the two men agreed on a two-point program: (1) reoccupation of all territory useful for colonization, and (2) creation of a public domain to be developed by Italian colonists. The following day Mussolini also received Volpi and approved the plan. Rapex, *L'affermazione*, p. 281.

51. See Volpi's introduction in *La rinascita della Tripolitania*, p. xx.

52. ACS, Presidenza del Consiglio dei Ministri, 1924, 17.4.3093, pp. 6-7.

53. For the following discussion see ibid., pp. 6-8; De Leone, *La colonizzazione*, 2:522-23; Miège, *L'impérialisme colonial italien*, pp. 178-79.

54. *Handbook on Cyrenaica* (Cairo, 1944), pp. 4-5; Mondaini, *Manuale di storia e legislazione coloniale*, 1:501-2.

55. *La rinascita della Tripolitania*, pp. 205, 226.

56. For the rationale behind Volpi's decrees and the procedures in implementing them, see Filippo Cavazza's article, "La politica della colonizzazione" in *La rinascita della Tripolitania*, pp. 187-238. Cavazza was in charge of the Colonization Office in Tripolitania under Volpi.

57. See especially Comitato Rappresentativo Italiano Tripoli, *L'Italia in Libia dal 1911-1942;* L. M. Bologna, "Report to the Government of Libya on Settlement Planning," ETAP, FAO Report no. 732 (Rome: FAO, 1957). The Comitato Rappresentativo was one of the Italian political organizations that developed in Tripolitania after World War II to defend Italian interests in Libya.

58. The Ottoman Land Code of 1858, on which the land tenure—modified by local custom—in Tripolitania and Cyrenaica was based, distinguished between five types of property: *waaf, mulk, miri, metruke, mawat.* Except for *mulk* (private property in absolute ownership) and *waaf* (the landed endowments of religious foundations), the state claimed authority over all the lands under its sovereignty. The other three categories distinguished the nature of

the right of usufruct by an individual or a collective group. For a brief description of the land code, see "Land Tenure: Eastern Europe and Near East," *Encyclopedia of Social Sciences* (New York, 1937), 9:102. The text of the code is most readily available in G. Young, *Corps de Droit Ottoman* (Oxford: Oxford University Press, 1905-6), 7 vols. See also A. N. Poliak, "Classification of Lands in Islamic Law and Terms," *American Journal of Semitic Languages and Literature* 57 (1940): 50-62.

59. G. Mondaini, *La legislazione coloniale italiana nel suo sviluppo storico e nel suo stato attuale (1881-1940)* (Milan, 1941), p. 733.

60. *La rinascita della Tripolitania,* p. 208.

61. Ibid.

62. Evans-Pritchard, *The Sanusi,* p. 222; A. Piccìoli, *La nuova Italia d'Oltremare,* 2d ed. (Rome, 1933), 2:548. Some 9,124 hectares were acquired by natural right, 43,441 hectares by purchase, expropriation, or renunciation, 62,225 by confiscation of the Sanusi estates, and 6,000 hectares from rebels and persons fighting in "patriotic" bands.

63. "La colonizzazione in Tripolitania nel 1923," *Rivista della Tripolitania* vol. 1 (March 1924). This article is signed "Ufficio di Colonizzazione." However, the article bears a close resemblance to Cavazza's article in *La rinascita della Tripolitania,* and Cavazza was in charge of the Colonization Office.

64. Ibid., p. 17.

65. Piccìoli, *La nuova Italia,* p. 420; Evans-Pritchard, *The Sanusi,* pp. 222-23.

66. In Cyrenaica, for instance, where legislation similar to Volpi's operated after 1928, the notices or signs announcing incorporation of lands into the public domain were usually posted in the Land Office or in the cities—seldom near the lands themselves. Hence, even if a Libyan could read, he was unlikely to see the sign. Evans-Pritchard, *The Sanusi,* pp. 222-23.

67. "La colonizzazione in Tripolitania nel 1923," *Rivista della Tripolitania,* p. 15; Cavazza, "La politica della colonizzazione," pp. 206-07.

68. "La colonizzazione in Tripolitania," pp. 7-9.

69. IAO-OR f. 1362, no. 23, "Relazione riservata 13-11-1923 a S.E. il Governatore: Espropriazione terre steppiche indemaniamento terreni." This remarkably frank report is unsigned, but it is included among Cavazza's papers at the IAO-OR and most likely was written by him.

70. The Consiglio Superiore Coloniale (CSC), created under provisions of the RD 31 December 1922, combined the functions of two earlier administrative and advisory bodies. One (the Consiglio Coloniale) antedated the creation of the Colonial Ministry and acted as the chief advisory body to the Foreign Ministry when it was in charge of the colonies. The other (Comitato Superiore Amministrativo) was created in 1914 to deal specifically with the administration of Tripolitania and Cyrenaica. The CSC was composed of a variety of legislators, administrators, and individuals influential in colonial circles. Among the many bodies and interests represented were the merchant marine, customs, aviation, justice, foreign affairs, agriculture, public health, internal emigration and migration, and the Italian Colonial Institute. For expert opinion, the CSC could rely on a panel of eight specialists, three former governors in the colonies or high colonial officials, and five experts who had distinguished themselves through their research on colonial matters or by their economic and commercial activities in the colonies. The CSC was divided into three sections: (1) administrative and legal affairs; (2) economic and financial matters; (3) matters not included in the business of the first two. In general the

sections deliberated individually and were summoned to a general session only for matters of special importance or to reexamine the opinions handed down by a particular section. The variety of problems on which the CSC gave its opinion was enormous. There was virtually no piece of legislation on colonial matters which was not brought before the CSC. On the other hand, the CSC's opinion was advisory and its recommendations were not always followed. C. Bertelli, *Consiglio Superiore Coloniale e Consiglio di Stato* (Rome: Edizione Oriente e Colonie, 1939).

71. IAO-OR f. 1362, no. 25, "Raccolta di relazioni, atti, decreti e pubblicazioni riguardanti la colonizzazione in Tripolitania."
72. ASMAI, CSC, cart. 1, no. 27, 12-10-23.
73. IAO-OR f. 1362, no. 25.
74. ASMAI, CSC, cart. 1, no. 27, 12-10-23.
75. Rapex, *L'affermazione*, p. 325.
76. IAO-OR f. 1362, no. 25.
77. IAO-OR f. 1362, no. 18. Italics in the original text.
78. G. Leone, "Agricoltura e colonizzazione nella Tripolitania e nel sud-Tunisino," *Bollettino di Informazione* 10 (September–October 1922): 585-95.
79. Despois, *La colonisation italienne*, p. 53.
80. *La rinascita della Tripolitania*, pp. 213-14.
81. Ibid., pp. 232-34.

Chapter 4

1. Mussolini, *Opera omnia*, 22:115.
2. Ibid., p. 114.
3. J. L. Miège, *L'impérialisme colonial italien* (Paris, 1968), pp. 138-41; J. L. Glanville, "Colonialism in the New Italy," *Arnold Foundation Studies in Public Affairs* vol. 2 (spring 1934).
4. R. De Felice, *Mussolini il rivoluzionario* (Turin, 1965), chap. 10; Miège, *L'impérialisme colonial italien*, p. 127.
5. For the following indications on Fascist themes and slogans, see Miège, *L'impérialisme colonial italien*, pp. 127-28; L. Preti, *Impero fascista: Africani ed ebrei* (Milan, 1968); C. Hollis, *Italy in Africa* (London, 1941), p. 14.
6. Federzoni (1878-1967) also held the key post of minister of the interior from 1924 to 1926. In 1928 he was named senator. The following year he became president of the Senate and in 1931 editor of *Nuova Antologia*, then became president of the Italian Academy in 1938. He was a member of the Grand Council in 1943 and voted with the majority to depose Mussolini. For his defense of the role of Nationalism in restraining the extreme elements of Fascism, see his memoirs, *Italia di ieri per la storia di domani* (Milan: Mondadori, 1967).
7. Cantalupo (b. 1891), a Neapolitan, had also collaborated on the *Idea Nazionale*. Following his term as colonial undersecretary, he founded *L'Oltremare* (1928) one of the most influential of the colonialist journals. He served as ambassador to Brazil (1933) and to Spain (1936). After the war he became influential in monarchist circles.
8. F. Coppola, "Italy in the Mediterranean," *Foreign Affairs* 1 (15 June 1923): 105-14. Coppola (b. 1878), a Neapolitan, was one of the founders of the Nationalist party, together with Corradini, Federzoni, and others. In 1918, he founded an influential political journal *Politica* with Alfredo Rocco,

another ex-Nationalist and future Fascist minister of justice. Coppola became a professor of diplomacy and diplomatic history at the University of Perugia in 1929.

9. Ibid., p. 114.
10. Miège, *L'impérialisme colonial italien*, pp. 145–47.
11. Ibid., pp. 167–68.
12. R. Cantalupo, *L'italia musulmana*, 3d ed. (Rome, 1932), p. 165.
13. After World War I, Italy experimented with partial "home rule" in Libya. On 31 October 1919, two separate statutes were prepared for Cyrenaica and Tripolitania. Each province had a separate parliament, a government council, and local councils to help the Italian administration govern in accordance with local traditions and customs. The Cyrenaican parliament was composed of some sixty members, mainly tribal sheiks elected by their followers and three Italians representing the Italian community. A total of five sessions were held before the parliament was disbanded in 1923 in accordance with the Fascist "hard line" policy. M. Khadduri, *Modern Libya* (Baltimore, 1963), pp. 17–18; G. Mondaini, *Manuale di storia e legislazione coloniale* (Rome, 1927), 1:391–94, 492–95.
14. E. Nolte, *Three Faces of Fascism* (New York, 1969), pp. 291–92. According to Nolte: "Nothing occupied Mussolini's mind as much as the 'demographic problem' and nothing had disappointed him as much as the failure of his attempts to solve it." For Nolte, "it is very probable" that the "demographic problem" provided "the crucial motivation" for the rapprochement with Germany.
15. Mussolini, *L'agricoltura e i rurali* (Rome, 1931), pp. 88–89.
16. M. Neufeld, *Italy: School for Awakening Countries* (Ithaca, N.Y., 1961), pp. 417–18.
17. L. Salvatorelli and G. Mira, *Storia d'Italia nel periodo fascista* (Turin, 1964), p. 571.
18. A. Oblath, "Italian emigration and colonization policy," *International Labor Review* 23 (June 1931): 805–34.
19. Neufeld, *Italy*, p. 418.
20. L. Preti, *Impero fascista*, pp. 17–18.
21. *L'Azione Coloniale* vol. 1 (28 June 1931).
22. Mussolini, *L'agricoltura e i rurali*, pp. 109–10.
23. On Fascist land reclamation and agricultural policy: M. Bandini, *Cento anni di storia agraria italiana* (Rome, 1963); L. Rosenstock-Franck, *L'economie corporative fasciste en doctrine et en fait* (Paris, 1934); A. Serpieri, *La struttura sociale dell'agricoltura italiana* (Rome, 1947); C. T. Schmidt, *The Plow and the Sword: Land, Labor and Property in Fascist Italy* (New York, 1938); C. T. Schmidt, *The Corporate State in Action* (New York, 1939).
24. Sir Ivone Kirkpatrick, in his biography *Mussolini, A Study in Power* (New York, 1964) comments that the Pontine Marshes were "the most striking and valuable legacy bequeathed to the Italian people by Mussolini" (p. 275). Kirkpatrick was more than a casual visitor. He served with the British embassy in Rome from 1930 to 1933.
25. A. Serpieri, *La bonifica in storia e dottrina* (Bologna [1947]), pp. 1–3.
26. G. Salvemini, *Under the Axe of Fascism* (New York, 1936), pp. 265–71; L. Rosenstock-Franck, *L'economie corporative fasciste* (p. 336) cites statistics that show 1.1 million hectares under reclamation in 1922. Of this

area, 597,000 hectares had been completed and 623,000 were still under development. Within the areas of reclamation, between 1882 and 1921 the mortality from malaria had been reduced to one-seventh, the population had increased by 64 percent, and the value of agricultural production and livestock had shown impressive gains.

27. Bandini, *Cento anni*, pp. 156–62.
28. G. Carocci, *La politica estera dell'Italia Fascista (1925–28)* (Bari, 1969), p. 11.
29. L. Federzoni, "Il fascismo per le colonie," *Rassegna Italiana* 6 ser. 2 (October 1923): pp. 605–8.
30. ORIG, T-586 (1134) 070545.
31. Ibid.
32. APCD, *Discussioni*, 13 March 1925, pp. 2533–35.
33. A. Carocci, *La politica estera*, pp. 4–5.
34. Federzoni, "Il fascismo per le colonie," pp. 605–08.
35. C. Gulinelli, in *L'Oltremare* 2 (November 1928): 418.
36. *L'Oltremare* 2 (July 1928): 270–72; *L'Oltremare* 2 (August 1928): 298. Among the schemes suggested were (1) a pooling of government life insurance policies which officers had received during their World War I military service. Instead of accepting the cash value of the policy or waiting for its maturity in 1948, the owners of these policies were invited to invest in a corporation that would engage in some aspect of Libyan development; (2) a *federale* of Milano, Mario Giampaoli, planned to sell shares at fifty lire apiece for a company that would operate in Cyrenaica; (3) a tax of twenty-five lire on one million Fascist party members to raise twenty-five million lire for Somalia.
37. P. Bignami, *Tra i colonizzatori in Tripolitania* (Bologna, 1931), pp. 268–69.
38. ACS, PCM, 1926, 17.4.3108; *Diari De Bono*, vol. 26 (13 July 1926 entry).
39. ACS, PCM, 1927, 17.4.1681; *Diari De Bono*, vol. 26 (22 September 1926 entry).
40. ASMAI, CSC, cart. 5, no. 330, 16–17 December 1927. Armando Maugini (1891–   ), born in Messina, was one of the chief technical advisers to the Colonial Ministry and a major architect of the Libyan colonization. For many years he was also director of the Istituto Agronomico per L'Oltremare in Florence, one of Italy's leading centers for the study of tropical agriculture and a major training ground for agricultural technicians. Maugini was familiar with Cyrenaica, since he had served there during World War I and afterward had organized the colony's agricultural technical services. His early writings indicate his opposition on technical grounds to any large-scale intensive colonization with state support. In 1932, however, he was called upon to draw up plans for the mass colonization in Cyrenaica. Like most of his colleagues, he gave his qualified—and somewhat grudging—approval to the regime's plans, realizing that they were politically motivated. Once the course of the colonization had been set, Maugini threw himself wholeheartedly into the struggle to realize the government's programs.
41. "La colonizzazione in Tripolitania nel 1923," *Rivista della Tripolitania*, vol. 1 (March 1924).
42. See the polemic in *L'Oltremare* 2 (June 1928): 212, between A. Maugini,

one of the chief technical authorities on Libyan agriculture, and R. Cantalupo, the *Oltremare's* editor and a former colonial undersecretary.
43. *L'Oltremare* 2 (February 1928): 64.
44. "La colonizzazione in Tripolitania nel 1923," pp. 23-24.
45. ORIG, T-586 (1134) 070574. (Underlining in the original text.)
46. Ibid., 070572-576.
47. Ibid.
48. The speech is reprinted in L. Federzoni, *A.O. "Il Posto al Sole"* (Bologna, 1938), p. 114.
49. Ibid.
50. E. De Cillis, "Gli aspetti e le soluzioni del problema della colonizzazione agraria in Tripolitania," *Primo Congresso Agricolo Coloniale a Tripoli (2-6 maggio 1928)* (Rome 1928), pp. 1-20.
51. E. De Bono, "Le mie idee sulla colonizzazione," *L'Oltremare* 2 (August 1928): 293-95; Feliciano Bianchi, "Per la trasformazione fondiaria in Tripolitania," *L'Agricoltura Coloniale* 22 (October 1928): 373-75.
52. ASMAI, CSC, cart. 5, no. 330 (16-17 December 1927): CSC, cart. 5, no. 40 (5-6 April 1928).
53. ASMAI, CSC, cart. 5, no. 40 (5-6 April 1928).
54. Ibid.
55. Ibid.
56. For a text of the legislation see: Governo della Libia, Direzione di affari economici e colonizzazione, *Norme relative alla colonizzazione in Libia* (Tripoli, 1939). The following summary of the operations of the 1928 laws is based on J. Despois, *La colonisation italienne en Libye* (Paris, 1935), pp. 56-61.
57. IAC, *La colonizzazione agricola della Tripolitania* (Rome, 1947), p. 61, 138.
58. Ibid.
59. A. Picciòli, *La nuova Italia d'Oltremare*, 2d ed. (Rome: Mondadori, 1933), 1:474. 476.
60. From the time of the Italian occupation to the end of 1932, 23,006 hectares, or about 19 percent of the land in concession, had been revoked by the government. Picciòli, *La nuova Italia*, 1:422.
61. Despois, *La colonisation italienne*, p. 61.
62. Ibid.
63. Picciòli, *La nuova Italia*, 1: 445. The contributions were divided in the following manner:

Wall construction	8,721,839
Fencing	116,281
Water systems	9,818,577
Agricultural machinery	800,375
Dry tree cultures	13,659,904
Irrigated cultures	1,927,700
Reforestation of dunes	541,070
Colonist families	212,859
Total	35,798,605

64. At the end of 1932 the state had contributed: 1,806 lire/hectare for small concessions—those of less than 75 hectares; 828 lire/hectare for medium-sized concessions of 75-400 hectares; 572 lire/hectare for large concessions (400 hectares and above). However, the figures also showed that the small

concessions were the most fully developed, with 71.5 percent of their area under development, while the medium-sized lots had developed 58.8 percent of their area and the large concessions had developed 40.8 percent of their land. Despois, *La colonisation italienne*, p. 63; Piccioli, *La nuova Italia*, 1: 446, n. 1. The distribution of concessions according to size was as follows: out of a total of 486 concessions, 324 (66%) were small; 98 (20%) were of medium size; and 64 (14%) were large.

65. Despois, *La colonisation italienne*, p. 63.

66. The following is based on Miège, *L'impérialisme colonial italien*, pp. 186-87.

67. ACS, PCM, 1925, 1.3-4.987.

68. ACS, PCM, 1926, 1.3-4.3768.

69. Ibid. (Underlining in original text.)

70. ACS, *Diari De Bono*, vol. 29 (5 September, 7 September 1927), vol. 35 (21 November, 29 November 1929).

71. ACS, *Diari De Bono*, vol. 35 (11 November 1929); ORIG, T-586 (1295) 112806-809.

72. Ibid., 112801-805.

73. Interview with G. Minnucci, 1 August 1971.

74. See, for instance, D.G. 31 March 1933, no. 3200; Governo della Tripolitania, Direzione degli Affari Economici e della Colonizzazione. "La colonizzazione demografica progressiva in Tripolitania" (Tripoli, March 1933). In order to get his subsidies, the concessioner had to be sure that his families were "authentic peasants" (*autentici contadini*) and the government could ask the concessioner to produce documents about the family's background before coming to the colony.

75. For the following, IAO-OR, f. 2258. U. Marroni, "Appunti sulla colonizzazione in Tripolitania (1933)."

76. For a portrait of the colonists see Despois, *La colonisation italienne*, pp. 94-95. Bignami, *Tra i colonizzatori*, pp. 105-72, describes individual concessions.

77. Among the political figures with a concession in Cyrenaica was Amerigo Dumini, implicated in the Matteoti affair.

78. Marroni was concerned that in a few years the vineyards in Libya would meet local needs and export would be extremely difficult. He favored a possible shift toward table grapes. Bartolozzi argued that vineyards were not the mainstay of the colonization and that Tripolitania's wine surplus would always be small. In 1933 Tripolitania was not close to self-sufficiency and needed to import olives and olive oil from Tunisia as well as 40,000 hectoliters of wine. Both experts doubted that Libya's agricultural production would ever reach a scale large enough to compete seriously with Italy. IAO-OR f. 1087 (1933), E. Bartolozzi, "La pretesa concorrenza della Tripolitania alla Madrepatria"; U. Marroni, "Su qualche aspetto tecnico della colonizzazione agraria in Tripolitania," *L'Agricoltura Coloniale* 24 (1935): 14-19.

79. D. De Micheli, "L'Azienda agricola coloniale De Micheli nella Gefara," *Bonifica e Colonizzazione*, 3 (March 1939): 7.

80. A wealthy businessman and patriot who lived for many years in Argentina and Brazil, Lincoln Nodari was known for his efforts to introduce new plants and crops to Libya. Through Badoglio, whom he met in Rio de Janeiro

in 1925, Nodari was presented to Mussolini. The Duce showed great interest in Nodari's experiments, since Nodari claimed that if they were successful Italy could be self-sufficient in sugar, cellulose, alcohol, meat, and starches. Agricultural experts were generally skeptical of his claims. After a first cycle of experiments between 1925 and 1928, Nodari returned to South America. In 1936 he revisited Libya and made highly critical comments about the progress of the colonization, especially about the role of the ECL. Nodari favored a colonization based on large private firms modeled after the United Fruit Company. Lincoln Nodari, *Nuovi orizzonti agricoli della Libia* (Rome, 1937). In ACS, *Diari De Bono,* vol. 26, (entries for 16 July, 17 September, 13 October 1926) De Bono followed the experiments with great interest and exclaimed, "it would be too beautiful" if the ones with the manioc (also known as cassava) worked out.

81. M. Borghi, *Got-es-Sultan* (Naples, 1934), pp. 36–40.

82. G. Palloni, *I contratti agrari degli Enti di Colonizzazione in Libia* (Florence, 1945), pp. 24–26. At the 1928 Congress of Agricultural Technicians in Tripoli the scarcity of Libyan labor had been used as a rationale for favoring the government's demographic goals. The labor shortage was raised again by colonial experts at the First Congress of Colonial Studies, held in 1931 at Florence. One proposal was to import blacks as agricultural labor. P. Battara, "Il movimento demografico della Tripolitania in rapporto allo sviluppo agrario," *Atti del Primo Congresso di Studi coloniali* (Florence, 1931), 4:80–82.

83. *L'Avvenire di Tripoli,* 4 (14 February 1931): 1.

84. The *enzel* is a perpetual leasehold. The concessioner has use of the land as long as he pays rent to the proprietor. According to the contract, the rent can be fixed or variable. If the rent is variable, it usually depends on the production of the land. The contract was often used by religious organizations with extensive properties. A Sanusi *zawia* near Barce, for instance, granted one thousand hectares to the colonial government at a fee of five lire/hectare for an indefinite period beginning in 1925. The Italians then subdivided the land for colonists. The *mgarsa* provided that the proprietor would give his land in concession with the understanding that the concessioner would make certain improvements. At the end of a stipulated period, the proprietor and concessioner would divide the improved land between them. This contract was often used to create small irrigated gardens in the oases of Tripolitania. E. Savarese, *Le terre della Cirenaica secondo la legislazione fondiaria ottomana* (Benghazi, 1928), 2 vols., II: 167–70.

85. IAO-OR, f. 2122, A. Romanini, "Notizie sulla colonizzazione in Tripolitania"; M. Finocchiaro, *La colonizzazione e la trasformazione fondiaria in Libia* (Rome, 1966).

86. Marroni, "Su qualche aspetto tecnico della colonizzazione agraria in Tripolitania," p. 16.

87. IAO-OR f. 2122, Romanini, "Notizie sulla colonizzazione in Tripolitania."

88. For the experiments at Tigrinna: Despois, *La colonisation italienne,* pp. 98–100; Picciòli, *La nuova Italia d'Oltremare,* 1:470–71; IAC, *La colonizzazione agricola in Tripolitania,* pp. 62–63; J. Soames, "Libya, Italy's North African Colony," *Geographical Magazine* 3 (May–October 1936): 317–33.

89. The following is based on IAO-OR, f. 4370, G. Trigona, "L'opera svolta dall'A.T.I.-Tigrinna (1936)."

90. ASMAI, CSC, cart. 13, n. 65 (10 May 1931); cart. 13, n. 82 (11 October 1931).
91. IAO-OR, f. 2638, G. Mazzocchi, "Relazione sul comprensorio Tigrinna in relazione all'attuale crisi (1954)."
92. Picciòli, *La nuova Italia d'Oltremare,* 1:468-69. Military colonization was a recurring topic of discussion throughout the years of Italian rule in Libya. Proponents pointed to Bugeaud's experiments in Algeria as well as to the Roman example. See C. Grillo, "Gli esperimenti coloniali nell'Africa neo-latina," *Rivista Internazionale di Scienze Sociali e Discipline Ausiliarie* 62: (1911): 433-62; 63 (1912): 30-64, 145-73, 449-77; 64 (1913): 29-42, 174-94, 309-32; and 65 (1914): 46-79. See also: N. M. Campolietti, "La colonizzazione militare dei romani," *Rivista Militare Italiana* 57 (September 1912: 128-48; Major D. Bartolotti, *La colonizzazione militare in Libia* (Padua, 1914): A. Franzoni, *Colonizzazione e proprietà fondiaria in Libia (con speciale riguardo alla religione, al diritto ed alle consuetudini locali* (Rome, 1912).
93. Ibid., pp. 470-71.
94. Ibid.
95. Ibid., pp. 556-57, 592.
96. IAO-OR, f. 2386, UCIA, "Relazione e progetto relativo al UCIA" (1930); IAO-OR, f. 2075, UCIA, "Relazione sulle origini e sulla sua attività (1933)."
97. V. Pisani, *Popolare la Libia: Perchè e Come* (Rome, 1933).
98. A. Maugini, "La colonizzazione della Cirenaica," in IAC, *Per le nostre colonie* (Florence, 1927), p. 141.

Chapter 5

1. Wright, for instance, writes " 'Demographic colonisation,' as it was called, was largely the brainchild of Italo Balbo": J. Wright, *Libya* (New York, 1969), p. 171.
2. C. Hollis, *Italy in Africa* (London, 1941), pp. 78-81; M. H. H. Macartney and P. Cremona, *Italy's Foreign and Colonial Policy (1934-37)* (Oxford, 1938), p. 284.
3. C. T. Schmidt, *The Plough and the Sword: Land, Labor and Property in Fascist Italy* (New York, 1938), p. 19. See also L. Rosenstock-Franck, *L'économie corporative fasciste en doctrine et en fait* (Paris, 1934), pp. 224-28; S. B. Clough, *The Economic History of Modern Italy* (New York, 1964), pp. 244-45.
4. J. L. Miège, *L'Impérialisme colonial italien* (Paris, 1968), pp. 195-99.
5. Quoted in Macartney and Cremona, *Italy's Foreign and Colonial Policy,* p. 285.
6. Governo della Tripolitania, "Notizie e cifre sul nuovo piano di colonizzazione della Libia," (Tripoli, 1939), p. 15; C. Basilici, "L'armata del lavoro," *Annali dell'Africa Italiana* 1 (December 1938): p. 757.
7. A. De Benedictis, "La colonizzazione demografica col metodo praticato dall'Ente per la Colonizzazione della Libia," in Sindacato Nazionale Fascista Tecnici Agricoli, *Agricoltura e impero* (Rome, 1937).
8. A full-length critical biography of Balbo remains to be written. The best short articles currently available are: "Balbo" article, Istituto della enciclopedia italiana, *Dizionario biografico degli Italiani* (Rome, 1963), vol. 5; and G. Bourgin, "Italo Balbo" in *Les techniciens de la colonisation* (Paris, 1947),

pp. 255–57. See also Luigi Federzoni's portrait in his memoirs, *Italia di ieri per la storia di domani* (Milan: Mondadori, 1967), pp. 150–65.

Numerous journalistic accounts—not always reliable—have been published in Italian popular magazines since World War II. See, for instance, Duilio Susmel, "La verità su Balbo," *Domenica del Corriere,* which appeared in weekly installments between 13 June and 4 July 1967.

9. Balbo's plane was shot down over Tobruk by Italian batteries on 28 June 1940. Stories still circulate that Balbo's crash was not an accident. Those who believe in a conspiracy theory offer a variety of explanations: the most imaginative is that a cuckold husband, victim of one of Balbo's amorous adventures, settled an old score; the more mundane view is that the Duce wanted to eliminate a dangerous political rival. From the available evidence, the accident theory is the only tenable one. Balbo appeared over Tobruk shortly after a British aerial incursion. The Italian batteries, imperfectly forewarned and still nervous from the British raid, fired on him. Balbo's generous but foolish handling of the situation—he attempted to land in order to assess the damage from the enemy raid—completed the tragedy. F. Pagliano, "L'ultimo volo di Italo Balbo," *Storia Illustrata* vol. 9, (June 1965).

10. R. Forti and G. Ghedini, *L'avvento del fascismo: Cronache ferraresi* (Ferrara: STET, 1923), p. 135.

11. C. Eylan, "Choses vues en Italie et en Libye," *Revue des Deux Mondes,* ser. 8, 32 (1 March 1936): 137.

12. G. Bucciante, *Vita breve di Italo Balbo* (Rome, 1941), p. 30.

13. R. Gilardi, "L'altro uomo: Italo Balbo," *Visto* 7 (1 February 1958): 18.

14. L. Nunzio, *Italo Balbo* (Predappio, 1940), p. 20.

15. I. Balbo, *Diario 1922* (Milan, 1932).

16. Eylan, "Choses vues," pp. 136–37.

17. H. Bailey, "The colonization of Libya," *Fortnightly Review* 151 (February 1939): 201.

18. For an admiring summary of Balbo's policies to 1936, see Spectator Libycus, *Due anni di governo del Maresciallo Balbo in Libia* (Tripoli, 1936).

19. C. Eylan, "Choses vues."

20. In 1936 a period of severe drought threatened to decimate the livestock in Tripolitania. Balbo organized a fleet of fifty ships to ferry some three hundred thousand head of livestock to Cyrenaica. During the return march to Tripolitania in the autumn, Balbo arranged for watering stations all along the route. Martin Moore, *Fourth Shore: Italy's Mass Colonization of Libya* (London, 1940), p. 174.

21. I. Balbo, "La politica sociale fascista verso gli Arabi della Libia" in Reale Accademia d'Italia, Fondazione Alessandro Volta, *Convegno di Scienze Morali e Storiche (4–11 October 1938)* (Rome, 1939), 1:734.

22. "Balbo" in "Enciclopedia bio-bibliografica Italiana," Milan: Istituto Editoriale Italiano Tosi (1941) (unpublished galley proofs in ASMAI collection), pp. 59–60.

23. I. Balbo, "La colonizzazione in Libia," *L'Agricoltura Coloniale* 33 (August 1939): 463–64.

24. For a brief sketch of the origins of the colonization companies, see G. Palloni, *I contratti agrari degli enti di colonizzazione in Libia* (Florence, 1945), pp. 34–40.

25. A well-publicized American example—complete with a personable military leader like Balbo—was the attempt in 1935 to settle about one thousand colonists from Michigan and Minnesota in Alaska's Matanuska valley. A. Stringer, "The Red-Plush Pioneers," *Saturday Evening Post* 208 (28 December 1935): 8; C. Ford and A. MacBain, "Uncle Sam's Icebox," *Collier's* 107 (4 January 1941): 28.

26. The Duce, for instance, commented to Eylan in 1935, "Now that you have visited the Pontine Marshes, you should go to Libya. You have seen how we colonize the water; over there you will see how we colonize the sand." Eylan, "Choses vues," p. 132.

27. The CMCI originated in 1926 as an advisory committee to the Ministry of Public Works. The committee was to deal with the problem of transferring the unemployed from overpopulated areas such as the Po Valley to the *mezzogiorno* and Sicily and Sardegna. When, in 1930, the Fascist Grand Council and the Corporation for Agriculture became concerned with the specific problem of the Po Valley, the committee became the CMCI and was given full autonomy to deal with the problem. Its powers were extended beyond metropolitan Italy to include all the national territories. The CMCI, in cooperation with the ONC, settled 2,215 families, or 19,048 individuals, between 1932 and 1936 in the area known as the Pontine Marshes, about 75,000 hectares some sixty kilometers south of Rome. See: "Migratorie, correnti," *Enciclopedia Italiana* (Milan, 1934), 23:258; L. Razza, "Le migrazioni interne e la colonizzazione," *Nuova Antologia*, vol. 67, fasc. 1438 (16 February 1932), pp. 532–39; *36 Anni dell'Opera Nazionale per i Combattenti 1919–1955* (Rome, 1955), pp. 62–74.

28. The CMCI contributed 5 million lire to the original endowment of 38 million lire that made up the Ente Cirenaica's patrimony. The rest was contributed by nine other banks and government credit and social security organizations as follows:

Commissione per le Migrazioni e la Colonizzazione Interna	l. 5.000.000
ICLE (Istituto di Credito per il Lavoro all'Estero)	5.000.000
Banco di Napoli	5.000.000
Banco di Sicilia	5.000.000
INA (Istituto Nazionale Assicurazioni)	5.000.000
Cassa Nazionale Assicurazioni Sociali	5.000.000
Cassa Nazionale Infortuni	2.000.000
Banca Nazionale del Lavoro	2.000.000
Consorzio Nazionale per il Credito Agrario di Miglioramento	1.000.000
Consorzio Provinciale Economico Corporativo del Regno	3.000.000
Total	l. 38.000.000

Palloni, *I contratti agrari*, p. 34, n. 2.

29. CDIA, *L'avvaloramento e la colonizzazione*, 3:334.

30. IAO-OR, f. 2176, A. Maugini, "Promemorie, relazioni e appunti vari sull' ECL" (May 1934 memorandum to Razza).

31. IAO-OR, f. 2176, A. Maugini, "Appunti per il Conte Durini (colloquio col Duce)," 25 March 1936.

32. CDIA, *L'avvaloramento e la colonizzazione*, 3:357–58.

33. E. E. Evans-Pritchard, *The Sanusi of Cyrenaica* (Oxford, 1949), pp. 219–20; O. Schmieder and H. Wilhelmy, *Die faschistische Kolonisation in Nordafrika* (Leipzig, 1939), pp. 151–82.

34. IAC, *La colonizzazione della Cirenaica* (Rome, 1947), p. 55.
35. IAC, *La colonizzazione agricola della Tripolitania* (Rome, 1947), pp. 64–73.
36. Ibid., 74–81.
37. Luigi Razza (1892–1935) became one of the regime's leading figures on agricultural labor problems. He was a Southerner (born at Catanzaro) who began his career as a Socialist newspaper editor. By 1914–15, however, he had come over to the side of the interventionists and served as editor of the *Popolo d'Italia*. Under Fascism, before becoming head of the CMCI, he served in various Fascist agricultural labor organizations. By 1935 he had become minister of public works. He died in a plane crash in Egypt on 7 August 1935, while on a flight to Asmara. One of the agricultural villages in Cyrenaica was named after him. G. Gattamorta, *Luigi Razza: L'uomo, l'opera* (Rome, 1936).
38. Lessona (b. 1891), born in Rome, took a degree in law and served as a cavalry officer in World War I. After the armistice he was personal secretary to General Diaz. As secretary of the Fascist Federation of the Ligurian Riviera and Savona, he became influential in Fascist politics around Genoa. He was elected a deputy in 1924. He served as undersecretary for industry (1924–29) and then as undersecretary for the colonies from 1929 to 1936. He served two brief terms as colonial minister in 1936–37 and then was ousted for political reasons. Among the cliques and rivalries that formed in Fascist colonial circles, Lessona was for a time allied with De Bono against Balbo. ORIG, T-586 (1114) 077402–077424. Lessona then received an appointment as professor of colonial history at the University of Rome. In recent years he has returned to public service as a senator with the MSI neo-Fascist party.
39. De Benedictis, "La colonizzazione demografica" credits Lessona with having "accelerated the process" of orientation toward state-directed colonization; Maugini also credits Lessona and the newspaper *L'Azione Coloniale,* edited by Marco Pomilio, with spearheading a campaign to reorient colonization policy. IAO-OR, f. 2009.
40. A. Lessona, "Il popolamento della Libia" and "Lo stato fascista e l'economia coloniale," in *Scritti e discorsi coloniali* (Milan, 1935), p. 71.
41. A. Lessona, "Il popolamento della Libia," p. 77.
42. L. Bongiovanni, "Demografia, metodo e credito," *L'Oltremare* 2: (March 1928): 102–5; P. Gaetano Venino, "Un progetto di colonizzazione libica," *L'Oltremare* 2: (July 1928): 270–72.
43. A. Lessona, "Lo stato fascista e l'economia coloniale," pp. 49–50.
44. A. Lessona, "Agricoltura tripolitana," in *Scritti e discorsi coloniali* (Milan, 1935), p. 130.
45. Ibid.
46. Lessona, "Il popolamento della Libia," pp. 71–72.
47. E. L. Guernier, *L'Afrique, champ d'expansion de l'Europe* (Paris, 1933).
48. A. Lessona, "L'Africa nella politica europea," in *Scritti e discorsi coloniali* (Milan, 1935), p. 174.
49. P. D'Agostino Orsini di Camerota, *Eurafrica: L'Europa per l'Africa, l'Africa per l'Europa* 2d ed. (Rome, 1934), p. 96.
50. A. Lessona, 'L'Africa nella politica europea," p. 174.
51. Corrado Massi, "La Transahariana," *L'Oltremare* 2: (July 1928): 259–62; 2: (August 1928): 303–9; Massimo Salvadori, "La Libia e le comunicazioni transahariana," *L'Oltremare* 2: (June 1930): 230–33.

52. I. Kirkpatrick, *Mussolini: A Study in Power* (New York, 1964), pp. 306-7.
53. IAO-OR, f. 2176, "Relazione e proposte circa l'ordinamento e l'attività dell'Ente per la Colonizzazione della Cirenaica." This report was prepared in August 1932 by Maugini for Luigi Razza.
54. IAO-OR, f. 2176, "Relazione e proposte circa Ente Cirenaica," p. 5.
55. IAO-OR, f. 2258, U. Marroni, "Appunti sulla colonizzazione in Tripolitania."
56. IAO-OR, f. 2176, Maugini, "Promemorie, relazioni e appunti vari sull'ECL."
57. Ibid.
58. IAO-OR, f. 2176, Maugini, "Promemorie, relazione e appunti vari sull' ECL."
59. Ministero dell'Africa Italiana. Ufficio studi. Servizio statistico. T. Mascaro and G. Palloni, "Primo censimento generale delle aziende agrarie della Libia al 21 aprile 1937," *Bollettino statistico dell'Africa Italiana,* (Rome 1941), 4:10-13.
60. Mascaro and Palloni, "Primo censimento generale," p. 17. The census refers to the four "provincie" or provinces of Tripoli, Misurata, Benghazi, and Derna. Strictly speaking, these areas did not become provinces of the mother country until January 1939 almost two years after the census was taken.
61. Ibid., pp. 18-21.
62. Ibid., p. 18.
63. Ibid., p. 26.
64. Quoted in A. Piccìoli, *La nuova Italia d'Oltremare,* 2d ed. (Rome: Mondadori, 1933), 1: 619.
65. A. Lessona, "La colonizzazione demografica in Libia," *L'Agricoltura Coloniale* 30 (February 1936): 52.
66. Mascaro and Palloni, "Primo censimento generale," table 12, pp. 54-55; CDIA, *L'avvaloramento e la colonizzazione,* 3: 369-75.
67. IAC, *La colonizzazione agricola della Tripolitania,* pp. 150-51.
68. IAC, *La colonizzazione agricola della Tripolitania,* p. 113, 150; CDIA, *L'avvolaramento e la colonizzazione,* 3:191.
69. IAC, *La colonizzazione in Cirenaica,* p. 16, 18; CDIA, *L'avvaloramento e la colonizzazione,* 3: 373-75.

Chapter 6

1. G. Volpe, "L'Italia degli emigranti," *L'Italia che fu* (Milan, 1961), pp. 123-24.
2. L. Federzoni, *Italia di ieri per la storia di domani* (Milan: Mondadori, 1967), p. 154.
3. J. L. Miège, *L'impérialisme colonial italien* (Paris, 1968), p. 263.
4. For the subdued and conciliatory tone of his speeches during the Libyan trip, see Mussolini, *Opera omnia,* 28:140-51.
5. The trip was also widely interpreted as a tribute to Balbo's accomplishments as governor. *L'Afrique Française* 47 (April 1937): 208.
6. E. D. O'Brien, "With the Duce in Libya," *English Review* 64 (May 1937): 556-57.
7. Legally, the status of the companies did not change. In theory, the companies could go ahead with their operations under the 1928 legislation, enjoying the same financial benefits and responsibilities as any other private concessioner.

In practice, as Palloni remarks, there were many "misunderstandings" since it was often assumed that the government's demographic goals had first priority over the other activities of the companies. G. Palloni, *I contratti agrari degli enti di colonizzazione in Libia* (Florence, 1945), pp. 37–40.

8. E. E. Evans-Pritchard, *The Sanusi of Cyrenaica* (Oxford, 1949), pp. 209–10; C. Giglio, *Colonizzazione e decolonizzazione* (Cremona, 1964), pp. 356–57.

9. Italo Balbo, "Politica sociale fascista verso gli Arabi della Libia," Reale Accademia d'Italia, *Convegno Volta (4–11 October 1938)* (Rome, 1939), 1: 748.

10. The new status meant that there were three categories of citizenship: Italian citizens (*cittadini metropolitani*), limited to Italian colonists and officials; the special citizenship (*cittadini italiani speciali*) for the Libyan elites; the general citizenship for Libyans (*cittadini italiani libici*) for the rest of the indigenous peoples. Balbo wanted Italians and Libyans to have the same legal status, a courageous and controversial proposal in view of the regime's racist and anti-Semitic campaigns which began in 1938. Balbo's proposals, however, were turned down by the Grand Council. G. Bottai, *Venti'anni e un giorno (24 luglio 1943)*, (Milan, 1949), p. 121; *Ciano's Hidden Diary 1937-38*, trans. Andreas Mayor (New York, 1953), p. 184.

11. The candidate had to be at least eighteen years old and without a prison record. In addition he had to have served in the army or belong to a Fascist youth organization or have performed a patriotic service for Italy or read and write Italian. See also E. E. Evans-Pritchard, *The Sanusi*, p. 217.

12. ACS, Partito Nazionale Fascista, Situazione politica delle provincie b. 5 (Misurata)

13. G. L. Steer, *A Date in the Desert* (London, 1939), pp. 163–65; E. W. Polson-Newman, "The Italians in Libya," *English Review* 58 (April 1934): 447–48; C. Eylan, "Choses vues en Italie et en Libye," *Revue des Deux Mondes*, ser. 8, 32 (1 March 1936): 141.

14. An official pamphlet published by the Italian Library of Information, New York (1940), *The Italian Empire, Libya*, lists the four shores as Ligurian, Tyrrhenian, Adriatic, and Libyan. More likely, however, Italians considered the Ionian Sea rather than the Ligurian as part of the quartet. I have been unable to trace any precise origin of the term.

15. The model was quite similar to Algeria. Libya thus became Italy's nineteenth region, subdivided—as Algeria was—into four metropolitan provinces. The Fezzan remained a military territory. The four northern provinces were governed by prefects, all subject to the authority of the governor-general. However, the Italian governor-general was dependent on the Ministry of Italian Africa and not on the Ministry of the Interior as was the case in Algeria. Giglio, *Colonizzazione e decolonizzazione*, p. 356.

16. Governo della Tripolitania, "Notizie e cifre sul nuovo piano di colonizzazione della Libia" (Tripoli, 1939), p. 15; C. Basilici, "L'armata del lavoro," *Annali dell'Africa Italiana* 1 (December 1938): 757.

17. Governo della Tripolitania, "Notizie e cifre," pp. 17–18. For an analysis of the selection process see chapter 8.

18. I. Balbo, *Diario 1922* (Milan, 1932), p. 81.

19. In describing how he managed to keep such discipline and control among his heterogeneous mass of blackshirts, Balbo wrote in his diary, "To those who asked me what the secret was to such a perfect voluntary organization,

I answered: first the example, second discipline." Balbo, *Diario 1922*, pp. 10–11.

20. Balbo's preparations for the Duce's 1937 visit began the year before. Thanks to Balbo's meticulous organization, cheering nomads lined the roadsides of the Littoranea as Mussolini inaugurated the new highway. Visitors were astonished to find themselves sipping chilled wines at multicourse banquets, served by white-gloved waiters—in the midst of the Sirte Desert. Balbo also arranged to have officers from his staff who spoke foreign languages available to accompany visitors—especially foreign journalists. Many of these gestures, tried in 1937, were repeated for the mass migration of 1938. The effect was almost always a "good press" abroad as well as at home. E. D. O'Brien, "With the Duce in Libya, pp. 550–58; Ugo Ojetti, "L'arco sulla litoranea," in *Cose viste* (Florence, 1960).

21. The following description is based on Martin Moore's impression as recorded in his *Fourth Shore: Italy's Mass Colonization of Libya* (London: 1940). Moore accompanied the 1938 expedition as a correspondent for the London *Daily Telegraph*. See also Basilici, "L'Armata del lavoro." The colonists' reaction was recorded in letters reprinted by *L'Azione Coloniale*, "I coloni scrivono," 5 January 1939, p. 8.

22. L. Bongiovanni, "Colonizzazione demografica in Libia," Senato del Regno (Rome, 1939).

23. G. Volpe, *Storia del movimento fascista* (Rome, 1939), p. 230.

24. This work by Adriano Grande won a grand prize of 1,500 lire in a contest sponsored by the *Bargello* of Florence. The contest attracted 874 entries. *L'Azione Coloniale*, 30 November 1939.

25. This was the VIII Congresso Internazionale di Agricoltura Tropicale e Subtropicale. Just before the sailing of the colonists in 1938, the Volta Congress, sponsored by the Italian Royal Academy, was convened in Rome (4–11 October) to discuss colonial development in Africa by European nations. Federazione Internazionale di Tecnici Agricoli, *VIII Congresso Internazionale di Agricoltura Tropicale e Subtropicale* (Rome, 1939), 2 vols.; Reale Accademia d'Italia, Fondazione Alessandro Volta, *Atti del Convegno* (Rome, 1939), 2 vols.

26. H. Bailey, "The colonization of Libya," *Fortnightly Review* 151 (February 1939): 201.

27. New York *Herald Tribune*, 9 November 1938, p. 2.

28. W. C. Lowdermilk, "Colonization De Luxe in Italian North Africa," *American Forests Journal* 46 (July 1940): 315–17.

29. H. N. Brailsford, "Blackshirts in Libya," *New Republic* 98 (8 March 1939): 125.

30. Lowdermilk, "Colonization De Luxe," p. 316.

31. Bailey, "Colonization of Libya," p. 201.

32. Ibid.

33. Steer, *Date in the Desert*, p. 157, for example, was generally critical and skeptical of the Italian effort; yet he concluded that "short of a world war" the colonization would succeed, "for it is carried through with the determination of the state and the personal enthusiasm of Marshal Balbo."

34. After the second emigration of 1939, the Duce grumbled again, Ciano noted in his diary. Apart from the Duce's humors, there was a practical reason for objecting to the publicity. With the attention that was showered on them, the colonists tended to develop an exalted image of themselves. At

Littoria, in the area reclaimed from the Pontine Marshes, "the peasants at one moment refused to work because they thought their role was to be purely representative," Ciano wrote. *Ciano's Hidden Diary (1937–38)*, p. 191; *Ciano's Diary (1939–43)*, ed. M. Muggeridge (London, 1947), pp. 4–5.

35. Moore, *Fourth Shore*, pp. 15–17.
36. T. Philipps, "Italy's Mass Colonization of Libya," *Journal of the Royal African Society* 139 (April 1940): 131.
37. The comment in *Newsweek*, for instance, was: "Of more immediate effect, Mussolini will have the benefit of an Italian population settled near the Egyptian border." *Newsweek*, 7 November 1938, p. 12.
38. *Ciano's Diary 1939–43*, pp. 4–5.
39. ORIG, T-586 (410) 003888.
40. J. Leyder, "Voyage en Libye, remarque sur le colonat Italien," *Bulletin de la Société Royale Belge de Géographie*, 63, fasc. 3 (1939), pp. 227–28.
41. Lowdermilk, "Colonization De Luxe," p. 331.
42. I. Balbo, "La colonizzazione in Libia," *L'Agricoltura Coloniale* 33 (August 1939): 465.
43. IAO-OR, f. 2178 contains a Maugini memorandum with the notation, "compiled in Tripoli 8 January 1939 at the request of Marshall Balbo." The memorandum is in the form of possible replies to objections about the need for continuing with intensive colonization. Intensive colonization is necessary because only intensive labor can effectively develop Libya's meager agricultural resources, Maugini notes. To objections about costs and possible competition of Libyan products with metropolitan produce, Maugini's advice is to stress the social and political benefits of the colonization over mere economic calculus. He adds that the Libyan experience might be defended as a model for colonization in the rest of the empire, not only as an organizational precedent, but also as a possible source for future experienced colonists.
44. Bozze di stampa per i Giornalisti. "Notizie sulla seconda phase della colonizzazione intensiva della Libia." 1939.
45. For the colonists' reaction in 1939, "Vengo con questa mia. . . ," *L'Azione Coloniale*, 19 January 1940, p. 8.

Chapter 7

1. M. Moore, *Fourth Shore: Italy's Mass Colonization of Libya* (London, 1940), pp. 104–5.
2. For a discussion of water policies: CDIA, *L'avvaloramento e la colonizzazione*, 2:67–72; Comitato Rappresentativo Italiano Tripoli, *L'Italia in Libia dal 1911 al 1942* (Tripoli, 1948), pp. 59–62; "Report to the Government of Libya on Agriculture," Expanded Technical Assistance Program, FAO report n. 21 (Rome, 1952), 1: 165–66.
3. A. Desio, "Il petrolio libico," Centro Economico Italia Africa, Quaderno no. 17 (Milan, 1966); A. Desio, "Short history of the geological, mining and oil exploration in Libya" (Istituto di Geologia dell' Università degli Studi di Milano, ser. G., no. 250), Milan, 1968, pp. 100–105. As early as 1914, the Italians found traces of hydrocarbons in Libya while drilling wells at Sidi Mesri. Despite the pleas of some geologists for more intensive oil exploration, the government did little to support such programs, even when Desio discovered oil and refined a small amount from Mellaha Well no. 8 near Tripoli in June 1938. As an example of how limited the Italian program was,

Desio himself divided his time between his academic duties in Milan and his field trips to Libya. However, even with more financial support the Italians never had the resources or the techniques to proceed on the scale of the international oil companies when they made their major findings beginning in 1959.

4. BMA, Tripolitania, Department of Agriculture. *Survey of Land Resources in Tripolitania*. Prepared by Lt. Col. R. T. Robb (Tripoli, 1945), p. 102.

5. CDIA, *L'avvaloramento e la colonizzazione*, 3:70-71.

6. The following description of the projects is based on: CDIA, *L'avvaloramento e la colonizzazione*, 3:161-67; IAC, *La colonizzazione agricola della Tripolitania* (Rome, 1947), pp. 64-77. See also O. Schmieder and H. Wilhelmy, *Die faschistische Kolonisation in Nordafrika* (Leipzig, 1939). The total number of farms includes those which were cleared and on which families were settled in 1938-39.

The choice of names for the projects—usually reflecting Balbo's preferences —was quite eclectic: there were heroes of the Risorgimento (Crispi, Garibaldi), irredentist martyrs (Oberdan), Nationalist heroes (Corradini, d'Annunzio), martyrs and heroes of Fascism (Giordani, Bianchi), fallen comrades of Balbo's flying days (Maddalena). A few projects retained italianized versions of Arabic place names (Tarhuna, Hascian).

7. For a description of the housing: E. Bartolozzi, "Nuove costruzioni rurali in Libia" (Istituto Nazionale di Economia Agraria. Studi e monografie. no. 4 bis) (Rome, 1936); E. Bartolozzi, "Case rurali in Libia dell'Istituto nazionale Fascista della Previdenza Sociale," *L'agricoltura coloniale*, 34, n. 2 (1940), pp. 3-8; CDIA, *L'avvaloramento e la colonizzazione*, 3:343-44; INFPS, "L'attività dell'INFPS per la colonizzazione demografica in Libia," Relazione al Comitato Speciale per l'Assicurazione e Disoccupazione (Rome, 1939).

8. CDIA, *L'avvaloramento e la colonizzazione*, 3:154.

9. G. L. Steer, *A Date in the Desert* (London, 1939), p. 160.

10. Almost invariably those I interviewed spoke of the wheat fields.

11. For the projects in Cyrenaica see: CDIA, *L'avvaloramento e la colonizzazione*, 3:335-40; E. E. Evans-Pritchard, *The Sanusi of Cyrenaica* (Oxford, 1949), pp. 219-20; Schmieder and Wilhelmy, *Die faschistische Kolonisation*, pp. 159-77.

12. CDIA, *L'avvaloramento e la colonizzazione*, 3:343-44.

13. Ibid., p. 342.

14. Governo della Tripolitania, "Notizie e cifre sul nuovo piano di colonizzazione della Libia" (Tripoli, 1939), pp. 4-5; Report to the Government of Libya on Agriculture, Expanded Technical Assistance Program, FAO report no. 21 (Rome, 1952), 1:191.

15. W. C. Lowdermilk, "Colonization De Luxe in Italian North Africa," *American Forests* 46 (July 1940): 315-17; Refugee Economic Corporation, New York, *Quest for Settlement* (New York, 1948), p. 56.

16. IAC, *La colonizzazione della Cirenaica* (Rome, 1947), p. 29.

17. For the following see: IAO-OR, f. 2178, "A Sua Eccellenza il Maresciallo Italo Balbo" (18 February 1938; 5 December 1938).

18. Moore, *Fourth Shore*, p. 220.

19. H. N. Brailsford, "Impressions of Tunis and Libya," *International Affairs* 18 (May 1939): 374.

20. "Vengo con questa mia. . .," *L'Azione Coloniale*, 18 January 1940, p. 8.

21. Ibid.
22. "I coloni scrivono," *L'Azione Coloniale,* 5 January 1939.
23. "Vengo con questa mia..." *L'Azione Coloniale,* 18 January 1940.
24. CDIA, *L'avvaloramento e la colonizzazione,* 3:356.
25. For the following see: "Notizie sul funzionamento di un centro" in IAO-OR f. 2176. The schedule for all working males varied with the seasons. During the winter the men worked from 7 to 12 in the morning and from 2 to 5 in the afternoon. The summer schedule, because of the intense heat, was 6 to 11 in the mornings and 4 to 7 in the afternoons.
26. For a description of the *capo zona's* functions see IAO-OR, f. 2176 "Notizie sul funzionamento di un centro"; CDIA, *L'avvaloramento e la colonizzazione,* 3:336. In addition to the *capo zona* and his assistants, the colonization companies typically employed the following personnel for each zone: a surveyer, an accountant, a storeroom keeper and his assistant, typist and office clerk, an assistant in charge of livestock, a blacksmith and carpenter, each with assistants; a mechanic; a chauffeur; an Arab stableboy or groom; and an Arab watchman who also served as an interpreter.
27. G. Palloni, *I contratti agrari degli enti di colonizzazione in Libia* (Florence, 1945) is the most comprehensive study of the agricultural contracts in Libya. In the appendix to this work Palloni has included the actual contract forms which were used by the companies.
28. Ibid., p. 68.
29. Ibid., pp. 90-103.
30. Ibid., pp. 116-17.
31. CDIA, *L'avvaloramento e la colonizzazione,* 3:365.
32. Interview, G. Palloni, 12 August 1971.
33. IAO-OR, f. 2176 "Notizie sul funzionamento di un centro"; IAO-OR, f. 2240, G. Minnucci, "Cinque anni di colonizzazione in Cirenaica."
34. Although the potential for infectious diseases was high with such large numbers of people coming together in a new environment, the colonists generally led healthy lives. An INFPS report mentions an epidemic of trachoma in 1937-38 which was eliminated after two months, some scattered cases of children's diseases (measles, scarlet fever), and a case of typhoid in February 1939. Minnucci listed some isolated cases of diphtheria, typhus, and tuberculosis in Cyrenaica. Despite the dangers of bites from vipers, asps, and scorpions, he heard of only three cases in five years. INFPS, "L'attività dell' INFPS per la colonizzazione demografica in Libia," pp. 21-22; IAO-OR, f. 2240, Minnucci, "Cinque anni di colonizzazione in Cirenaica."
35. Steer, *A Date in the Desert,* p. 161.
36. For instance, a troupe of opera artists presented a mixed program of opera and popular songs to the colonists at the village of Oberdan after first playing in Benghazi; similarly, a Venetian comic, Emilio Baldanello, did a show at the village of Crispi after playing in Tripoli (*L'Azione Coloniale,* 25 April 1940, p. 1.)
37. The king visited Libya for ten days in 1938 (21-31 May). His itinerary on 27 May included the villages of Tarhuna and Breviglieri in Tripolitania. On 30 May he visited Maddalena, Razza, and Beda Littoria in Cyrenaica. Steer reported seeing a brushwood enclosure where the king stayed during his visit to Crispi (*Date in the Desert,* p. 162).
38. IAO-OR, f. 2664, A. Marassi, "La colonizzazione demografica in Tripolitania nella attività dell'INFPS," pp. 71-74.

39. IAO-OR, f. 2176, A. Maugini, "Pro-memorie, relazioni, e appunti vari sull' ECL," contains the Balbo letter with the colonists' complaints.

40. IAO-OR, f. 2176 "Notizie sul funzionamento di un centro."

41. IAO-OR, f. 2081, A. Chiappini, "Considerazioni sulla colonizzazione agrario-demografica dal 1933-42," pp. 45-46.

42. Interview with G. Palloni, 12 August 1971.

43. IAO-OR, f. 2664, Marassi, "La colonizzazione demografica in Tripolitania nella attività dell'INFPS," pp. 73-74.

44. Steer, *Date in the Desert*, p. 162.

45. Interviews with Sig. Pino Fazio of Rome and with former colonists now living in Sacida (Anzio), August 1966.

46. P. Rossi, *Libye* (Lausanne, 1965), p. 37.

47. Ibid.

48. Ibid.

49. R. Graziani, *Libia redenta* (Naples, 1948), p. 265.

50. M. Pomilio, *Apriamo lo scatolone di sabbia* (Rome, 1935), p. 56.

Chapter 8

1. The two chief training centers for technical experts who directed the projects were the Regio Istituto Superiore Agrario at Portici and the Istituto Agricolo Coloniale in Florence (now known as the Istituto Agronomico per l'Oltremare). Since both schools trained experts in tropical agriculture, it was inevitable that to some extent these institutes became centers for the diffusion of colonial propaganda. For a brief sketch of the two institutes: A. Picciòli, *La nuova Italia d'Oltremare* (Rome, 1933), 1:625-27; and A. Maugini, *Sviluppo agricolo e progresso sociale dei paesi tropicali* (Florence, 1966), pp. 557-68.

2. For a concise summary of the technical expert's dilemma, see Maugini's preface to G. Palloni, *I contratti agrari degli enti di colonizzazione in Libia* (Florence, 1945), p. 5.

3. Ibid., p. 119.

4. IAO-OR, f. 2236, E. Ciulli, "Notizie sul villaggio di Garibaldi e sulla colonizzazione in Tripolitania" (21 November 1947).

5. U. Marroni, "Considerazioni sull'opera svolta dall'ente per la colonizzazione della Libia," *Rivista di Agricoltura Subtropicale e Tropicale*, vol. 41 (1947), nos. 1-3.

6. IAO-OR f. 2252, A. Tucci, "Considerazioni sui cessionari" (30 September 1945), p. 15.

7. Palloni, *I contratti agrari*, p. 121.

8. Ibid.

9. IAO-OR f. 2236, Ciulli, "Notizie sul villaggio di Garibaldi."

10. IAO-OR f. 2176, A. Maugini, "Relazione e proposte circa l'ordinamento e l'attività dell'ente per la colonizzazione della Cirenaica."

11. IAO-OR f. 2252, Tucci, "Considerazioni sui cessionari," p. 15. Ciano makes a similar remark that the publicity induces the colonists to see themselves as "official personages sent by the regime to cut a fine figure." *Ciano's Hidden Diary, 1937-38*, trans. Andreas Mayor (New York, 1953) p. 191.

12. Interview with G. Palloni, 12 August 1971.

13. IAO-OR f. 2100, "Promemoria sulla situazione dei comprensori di colonizzazione della Tripolitania."

14. INFPS, "L'attività dell'INFPS per la colonizzazione demografica in Libia," Relazione al Comitato Speciale per l'Assicurazione e Disoccupazione (Rome, 1939).

15. Ibid., p. 39.

16. Palloni, *I contratti agrari*, pp. 127–28.

17. IAO-OR f. 2176, Maugini, "Relazione e proposte."

18. Ibid.

19. IAO-OR f. 2236, Ciulli, "Notizie sul villaggio di Garibaldi, p. 3.

20. IAO-OR f. 2081, A. Chiappini, "Considerazioni sulla colonizzazione agrario-demografica dal 1933–42."

21. IAO-OR f. 2236, Ciulli, "Notizie sul villaggio di Garibaldi."

22. IAO-OR f. 2176, A. Maugini, "Pro-memorie, relazioni, e appunti vari sull' ECL."

23. IAO-OR f. 2081, Chiappini, "Considerazioni sulla colonizzazione," p. 39; Interview, A. Marassi, 7 August 1971.

24. IAO-OR f. 2240, G. Minnucci, "Cinque anni di colonizzazione in Cirenaica," p. 200; A. De Benedictis, "La colonizzazione demografica col metodo praticato dall'Ente per la Colonizzazione della Libia," in Sindacato Nazionale Fascista Tecnici Agricoli, *Agricoltura e impero* (Rome, 1937); Palloni, *I contratti agrari*, pp. 59–62.

25. IAO-OR f. 2081, Chiappini, "Considerazioni sulla colonizzazione," pp. 38–39,

26. IAO-OR f. 2176, Maugini, "Relazione e proposte."

27. IAO-OR f. 2240, Minnucci, "Cinque anni di colonizzazione in Cirenaica."

28. IAO-OR f. 2081, Chiappini, "Considerazioni sulla colonizzazione," pp. 36–38.

29. IAO-OR f. 2923, E. Casini, "Sguardo panoramico sullo stato attuale della colonizzazione italiana in Tripolitania" (1950), p. 44.

30. Presidenza del Consiglio dei Ministri, Commissariato per le Migrazioni e la Colonizzazione, *Le migrazioni nel regno e nell'Africa Italiana, 1937–38* (Rome, 1938), p. lxxiv.

31. M. Moore, *Fourth Shore: Italy's Mass Colonization of Libya* (London, 1940), p. 20.

32. *L'Azione Coloniale*, 26 October 1939.

33. Moore, *Fourth Shore*, p. 27. Moore writes of the colonization as a "gold rush" for the peasants, who were eager for land. Peasants familiar with reclamation projects did not need any "superhuman effort of faith to have confidence in farms won from the sand," he writes.

34. Carlo Levi, who learned to know the peasants of Lucania well during his political exile, wrote that "in spite of all that was promised, they [the peasants] saw no openings for themselves in the mythical and ill-gotten new land. The thought of Africa did not even cross their minds as they went down to the banks of the Agri." C. Levi, *Christ Stopped At Eboli* (New York, 1965), pp. 225–26.

35. ASMAI, CSC, Cart. 5, no. 4 (5–6 April 1928).

36. According to Federzoni, Balbo saw to it personally that "the Party's criteria did not prevail over the moral, physical and technical qualifications of the families." L. Federzoni, *Italia di ieri per la storia di domani* (Rome: Mondadori, 1967), pp. 154–55.
Officially, the families were chosen according to the following characteristics:

—families of authentic peasants with eight or more members

—sound physical condition of all members (each colonist was checked for general physical fitness, tuberculosis, and trachoma)

—sound moral character of all members

—Fascist party membership (in exceptional cases, if the father was not a party member, the family could be accepted as long as the other members belonged to appropriate Fascist organizations)

—illiterates were not acceptable

—family was to have had previous experience as small landowners, sharecroppers, or agricultural day laborers.

Governo della Tripolitania, "Notizie e cifre sul nuovo piano di colonizzazione della Libia" (Tripoli, 1939), pp. 17–18.

37. Interview with G. Minnucci, 31 July 1971, Macerata. Many of the reports in the IAO-OR also complain about the poor selection. Cf. f. 2664, 2923, 2236.

38. See tables 3–4, pp. 141, 179.

39. For these reports see ACS, Partito Nazionale Fascista, "Situazione politica delle provincie," busta 11 (Padova, 1928–42); busta 26 (Treviso)

40. Interview with G. Minnucci, 31 July 1971.

41. INFPS, "L'attività dell'INFPS per la colonizzazione demografica in Libia," p. 20.

42. ACS, PCM 1937–39, fasc. 17.4.23. The letter also remarks that the INFPS planned to rely on its own regional offices rather than the CMCI for selecting the colonists for INFPS projects.

43. IAO-OR f. 2081, Chiappini, "Considerazioni sulla colonizzazione," pp. 36–38.

44. IAO-OR f. 2664, A. Marassi, "La colonizzazione demografica in Tripolitania nella attività dell'INFPS," p. 29.

45. M. Pomilio, *Apriamo lo scatolone di sabbia* (Rome, 1935), pp. 59–60.

46. IAO-OR f. 2236, Ciulli, "Notizie sul villaggio di Garibaldi."

47. Interview with G. Palloni, 12 August 1971.

48. IAC, *La colonizzazione agricola della Tripolitania* (Rome, 1947), p. 130.

Chapter 9

1. Official figures for 1939 showed a total population of 908,628 including estimates of the nomadic populations. The Libyans totaled 800,223 and the Italians 108,405. The population was clustered in Tripoli province, which accounted for 419,344, or nearly half the total population. Tripoli province together with Misurata accounted for nearly two-thirds of the colony's total population. Istituto Fascista dell'Africa Italiana, *Annuario dell'Africa Italiana* (Rome, 1940), p. 40.

2. According to the 1936 Italian census, 78 per cent of the population was of Arab or Arab-Berber stock. The minorities included Berbers (70,000), Turk-Berbers (*Cologhla*) (35,000), Negroes (30,000), and Jews (28,500). C. L. Pan, "The Population of Libya," *Population Studies* 3 (June 1949): 102–3.

3. Ibid., p. 114.

4. G. Fowler, "Italian Agricultural Colonization in Tripolitania, Libya" (Ph.D. dissertation, Department of Geography, Syracuse University, 1970), 9:74.

5. On the basis of the sketchy data available, Pan estimates a birthrate of 40/1,000 and a death rate of 35/1,000 or a natural increase of 5/1,000 annually for the Libyans. From other data and comparisons with neighboring

countries, she concludes that a natural increase of 0.5 percent to 1.5 percent seems reasonable for the Libyans. The Italians, however, may have had a natural increase of 20/1,000, or 2 percent, and even higher. The limited data on the ECL villages of Cyrenaica between 1935–39, indicate an average annual natural increase of 24.6/1,000. Pan, "Population of Libya"; E. Scarin, *L'insediamento umano nella Libia occidentale* (Ufficio studi del ministero dell'Africa Italiana), 1940, p. 66; IAC, *La colonizzazione della Cirenaica* (Rome, 1947), p. 22.

6. For the following description see: "Report to the Government of Libya on Agriculture," ETAP, FAO Report n. 21 (Rome, November 1952), 1; IAC, *La colonizzazione agricola della Tripolitania* (Rome, 1947), pp. 8–10; V. B. Sullam, "The Agriculture of Northern Libya," *Foreign Agriculture*, vol. 8 (July 1944); CDIA, *Territorio e popolazioni*, 1:317–21.

7. A 1936 Italian census classified 16 percent of the indigenous population as nomadic or seminomadic. Yet, as the Italians admitted, the figure meant little, for even those who were classified as "stable" often shifted temporarily from their normal residences in oases. CDIA, *Territorio e Popolazioni*, 1:317–18.

8. IAO-OR f. 1966, Ufficio agrario, Bengasi, "Le condizioni attuali delle forme stabili di agricoltura indigena nella provincia di Bengasi e proposte relative al RD 3 aprile 1937," p. 8.

9. D. Prinzi, "I rapporti di lavoro nella agricoltura indigena della Tripolitania" (Florence: Istituto Agronomico coloniale Italiano, 1936), p. 40.

10. Prinzi, "I rapporti di lavoro nella agricoltura indigena, pp. 7–8; IAC, *La colonizzazione agricola della Tripolitania*, pp. 8–10; F. Coletti, *La Tripolitania settentrionale e la sua vita sociale* (Bologna, 1923), pp. 229–32.

11. Pan, "Population of Libya," p. 100.

12. F. Coletti, *La Tripolitania settentrionale e la sua vita sociale*, p. 57.

13. Prinzi, "I rapporti di lavoro nella agricoltura indigena," p. 54.

14. IAC, *La colonizzazione agricola della Tripolitania*, pp. 11–19.

15. IAO-OR f. 2089, A. Folco-Zambelli, "Rapporto sulla colonizzazione mussulmana" (2 February 1943).

16. IAC, *La colonizzazione agricola della Tripolitania*, pp. 17–18; *Italy and the Mohammedans of Italian Africa* (Rome, 1940), pp. 68–69; M. Moore, *Fourth Shore: Italy's Mass Colonization of Libya* (London, 1940), p. 193.

17. For the following, see: IAC, *La colonizzazione agricola della Tripolitania*, pp. 16–19; 22–24; IAC, *La colonizzazione della Cirenaica*, pp. 11, 15, 22; CDIA, *L'avvaloramento e la colonizzazione*, 3:183–84, 383–88.

18. "Notizie sulla seconda fase della colonizzazione intensiva della Libia." *Bozze di stampa per i giornalisti* (Tripoli, 1939), pp. 2–3.

19. ASMAI, Schedario di nomi propri, pos. 180/22, no. 71.

20. ASMAI, CSC, art. 27, no. 52 (27 April 1938).

21. The villages for sedentary agriculture planned for Cyrenaica by about 1940 were El Fager, or Alba (Dawn); Zahra, or Fiorita (Flowering); Gedida, or Nuova (New), and Mansura, or Vittoriosa (Victorious). The pastoral villages were Nahiba, or Risorta (Resurrected), and Chadra, or Verde (Green). In Tripolitania two villages for sedentary agriculture were planned: Mahamura (Garden City), later named after Balbo, and Naima, or Deliziosa (Delightful). The Italians were not consistent in referring to a village by its Italian or its Arabic name. The only villages occupied by the time the war broke out were El Fager and Zahra in Cyrenaica and Mahamura in Tripolitania.

22. IAO-OR f. 2237, A. Folco-Zambelli, "Cause della decadenza dell'agri-

coltura indigena e sue possibilità di miglioramento"; IAO-OR f. 2232, A. Fantoli, "Relazione della missione in Libia del Capo Servizio Meteorologico" (20 February–10 May 1947), pp. 1–9.

23. IAO-OR f. 2089, Folco-Zambelli, "Rapporto sulla colonizzazione mussulmana."

24. IAO-OR f. 2091, C. Manni, "Promemoria sulla colonizzazione mussulmana" (26 January 1942).

25. Ibid., p. 8. For instance, the families took such poor care of the livestock with which they were provided that half of the original one hundred camels died. The reaction of the colonists was simply to demand replacements from the Ente.

26. The oases in Cyrenaica were developed almost exclusively by descendants of emigrants, either Berbers from Augila or slaves from the Sudan. IAO-OR f. 1966, Ufficio Agrario, Bengasi, "Le condizioni attuali delle forme stabili di agricoltura indigena nella provincia di Bengasi e proposte relative al RD 3 aprile 1937."

27. IAO-OR f. 2232, Fantoli, "Relazione della missione in Libia del Capo Servizio Meteorologico," p. 77.

28. IAC, *La colonizzazione della Cirenaica*, p. 30; CDIA, *L'avvaloramento agricolo e zootecnico della Tripolitania e della Cirenaica* p. 386; Maugini visited the villages of Alba and Fiorita in 1939 and remarked that he had an "excellent impression" of them. IAO-OR f. 2178, A. Maugini, "Appunti e relazioni varie sulle missioni compiute in Libia dal Prof. Maugini."

29. Personal interview with G. Minnucci, July 1971, Macerata.

30. In his study Fowler concluded that the Italian agricultural colonization in Tripolitania did not result in massive displacement of indigenous peoples. "The areas which the Italians appropriated were sparsely populated and were generally used as seasonal campsites (summer) by Libyans engaged in pastoral activities. No estimate of the total population affected was ever published and none can be derived from the available data." Fowler, "Italian agricultural colonization in Tripolitania," pp. 456–57. See also G. L. Fowler, "Italian Colonization of Tripolitania," *Annals of the Association of American Geographers* 62 (December 1972): 627–40.

31. IAC, *La colonizzazione della Cirenaica*, p. 20; Pan, "Population of Libya," *Population Studies* 3 (June 1949): p. 115.

32. Pace's official report lists an estimated population of 55,350 in the five camps scattered throughout Cyrenaica, out of a total population, according to the 1931 census, of 136,215. Gen. Guglielmo Nasi, the vice-governor for Cyrenaica, in a frank report to Balbo in 1934, described the camps as "veri e propri campi di concentramento" (genuine concentration camps). However, in fairness to the Italians, the term can be misleading, for the camps were nothing like the Nazi models. One camp only was concerned with the detention of real political prisoners. The Libyans were in no way used as slave labor, nor was there ever any attempt at genocide. The interns were recruited to work on public works projects at wages—according to the Italians—sufficient to support their families and even allow some savings. The Libyans were also encouraged to develop small plots of land and to continue with their customary pastoral activities. The Italians furnished medical aid and educational facilities. IAO-OR f. 2077, G. Nasi, "Situazione politico-economica delle popolazioni indigene della Cirenaica"; B. Pace, *La Libia nella politica fascista* (Messina and Milan, 1935), pp. 83–107.

33. A. Maugini, "La pianura di Merg," *Rivista della Tripolitania* 1, n. 4

(1925), p. 262; E. E. Evans-Pritchard, *The Sanusi of Cyrenaica* (Oxford, 1949), p. 225. Maugini, in his 1933 report to Razza outlining the program for the future Ente Cirenaica, recommended that the bedouins, who had been deported to camps in southern Cyrenaica by Graziani, not be allowed to return to the Gebel. He proposed an alternate system of reservations for pasture.

34. IAO-OR f. 2239, G. Loris, "Breve relazione sull'attività svolta dall'ECL in Cirenaica dalla costituzione a tutto il 1942."

35. Ibid., p. 48.

36. IAO-OR f. 2176, A. Maugini, "Promemorie, relazioni e appunti vari sull'ECL."

37. IAO-OR f. 2081, A. Chiappini, "Considerazioni sulla colonizzazione agrario-demografica dal 1933–42," pp. 78–79.

38. Ibid., pp. 73–76.

39. ORIG, T-586 (409) 003636, describes a raid against the village of Luigi di Savoia which resulted in four colonists dead and considerable looting and destruction. The loot included the village priest's robes, which were returned for a ransom of two thousand lire.

40. IAO-OR, f. 2081, Chiappini, "Considerazioni sulla colonizzazione agrario-demografica," p. 82.

41. Fowler, "Italian Agricultural Colonization in Tripolitania," 9:73.

42. IAO-OR f. 2232, Fantoli, "Relazione della missione in Libia del Capo Servizio Meteorologico". Fantoli cited two examples of Libyans who were benefiting from the opportunities the Italians offered in agriculture. One Libyan had served as a medical aid with the Libyan troops and the other had worked for thirteen years on an Italian concession.

43. IAC, *La colonizzazione agricola della Tripolitania*, pp. 22–23.

44. Governo della Tripolitania, "Notizie e cifre sul nuovo piano di colonizzazione della Libia" (Tripoli, 1939), p. 15.

45. INFPS, "L'attività dell'INFPS per la colonizzazione demografica in Libia," Relazione al Comitato Speciale per l'Assicurazione e Disoccupazione (Rome, 1939), p. 7.

46. "Primo censimento generale delle aziende agrarie metropolitane della Libia al 21 aprile 1937-XV," *Bollettino Statistico dell'Africa Italiana* 4 (January–February 1941), table 12; IAC, *La colonizzazione agricola della Tripolitania*, p. 124.

47. IAO-OR f. 2176, A. Maugini, "Pro-memorie, relazioni, e appunti vari sull'ECL."

48. Prinzi, "I rapporti di lavoro nella agricoltura indigena della Tripolitania," p. 40; IAO-OR f. 2664, A. Marassi, "La colonizzazione demografica in Tripolitania nella attività dell'INFPS," p. 76.

49. IAO-OR f. 2236, E. Ciulli, "Notizie sul villaggio di Garibaldi e sulla colonizzazione in Tripolitania," pp. 7–8.

50. P. Bignami, *Tra i colonizzatori in Tripolitania* (Bologna, 1931), pp. 272–73.

51. Prinzi, "I rapporti di lavoro nella agricoltura indigena della Tripolitania," p. 40.

52. Ibid., p. 246.

53. F. Coletti, *La Tripolitania settentrionale e la sua vita sociale*, p. 246. In hopes that the Libyans would work steadily for longer periods, the Italians experimented with cutting wages. The policy had little or no effect. Interview with G. Palloni, August 1971.

54. Prinzi, "I rapporti di lavoro nella agricoltura indigena," pp. 11-12.
55. R. S. Harrison, "Migrants in the City of Tripoli, Libya," *Geographical Review,* 57 (July 1967): 405-6.
56. *Ciano's Diary (1939-43),* ed. M. Muggeridge (London, 1947), p. 489.
57. FAO. Report to the Government of Libya. Development of Tribal Lands and Settlements Project. *General Report* (Rome, 1969), 1:159-64.
58. Government of Libya, National Agricultural Settlement Authority. *Land Policy in the Near East* (Rome, 1967), p. 145.

Chapter 10

1. Official 1939 estimates show a population of 108,405 Italians. With additional immigration, Pan estimated a total of 140,000 by the end of 1940. *Annuario dell'Africa Italiana* (1940), p. 40; C. L. Pan, "The Population of Libya," *Population Studies* 3 (June 1949): 113.
2. The population of Algeria in 1954 was 8.9 million, of which about 11 percent were Europeans. R. Gallissot, *L'économie de l'Afrique du Nord* (Paris, 1964), pp. 59-61.
3. The Italian population in Tunisia in 1936 totaled about 94,000. This figure does not include the large numbers of Italians who became naturalized French citizens (18,000 during the decade 1921-31). E. M. Kulischer, *Europe on the Move* (New York, 1948), p. 224.
4. J. L. Miège, *L'impérialisme colonial italien* (Paris, 1968), p. 251.
5. IAC, *La colonizzazione della Cirenaica* (Rome, 1947), p. 20; IAC, *La colonizzazione agricola della Tripolitania* (Rome, 1947), pp. 113-17. In Tripolitania, 15,000 of the 24,000 colonists had been settled by the two colonization companies. In Cyrenaica, the ECL had settled 13,000 of the 15,000 colonists.
6. Interview with G. Palloni, 10 August 1971.
7. The estimate is based on the amount of labor needed to fully develop the agricultural zone of about 200,000 hectares in Tripolitania. G. Trigona, "Nuove possibilità di lavoro e di benessere create dalla colonizzazione agricola italiana in Tripolitania," *Rivista di Agricoltura Subtropicale e Tropicale* 42 (April-June 1948): 92-98. Cf. IAC, *La colonizzazione agricola della Tripolitania,* pp. 121-25.
8. Maugini's opinions can be seen in an angry letter, dated 1 September 1945, to the Ministry of Italian Africa about speculative newspaper reports describing a plan to settle some forty thousand Poles in Libya. The potential colonists were Poles living in England and members of the Polish army stationed in Italy. Maugini claimed that such a project would fail because no more land for colonization was available. The only result would be to disturb the remaining Italian colonists and to excite the Libyans. IAO-OR f. 2195, A. Maugini, "Trasferimento di coloni polacchi in Libia."
9. IAO-OR f. 2176, A. Maugini, "Promemorie, relazione, e appunti vari sull' ECL." The colonists at Gioda arrived with the *Ventimila* in 1938. Their water system, however, was not completed until 1940. For nearly two years, the families stayed busy clearing the land and digging holes to plant windbreaks. Winds and shifting sands frustrated their efforts. Morale sagged so much that in April 1941 it was recommended that most of the colonists be transferred to more successful settlements.
10. The annual crude rate of natural increase in the ECL villages of Cyrenaica between 1935 and 1939 varied from a high of 29.8/1,000 to a low of 20.6/

1,000, with an average of 24.6/1,000. One British observer commented that
"the prolific birthrate threatened to saddle the county with a superfluity of
farming families. Some colonists' houses contained in 1938 no less than three
married couples, the total family reaching 18 persons in three rooms." IAC,
La colonizzazione della Cirenaica, p. 22; D. H. Weir, "Italian Colonization,"
Handbook on Cyrenaica, 11 (Cairo: British Military Administration, 1944–
47), p. 18.

11. IAO-OR f. 2253, U. Marroni, "Il beneficio derivato all'economia agricola
indigena dalla colonizzazione metropolitana in Tripolitania" (November
1946).

12. IAO-OR f. 2081, A. Chiappini, "Considerazione sulla colonizzazione
agrario-demografica dal 1933–42," p. 59.

13. IAC, *La colonizzazione agricola della Tripolitania*, p. 116.

14. IAC, *La colonizzazione della Cirenaica*, p. 21.

15. The olive plantings provide an indication of the magnitude of the Italian
effort. A Turkish census of 1910 for Tripolitania gave an estimate of 110,000
trees. By 1937 this total had increased to 2.4 million trees, of which about
1.6 million were Italian and 828,600 were planted by Libyans. By 1940 the
Italians had increased their plantings to 2.2 million, and one agricultural
expert estimated that total Libyan and Italian plantings would reach 4
million trees by 1943. The majority of these trees were far from mature, but
within a decade it was estimated that the olives counted under the 1937
census would be able to produce 63,000 to 83,000 quintals of olive oil
annually, or about three to four times the average annual imports needed
between 1929 and 1938. Within twenty-five years of the 1943 plantings,
it was estimated that olive oil production could increase to 100,000 quintals.
G. Vivoli, "L'olivicoltura mondiale con particolare riguardo a quella africana," *Gli annali dell'Africa Italiana*, 4, no. 1 (1941): 209–18.

16. IAC, *La colonizzazione della Cirenaica*, pp. 33–35; IAC, *La colonizzazione
agricola della Tripolitania*, pp. 106–12.

17. For the following trade figures see Istituto Fascista dell'Africa Italiana,
Annuario dell'Africa Italiana (Rome, 1940), pp. 248–50.

18. For the period 1934–38, Libyan imports included 49,280 metric tons of
wheat flour: 8,030 metric tons of barley; 62,800 hectoliters of wine, 8,300
hectoliters of olive oil, and 40 metric tons of tobacco. Statistics for the war
period are not available. International Institute of Agriculture, *International Yearbook of Agricultural Statistics 1941–42 to 1945–46*, vol. 2
(International Trade) (Rome, 1947), tables 2, 6, 20, 21, 27.

19. For the following see: Miège, *L'impérialisme colonial italien*, p. 252;
W. G. Welk, *Fascist Economic Policy* (Cambridge, 1958), pp. 222–23.

20. The taxes were levied on corporations and real property. In the meantime
the public debt increased from 102.2 billion lire in 1934 to 145.8 billion lire
in 1939. Real wages are estimated to have dropped 26 percent. To raise more
capital for colonial investment the Italians looked for financial support both
in Germany and in England. Cf. Miège, *L'impérialisme colonial italien*,
p. 252; S. B. Clough, *The Economic History of Modern Italy* (New York,
1964), p. 259.

21. For the following see *Memorandum sulla situazione economica e finan-
ziaria dei territori italiani in Africa* (Rome, 1946), p. 4. These figures are
probably low since they are meant to include only development costs of the
infrastructure—items such as roads, dams, harbors. They exclude military

expenses and extraordinary expenses that might have been authorized by colonial governments.

22. IAC, *La colonizzazione agricola della Tripolitania*, p. 128; IAC, *La colonizzazione della Cirenaica*, p. 29. These figures are not exact. They are intended to give a rough idea of the magnitude of the investment. They are an average of three different methods of estimating the investment: (1) the total investment of the state, directly and indirectly, plus the investment of private funds, (2) the average unit cost of developing various areas, and (3) the cost of each single improvement or transformation.

23. C. T. Schmidt, *The Plough and the Sword: Land, Labor and Property in Fascist Italy* (New York, 1938), p. 93. The Pontine Marshes absorbed 203 million lire during the fiscal years 1926–32; 223 million lire during the fiscal years 1932–34; and 600 million lire during the period 1 July 1934 to 1 March 1936. These figures do not include outlays for construction of cities in the district.

24. As a rule of thumb the state contributed 50 percent of expenses in credit, 25 percent in prizes, subsidies and state contributions. Private capital contributed only 25 percent. IAC, *La colonizzazione agricola della Tripolitania*, p. 128.

25. IAC, *La colonizzazione della Cirenaica*, p. 28.

26. In Cyrenaica, the average cost per hectare for the demographic farms was estimated at 10,000 lire. For private colonization, depending on the locale, the average costs per hectare were estimated to range from 4,000 to 8,000 lire. IAC, *La colonizzazione della Cirenaica*, p. 29.

27. IAO-OR f. 2178, "A Sua Eccellenza il Maresciallo Italo Balbo" (18 February 1938; 5 December 1938). See chapter 7 above.

28. IAO-OR f. 2306, "Ente per la Colonizzazione della Libia" (1949), p. 23.

29. G. Palloni, *I contratti agrari degli enti di colonizzazione in Libia* (Florence, 1945), pp. 130–33; IAO-OR, f. 2248, U. Marroni, "Relazione al bilancio consuntivo, 1946," pp. 12–14.

30. IAO-OR f. 2264, "Progetti di legislazione relativi alla colonizzazione agraria in Libia."

31. Interview with G. Palloni, 10 August 1971. According to Palloni, Balbo contemplated launching such a fund drive in early 1940 to ensure support for the future mass emigrations. However, his technical advisors dissuaded him on the grounds that there was no more suitable land available to extend the colonization.

32. L. Salvatorelli and G. Mira, *Storia d'Italia nel periodo fascista* (Turin, 1964), p. 1041. De Bono, who inspected the troops in Libya, complained about serious shortages of material and equipment in a report dated February 1940. Antitank weapons and mortars were in short supply, and many soldiers did not have a change of uniform or shoes, he reported. "It pains me to say it; but as far as equipment is concerned, the impression which our troops make is certainly not edifying," he concluded. ORIG, T-586 (465) 035326–035333.

33. Balbo died in a plane crash 28 June 1940, while flying over Tobruk. He was shot down by Italian antiaircraft batteries which mistook his plane for a British incursion.

34. "Libia," *Enciclopedia Italiana*, appendix 2, 1938–48, p. 198.

35. For the following see: IAO-OR f. 2239, G. Loris, "Breve relazione sull'attività svolta dall'ECL"; IAO-OR f. 2090, G. Minnucci, "Quello che è

avvenuto nei due mesi di occupazione inglese presso i villaggi dell'ECL";
IAO-OR f. 2102, ECL, "Relazione sulla seconda occupazione inglese della
Cirenaica."
36. F. J. Rennell Rodd, *British Military Admistration of Occupied Territories
in Africa during the Years 1941–47* (London, 1948), pp. 242–93; Ministero
della Cultura Popolare, *Che cosa hanno fatto gli inglesi in Cirenaica* (Rome,
1941); G. Scalfaro, *56 giorni di "civiltà" inglese a Bengasi* (Rome,
1941); G. Rossi, *Martirio di Bengasi sotto l'oppressione inglese* (Rome,
1942). Rennell Rodd is inclined to blame "certain elements among the local
population" for the "main breaches of law and order" that occurred on the
Gebel (*British Military Administration*, p. 37). Fascist publications blamed
Australian soldiers in particular, who acted from the "atavistic instincts"
derived from their convict ancestors (Scalfaro, *56 giorni di civiltà*, p. 176).
37. IAO-OR f. 2239, Loris, "Breve relazione sull'attività svolta dall'ECL,"
p. 38.
38. IAO-OR f. 2248, Marroni, "Relazione al bilancio ECL consuntivo 1946."
39. At the beginning of 1948 there were about 100 Italians left in Cyrenaica,
including twelve missionaries and forty-one nuns. *Enciclopedia Italiana,*
appendix 2, 1938–48, p. 623.
40. Rennell, *British Military Administration,* pp. 259–60.
41. IAO-OR f. 2232, A. Fantoli, "Relazione della missione in Libia del Capo
Servizio Meteorologico" (20 February–10 May 1947), pp. 73–74.
42. Ibid., pp. 22–24.
43. V. B. Sullam, "The Agriculture of Northern Libya," *Foreign Agriculture,*
8 (July 1944): 159–68; A. Rompietti, "La colonizzazione contadina in
Tripolitania," *Rivista di agricoltura subtropicale e tropicale,* 55 (January–
March 1961): 20–34.
44. IAO-OR f. 4371, G. Aiuti, "Rapporto Aiuti su Oliveti-Maamura e Azizia
e profughi Bianchi-Giordani-Micca," p. 2.
45. For the following see: IAO-OR f. 2175, U. Marroni, "Opera svolta a favore
dei coloni nel 1943–44 sotto l'occupazione Britannica."
46. British Military Administration, *Handbook of Tripolitania* (Cairo, 1947),
pp. 47–49.
47. R. L. Robb, "The Agriculture of Tripolitania with special reference to land
settlement" (BMA Tripolitania, December 1943), p. 32.
48. IAO-OR f. 2232, Fantoli, "Relazione della missione in Libia del Capo
Servizio Meteorologico," p. 20.
49. Comitato Rappresentativo Italiano Tripoli, *L'Italia in Libia dal 1911 al
1942* (Tripoli, 1948), p. 131.
50. IAO-OR f. 2923, E. Casini, "Sguardo panoramico sullo stato attuale
della colonizzazione italiana in Tripolitania; relazione per illustrare il
documento fotografico eseguito durante il viaggio 15 agosto–15 settembre,
1950," pp. 26–27.
51. For the following see Palloni, *I contratti agrari in Libia,* pp. 130–33.
52. IAO-OR f. 2252, A. Tucci, "Considerazioni sui cessionari" (30 September
1945).
53. IAO-OR f. 2084, "Rapporti dei capi zona sui poderi passati in proprietà
il 31 maggio 1942."
54. IAO-OR f. 2236, E. Ciulli, "Notizie sul villaggio di Garibaldi e sulla
colonizzazione in Tripolitania," pp. 4–6.
55. IAO-OR f. 4371, Aiuti, "Rapporto Aiuti su Oliveti-Maamura e Azizia."

56. For the following see: IAO-OR f. 2232, Fantoli, "Relazione della missione in Libia del Capo Servizio Meteorologico," pp. 22-24.
57. Ibid., pp. 23-31.
58. Ibid., p. 31.
59. British Military Administration, *Annual Report* (Tripoli, 1947), p. 42.
60. In 1946 the Italian population in Tripolitania totaled 49,536 out of a total population of 803,915. The second largest minority was the Jewish population of 28,031 and 2,757 were classified as "others." The Moslems totaled 732,591. The Italian agricultural population totaled 15,000 and was distributed as follows: ECL, 4,900; INFPS, 4,900; ATI, 1,300; private farms, 5,000. British Military Administration, *Handbook of Tripolitania,* appendix 1: p. 77.
61. IAO-OR f. 2232, Fantoli, "Relazione della missione in Libia del Capo Servizio Meteorologico, pp. 1-9.
62. Ibid., p. 2.
63. Ibid., p. 5.
64. For the following on repatriation see: Rennell *British Military Administration in Africa,* p. 467; British Military Administration, *Annual Report* (1947), p. 16; IAO-OR f. 2248, Marroni, "Relazione al bilancio consuntivo, 1946," pp. 12-14.
65. British Military Administration, *Annual Report* (1947), p. 42.
66. Eden had made a statement in the House of Commons on 4 October 1944 implying that Great Britain would oppose Italy's return to all of her colonies. When Italian premier Bonomi requested clarification of the statement, he was informed that the Eden statement was misunderstood. M. Khadduri, *Modern Libya* (Baltimore, 1963), p. 113.
67. G. H. Becker, *The Disposition of the Italian Colonies 1941-51* (Geneva, 1952), p. 125.
68. Università degli studi di Firenze, *Atti del convegno di studi coloniali* (Florence, 29-31 January 1946).
69. Becker, *Disposition of the Italian Colonies,* pp. 125-26.
70. U.S.Department of State, *Bulletin* 13, no. 333 (11 November 1945): 764-65.
71. Ibid.
72. Ibid.
73. C. Grove Haines, "The Problem of the Italian Colonies," *Middle East Journal,* 1: (October 1947): 417-31; H. S. Hughes, *The United States and Italy,* rev. ed. (Cambridge, 1965), p. 148.
74. Khadduri, *Modern Libya,* pp. 120-23.
75. Khadduri, *Modern Libya,* pp. 105-06; Council of Foreign Ministers, *Report of the Four Power Commission of Investigation for the Former Italian Colonies,* vol. 3, annex, pp. 12-15.
76. *Report of the Four Power Commission,* vol. 3, annex, pp. 4-5.
77. For the following summary of diplomacy, see Khadduri, *Modern Libya,* pp. 126-37; Becker, *Disposition of the Italian Colonies,* pp. 103-96.
78. United Nations, *United Nations Treaty Series,* vol. 49 (1950), no. 747, "Treaty of Peace with Italy, signed at Paris on 10 February 1947," pp. 126-235. Art. 79, par. 1 and 6c dealt with property rights (pp. 163-65).
79. United Nations, General Assembly, *Annual Report of the United Nations Commissioner in Libya* (A/1430, Sept. 1950) (New York, 1950), par. 28, p. 5.

80. For the text see *Yearbook of the United Nations, 1950* (New York, 1951), pp. 357–59.
81. Khadduri, *Modern Libya,* pp. 276–77.
82. For the official text, see Libya, *Official Gazette of the United Kingdom,* vol. 8, no. 5 (25 March 1958); Italy, Centro di Documentazione, *Italian Affairs: Documents and notes,* 9 (November–December 1962): 4136–37.
83. Rompietti, "La colonizzazione contadina in Tripolitania," p. 27.
84. IAO-OR, f. 560, A. Maugini, "Relazione sulla colonizzazione contadina della Tripolitania, 8/5/953."
85. On 21 January 1953, Italian diplomats stationed in Tripoli, representatives of the ECL and INFPS, and emigration officials met to discuss the plight of the colonists. To support the Italian—and Western European position—in the Mediterranean, the diplomats favored continuing support for the remaining colonists in Libya. The colonization companies, however, showed reluctance to continue shouldering the financial burden. The INFPS, for instance, argued that legally it had no authority to support projects which were now located in a foreign country. IAO-OR f. 131, folder 20, "Libia—rapporti sulla colonizzazione demografica."
86. IAO-OR, f. 560, Maugini, "Relazione sulla colonizzazione contadina della Tripolitania," appendix 1, p. 4. The status of each settlement is described in the appendixes to Maugini's report. See also: IAO-OR, f. 2923, Casini, "Sguardo panoramico sullo stato attuale della colonizzazione italiana in Tripolitania."
87. G. Fowler, "Italian Agricultural Colonization in Tripolitania, Libya" (Ph.D. dissertation, Department of Geography, Syracuse University, 1970), 10: 19–20.
88. Ibid., 10: 21–26.
89. Ibid.
90. In practice, the Libyan government was concerned with expelling the permanent, long-term resident Italian community. Large-scale Italian companies engaged in public works projects for the Libyan government or in the petroleum, shipping or airlines businesses were not disturbed. The employees of these firms and their families continue to live and work in Libya today. However, members of the "old" long-term resident community are not allowed to return to Libya.
91. There are no official figures on the number of farms or agricultural lands still in Italian hands at the time of the expulsion. The *Corriere della Sera* (23 July 1970, p. 2) estimated that 20,000 hectares—most of them in the form of large-scale model farms—were still in Italian hands at the time of the confiscation decrees.
92. Initially the Libyan government declared that it would pay compensation in the form of government bonds redeemable in fifteen years, but the Libyan state reserved the right to ask for damages caused by the Italian occupation. Later, the Libyan government announced that it would pay compensation *only* after it had recovered damages incurred under the Italian occupation. The value of the confiscated properties has been estimated at between 200 and 400 billion lire. (*Corriere della Sera,* 8 September 1970.)
93. The Italians, for instance, were prohibited from operating pharmacies or insurance and shipping agencies. Among the Italian properties nationalized were the Banco di Roma and Banco di Napoli branches. British and American air bases were also evacuated in March and June of 1971.

94. Ministero degli Affari Esteri, Comitato Consultivo degli Italiani all'Estero, *Verbali della IV Sessione (24-27 November 1970)*, p. 11.
95. A colonist at the village of Garibaldi, for instance, claimed that a Libyan official came to count his chickens every morning and took away all the eggs. *Corriere della Sera* (2 September 1970, p. 2.)
96. Ministero degli Affari Esteri, Comitato Consultivo degli Italiani all'Estero, *Verbali della IV Sessione,* p. 13.
97. This included a grant of 200,000 lire for each head of a family and 150,000 lire for each family member. In addition, the Ministry of the Interior offered an extraordinary subsidy of 100,000 lire for each family member. The colonists were entitled to free medical care for six months, various housing accommodations in camps or boarding houses or rest homes (for the oldest refugees). The government also provided the licenses or permits the refugees needed to resume practicing their trades, businesses, and professions in Italy. *Corriere della Sera,* 26 July 1970, p. 2.
98. *Corriere della Sera,* 25 July 1970, p. 2.

Chapter 11

1. R. L. Robb, "The Agriculture of Tripolitania with Special Reference to Land Settlement: Review of the Position Nine Months after British Occupation" (BMA Tripolitania, December 1943), p. 38.
2. G. Volpe, *Storia del movimento fascista* (Istituto per gli studi internazionali, 1939), p. 230.
3. F. C. Thomas, Jr., "The Libyan Oil Worker," *Middle East Journal* 15 (summer 1961): 246-76; R. W. Brown, "Libya's Rural Sector," *Africa Report* (April 1967), pp. 16-18.
4. "Report to the Government of Libya on Agriculture," ETAP, FAO Report no. 21 (Rome: FAO, November 1952), p. 73.
5. Quoted in L. Federzoni, *Italia di ieri per la storia di domani* (Milan: Mondadori, 1967), p. 17.

Bibliographical Essay

This essay describes the nature and location of the most important primary and secondary sources on which this study is based. For detailed references on specific problems, the reader should refer to the footnotes in the main text. Since bibliographical guides in English on the general topic of Italian colonialism are rare, I have also included some references to more general works in this field. The single most important and complete bibliography on all aspects of Libya—history, economy, politics, and natural environment—is R. W. Hill, *A Bibliography of Libya* (Department of Geography, University of Durham, 1959). Hans Schlüter's *Index Libycus: Bibliography of Libya, 1915–1956* (Boston, 1972) brings Hill's work up to date.

Primary Sources

The Osservatorio Rurale, or Rural Observatory, situated in the Institute for Overseas Agriculture (Istituto Agronomico per l'Oltremare) in Florence, provided the bulk of the unpublished material in this work. This collection of reports, papers, and correspondence related to agriculture and rural development in Italy's African colonies was begun in the days when the institute—then known as the Istituto Agricolo Coloniale, or Institute for Colonial Agriculture—was a major training center for the agricultural experts who were to provide technical direction to the colonization programs. The observatory was intended as a repository and reference collection for technical and scientific information. However, the documents often expand beyond technical problems to comment on broad social, political, and economic issues. Some of the most revealing material deals with the professional career of Professor Armando Maugini, for many years director of the institute and one of the major architects of the colonization programs in Italian Africa. These papers include Professor Maugini's recommendations for various colonization projects in both Libya and East Africa; his correspondence with agricultural experts working in the colonies—men who were often his former students at the institute; and his memorandums and position papers to officials in the Colonial Ministry. Thus the materials in the collection provide important insights into many aspects of life in the Italian colonies and into many facets of policymaking.

The records of the Italian Colonial Ministry (known first as the Ministero delle Colonie, and after the Ethiopian conquest as the Ministero dell'Africa Italiana) are preserved in the Archivio Storico dell'ex-Ministero dell'Africa

Italiana (ASMAI) at the Foreign Ministry in Rome. This vast collection dates back to the earliest days of Italian involvement in Africa during the Liberal period. However, as with any archive, there are many gaps. With the ASMAI in particular, many of the documents from the Fascist period were lost when the archive was shifted from Rome to Northern Italy during World War II. For this study, the ASMAI records of the Consiglio Superiore Coloniale and the collection of published and unpublished works of the Fascist Colonial Ministry's propaganda and information section were most valuable. Some of the Colonial Ministry's records were captured by the Allies at the end of World War II and were microfilmed. These records are available from Saint Antony's College, Oxford, and in the United States from the National Archives, in the series known as Official Records of Italian Government Agencies, 1922–44 (ORIG).

The Archivio Centrale dello Stato (ACS) in Rome contained the papers on the Presidenza del Consiglio dei Ministri and many of the original documents reproduced on the ORIG microfilm. The ACS material on leading colonial figures such as De Bono, Volpi, and Balbo, included in Mussolini's Personal Secretariat, is rich in accusations and rumors of personal scandals and vendettas, but meager on policymaking and day-to-day administration in the colonies.

Secondary Sources

Any investigation of the secondary literature on the colonization in Libya—and on Italian colonialism in general—must begin with the mammoth multivolume series *L'Italia in Africa*, published by the Italian Foreign Ministry's Comitato per la Documentazione delle Attività Italiane in Africa. More than twenty volumes have appeared to date in this series, which is intended to cover all aspects of the Italian colonial experience. Many of the authors contributing to the project are not professional scholars. Hence the series is of uneven quality and generally apologetic in tone. Nevertheless, *L'Italia in Africa*, when completed, is destined to become a standard reference in the field.

The volumes in the series which deal with economic and agricultural problems include a monograph on Libya, *L'avvaloramento agricolo e zootecnico della Tripolitania e della Cirenaica* (Rome, 1971), by P. Ballico and G. Palloni, two agricultural experts who spent much of their professional careers working in the colonies. In their study they stress the important contributions the colonization experience made to scientific knowledge. They also recall their disappointment at the reserved and hostile attitude of the indigenous peoples toward the Italian development plans.

For technical aspects of the colonization, Ballico and Palloni's study in the *Italia in Africa* series supersedes earlier works such as the two sketchy monographs produced by the Istituto Agricolo Coloniale, *La colonizzazione agricola della Tripolitania* (Rome, 1947) and *La colonizzazione della Cirenaica* (Rome, 1947) and A. Picciòli's propagandistic two-volume compendium *La nuova Italia d'Oltremare* (Milan, 1933). Both of the Istituto Agricolo Coloniale monographs, produced hastily after the war, in part to justify continued Italian sovereignty over Libya, are still useful for their statistical material. The volume on Tripolitania also contains interesting critical observations on political interference with the colonization programs.

Debates and discussions about technical aspects of the colonization—which ultimately had an effect on policymaking—can be followed in such periodicals as the Istituto Agricolo Coloniale's *L'Agricoltura Coloniale* and in the proceedings of Italian colonial congresses (published as the *Atti* of the Congresso di Studi Coloniali), which held meetings in Florence (1931), Naples (1934), and Florence-Rome (1937). G. Palloni, *I contratti agrari degli enti di colonizzazzione in Libia* (Florence, 1945) is valuable for its general observations on the colonization programs as well as the specific problem of the agricultural contracts. Foreign technical experts who visited the projects and concessions in Libya often discussed the colonization with far more candor than the Italian experts, restricted by political considerations, could permit themselves. Two of the best reports, sympathetic yet dispassionate, are Jean Despois, *La colonisation italienne en Libye* (Paris, 1935) and F. Vöchting, "Italienische Siedelung in Libyen," *Jahrbucher für Nationalekonomie und Statistik*, vol. 151, no. 2 (February 1940) and no. 3 (March 1940).

The speeches and writings of major colonial figures like Volpi, Federzoni, and Lessona show how the colonization in Libya fitted into the broader plans for Fascist expansion in the Mediterranean. When Volpi's term as governor of Tripolitania ended, his work was celebrated in a collection of essays entitled *La rinascita della Tripolitania* (Milan, 1926) to which Volpi himself made a contribution. Volpi's governorship is also discussed in R. Rapex, *L'affermazione della sovranità italiana sulla Libia* (Tientsin, 1937), a laudatory memoir by one of the governor's former aides. Another influential colonial figure during the Volpi and De Bono eras was Luigi Federzoni, who served two terms as minister of colonies. His articles and speeches, which were important indicators of colonization policy, are collected in *Venti mesi di azione coloniale* (Milan, 1926) and *A.O.: Il "Posto al Sole"* (Bologna, 1938). Alessandro Lessona, the colonial undersecretary who campaigned for increasing state intervention when the colonization faltered during the Depression, collected his many journal and newspaper articles in *L'Africa settentrionale nella politica mediterranea* (Rome, 1942) and *Scritti e discorsi coloniali* (Milan, 1935). *Per le nostre colonie* (Florence, 1927) is a remarkably sober and concise discussion of the colonization problem by a panel of politicians and agricultural experts attending a symposium sponsored by the Istituto Agricolo Coloniale. Many of the sharpest polemics over the progress of the colonization were carried on in colonialist journals of the period, such as *L'Oltremare* and *Rivista della Tripolitania*. *L'Agricoltura Coloniale*, published by the Istituto Agricolo Coloniale, although primarily devoted to technical aspects of the colonization, often contained important editorial statements about policy. The reaction of the concessioners to changes in policy can be traced in newspapers published in the colony, such as *Il Corriere di Tripoli*.

There are few general surveys of Italian colonialism to help the scholar place the colonization in Libya within the broader framework of the Italian colonial tradition. The best general survey currently available is J. L. Miège's *L'impérialisme colonial italien de 1870 à nos jours* (Paris, 1968). In this fine synthesis, marred only by an embarassing number of typographical errors, Miège touches on all aspects of Italian colonialism, and especially on the ideological theme of Italy's search for demographic outlets. Luigi Preti's *Impero fascista. Africani ed ebrei* (Milan, 1968) argues that the Fascist imperial myth—including the

rationale that Italy needed colonies to help resolve her demographic problems
—was largely derived from the ideology of the Nationalists. Two older surveys
which gradually will be superseded by volumes in the *L'Italia in Africa* series
are R. Ciasca, *Storia coloniale dell'Italia contemporanea* (Milan, 1938), and
Gennaro Mondaini, *Manuale di storia e legislazione coloniale del regno d'Italia*
(Rome, 1927). Ciasca, who focuses primarily on political-diplomatic and
military developments, is strongly nationalist in tone and ends on a triumphant
note with the Fascist conquest of Ethiopia. Mondaini concentrates heavily on
colonial legislation, but his book also contains nuggets of statistical information in footnotes.

The story of Italian colonialism in Libya from the Libyan view still remains to
be told. Italian ethnographers, anthropologists, and colonial officials, such as
Emilio Scarin, Ester Panetta, Enrico de Agostini, and many others, made
important investigations into the demographic patterns, folklore, and social
structure of the indigenous peoples. Italian agricultural experts and members
of scientific missions like the Franchetti expedition devoted much time and
attention to the indigenous peoples and attempted to assess the impact of the
Italian occupation on their lives. The best introduction to this literature is
through the appropriate sections in R. W. Hill's fundamental *Bibliography of
Libya* (Durham, 1959). Two works in English which deal at least partially with
the impact of the colonization of the indigenous peoples are E. E. Evans-
Pritchard's *The Sanusi of Cyrenaica* (Oxford, 1949) and John Wright's *Libya*
(New York, 1969). Evans-Pritchard, an English anthropologist, devotes an
angry chapter to the destructive impact which the Italian expropriation of
Sanusi lands brought on the bedouins. Wright, in a journalistic survey of Libya
from ancient times to the present, is somewhat more sympathetic to the
colonization in the three chapters he devotes to the Italian regime in Libya.

The politics and diplomacy of Libya's postwar struggle for independence have
been treated in numerous studies. Two of the best are Majid Khadduri's
political history, *Modern Libya: A Study in Political Development* (Baltimore,
1963) and Adrian Pelt, United Nations commissioner in Libya, *Libyan Independence and the United Nations* (New Haven, 1971).

Index

Adowa, Italian defeat at, 12, 16, 18, 19, 23
Africa, Italian empire in, 82-83, 102, 164-65
Agricultural Census (1937), 92, 97-100
Agricultural credit, 56, 104. *See also* Contracts, agricultural
Agriculture: industries related to Libyan, 163-64; and Italian investment in Libya, 63, 65, 70, 184; and Italian programs for Libyan peoples, 105, 147-53; and locale of Italian concessions in Libya, 97, 100, 144; and productivity of Italian farms, 162-63, 169; and subsidies to colonists and Libyans, 148, 170; traditional forms of Libyan, 144-57; and water resources, 24, 36, 38, 77, 113-15, 119, 120-21, 194 n.6. *See also* Contracts, agricultural; Crops; Farms; Land policies, Italian
Algeria, 65, 94, 161
Archaeology, 87
Argentina, 10, 18, 29
Artesian wells, 115
Association for the Progress of Libya, 175
Azienda Tabacchi Italiani (ATI), 76-78, 169. *See also* Tigrinna
Azizia, 45, 113, 115, 165

Badoglio, Pietro, 70, 80, 81, 83, 86
Balbo, Italo, 81, 86, 106, 109, 127, 162, 183, 184; attitude toward Libyan peoples, 87-88, 104, 210 n.10; career before governorship, 84-86; colonization plan for Libya, 88-89; contribution to colonization summarized, 84; criticized by technical experts, 133; death of, 166, 206 n.9; relations with

Mussolini, 85, 156; and *Ventimila,* 107-8
Banco di Roma, 42, 43, 79, 195 n.25
Barce, 79, 90, 121
Barzilai, Salvatore, 21
Barzini, Luigi, 26
"Battle of the births," 59, 60
Benghazi, 105, 146
Bengodi, Land of, 24, 111, 112, 134-35, 191 n.15
Bertolini Commission, 43, 44, 46, 56, 154
Bevione, Giuseppe, 24, 29
Bir Terrina, 141
Boccardo, Girolamo, 10
Bongiovanni, Luigi, 108
Bonifica integrale, 61
Bove, Giacomo, 11
British Military Administration (BMA), 167, 168, 169, 172, 173, 175, 176, 177
Bureaucracy, Italian colonial, 111, 112, 127, 132, 135, 152

Caetani, Leone, 26
Camperio, Manfredo, 9, 27
Cantalupo, Roberto, 58, 199 n.7
Capo zona, 124, 128, 137
Capitalist colonization, 12, 13, 96. *See also* Latifundia
Carducci, Giosuè, 17, 21
Carocci, Giampiero, 62
Carpi, Leone, 10
Cavazza, Filippo, 50, 55, 64-65
Cecchi, Antonio, 11
Ciano, Galeazzo, 109-10
Civilizing mission, 26, 30, 42, 148
Colajanni, Napoleone, 25
Cold War, 174-75
Colonial budget, Italian, 83, 164
Colonists, Italian: and agricultural con-